Philadelphia Flavor 2

Philadelphia Flavor 2

A *SECOND* HELPING OF ALL NEW RESTAURANT RECIPES FROM THE CITY AND THE SUBURBS

Connie Correia Fisher and Joanne Correia

Foreword by Pam Rainey Lawler
Founder of Philabundance

small potatoes press

**Dedicated to the C4 and S2 for giving to each
other the gifts of friendship and love. — J.C.**

And to all the parents who taught us how. — C.C.F.

ISBN: 0-9661200-8-6
Library of Congress Control Number: 2003096250

Printed in the United States

Small Potatoes Press
401 Collings Avenue
Collingswood, NJ 08108
856-869-5207

Visit us on the Web!
www.smallpotatoespress.com

10 9 8 7 6 5 4 3 2 1

Contents

Foreword

"Good food should not go to waste when so many of our neighbors are going hungry" came to be the motivation and driving force when I founded Philabundance in 1984, and remains so today.

During the past two decades, Philabundance has grown from those first few months in the back of my station wagon, picking up food from restaurants and caterers throughout Philadelphia, to collecting and distributing more than 15 million pounds of food to those in need in the Greater Philadelphia area through a network of over 200 agencies.

Many of the restaurateurs who have contributed recipes to *Philadelphia Flavor 2* were instrumental in the early days of Philabundance. They were aware of the problem of hunger and yet had no way to help provide their surplus perishable food to meet the need.

Philabundance provided the pick up and delivery service that moved their food to an agency that could best use it, just as we do today. The back of my station wagon became vans and then refrigerated trucks, and now we have grown to a 19,120-square-foot warehouse and seven refrigerated trucks. We may be larger and more sophisticated in our operations now, but we will continue to rely on the support of the restaurant community — those early pioneers — for donations of surplus food and prepared meals and for the hosting of events to continue to raise awareness of the problem of hunger and malnutrition in our region.

As you enjoy recreating these delicious dishes in your home or feast on them by patronizing these restaurants, you will also be helping to end hunger in our communities. Philabundance is honored to be designated as a recipient of proceeds from this delightful cookbook, and all of us appreciate the opportunity to share a bit of our story with you ... a story that continues, thanks to the generous support of so many.

Regards,
Pam Rainey Lawler
Founder, Philabundance

Editors' Letter

Anyone who has watched an episode of "The Restaurant" can attest to this ... things change quickly in the restaurant world. And the world of the Philadelphia restaurant scene is no exception. It is innovative, exciting, and ever changing.

We completed the first volume of *Philadelphia Flavor* in the summer of 1999 and sent the manuscript to the printer with high hopes. Before we got the finished books back from the printer, two of the participating restaurants had already closed! It's the nature of the industy. Restaurants open with a flourish and close with a whimper. Chefs move from stove to stove and state to state. A French menu becomes Cuban becomes New American becomes French. And our old standbys just get better and better. These unexpected and often fast paced changes are what makes dining and eating in the Philadelphia area fresh and exciting. These changes are also the reason for this new cookbook.

We are very excited about *Philadelphia Flavor 2*. At almost 400 pages, it's the biggest book we've ever compiled and certainly the most comprehensive. One hundred and fifty chefs contributed over 325 all new recipes, and we've included a dozen of our past favorites. Wine mavens paired many of these recipes with their favorite vintages, and some of the area's hippest bartenders shared their favorite cocktail concoctions. This book — with its quirky sandwich chapter — has a real Philly flavor that you'll love.

What *we* love is that with this book, we'll be able to contribute something to the community at large. We've teamed up with Philadabundance, and a portion of the profits from this book will help fight hunger.

So thanks to all of you who will use and enjoy *Philadelphia Flavor 2* and to the chefs who made this book possible. We invite you to settle in your kitchen, pull out your whisk, and discover the flavors of Philadelphia.

Best regards,
Connie Correia Fisher and Joanne Correia
Editors

Hors d'oeuvres

Tortilla Press Guacamole 10

Copa Guacamole and Chips 11

Pulled BBQ Pork Pot Stickers 12

Lobster Pot Stickers 13

Scallop and Shrimp Dumplings 14

Shau Mai Dim Sum 15

Crab and Lobster Roll 16

Seared Ahi Tuna Summer Rolls 17

Tuna Tartare with Sesame Chips and Soy Wasabi Drizzle 18

Big Eye Tuna Tartare 19

Hazelnut Crusted Calamari and Rock Shrimp 20

Bourbon Grilled Shrimp Skewers 21

Riverboat Shrimp 22

Classic Baked Clams Oregano 23

Chilled Monk's Mussels 24

Puffed Asparagus Spears 25

Grape Tomato and Goat Cheese Bruschetta 26

The Love Note 27

Tortilla Press Guacamole

Whisk Wisdom

The best way to tell if an avocado is ready to eat is to gently squeeze it in the palm of your hand. Ripe fruit will be firm but yield to gentle pressure. To speed the ripening process, place the fruit in a brown paper bag and store at room temperature until ready to eat (usually two to five days). If you add an apple to the bag, it speeds up the process even more.

Avocados are easy to peel when ripe. Cut the avocado in half and remove the big center seed. Begin at the small end and remove the skin with a knife or spoon. Avocados should be eaten immediately to retain a fresh green color. If you are preparing them in advance, sprinkle with lemon or lime juice, cover in an airtight container, and store in the refrigerator. If, after storage, the avocado has turned brown on top, remove and discard the top layer.

2 tablespoons minced onions
1 teaspoon minced jalapeño
1 teaspoon lime juice
1 teaspoon finely chopped cilantro
½ teaspoon salt
1 avocado
2 tablespoons diced tomato
4 ounces Pico de Gallo
Tortilla chips, warmed

Mash onion, jalapeño, lime juice, ½ teaspoon cilantro, and salt to form a paste.

Cut avocado in half and remove pit. Dice avocado in shell to ¼ inch and scoop into bowl with paste. Add remaining cilantro and diced tomato. Mix well.

Serve with Pico de Gallo and chips

Yields 2 servings

**Mark E. Smith, Chef/Owner
The Tortilla Press, Collingswood, NJ**

Copa Guacamole and Chips

Copabanana

Known for:
best margaritas and burgers in the city

Year opened:
1979

Most requested table:
#14 and 15

Menu:
Caribbean/South Western with Mexican flair

Chef:
John C. Hayden

Chef's training:
Academy Culinary Arts and 2 years formal training in Paris

Chef's hobbies/ accomplishments:
golf, automobilia/ won gold medal ACF ice carving competition

Chef's favorite ingredient:
all peppers — serranos, chilis, habaneros, etc.

Chef's favorite food:
New Orleans style from the old Cafe Nola

3 ripe Hass avocados
1 ripe jalapeño pepper, seeds removed and finely chopped
1 vine ripe tomato, finely chopped
½ small Spanish onion, finely chopped
½ cup chopped washed fresh cilantro
2 lemons
1 teaspoon "good" balsamic vinegar
1 teaspoon ground cumin
Kosher salt and fresh ground black pepper to taste
1 1-pound package uncooked 6-inch corn tortillas
3 cups vegetable oil

Cut avocados lengthwise to separate. Scoop flesh from skin and place in a nonreactive bowl. Add jalapeño pepper, tomato, onion, and cilantro to bowl. Squeeze lemons over top. Add vinegar and cumin. Mix with a fork to incorporate ingredients and break up avocados. Season to taste with salt and pepper.

Heat vegetable oil in a pot to 325°. Cut each tortilla into 4 to 6 pie wedges. Carefully place wedges into hot oil and fry for 3 to 4 minutes or until crisp. Season to taste. Enjoy chips and dip with friends! ☺

Yields 4 servings

**John C. Hayden, Executive Chef
Copabanana, Philadelphia, PA**

Pulled BBQ Pork Pot Stickers

Elements Cafe

Year opened:
2003

Most requested table:
window table

Menu:
New American small plates

Chef:
Fred Kellermann

Chef's training:
graduate of Greenbrier Hotel
Apprenticeship Program

**Chef's hobbies/
accomplishments:**
ACF Gold Medal winner, Mobil
4-star honoree

Chef's favorite ingredient:
jalapeños, ginger, and garlic—
anything that adds punch

Chef's favorite food:
mom's cooking

¼ cup adobe seasoning
2 tablespoons Cajun spice
2 tablespoons chile spice
1 teaspoon cayenne pepper
2 pounds boneless pork shoulder
1 onion
2 stalks celery
¼ cup minced garlic
2 quarts BBQ sauce (use your favorite)
¼ cup soy sauce
36 to 48 wonton skins

Combine first four ingredients. Rub pork with mixture and refrigerate for 4 hours.

Preheat oven to 325°. Brown pork on all sides in a braising pan over medium heat. Add onion, celery, garlic, and BBQ sauce. Add enough water to cover pork half way. Place uncovered in oven and cook for 3 hours or until fork tender. Remove pork. Strain and skim braising liquid. Add soy sauce to liquid. Keep warm until ready to serve.

Hand shred pork and mix with one-quarter of warm soy sauce. Place 1 tablespoon of pork mixture into each wonton wrapper. Fold wrapper and seal edges with a moistened fork.

Brown pot stickers on both sides in a fry pan. Serve with warm soy sauce for dipping.

Chef's note ... Blending Asian, Mexican, and Southern traits to make the perfect party hors d'oeurves or dinner appetizer.

Yields 12 servings

Frederick Kellermann, Chef/Owner
Elements Cafe, Haddon Heights, NJ

Lobster Pot Stickers

Did you know?

Dumpling wrappers are also called dumpling skins, shu mai skins, siu mai skins, and su my wrappers. Whatever the name, these thin, round wrappers are used to make dumplings in Chinese cuisine. While assembling the dumplings, keep the stack of wrappers moist by covering them with a damp towel. When stuffed, they can be steamed, boiled, or lightly fried. You can find dumpling wrappers fresh or frozen in several shapes and thicknesses, usually in 1-pound packages. They can be held in the refrigerator for up to a week or frozen for one to two months.

1 pound lobster meat, coarsely chopped
4 scallions, finely chopped plus 1 tablespoon chopped scallion
¼ cup crème of coconut
1 ounce fresh ginger, grated
1 pound dumpling wrappers, about 16 wrappers
1 egg beaten
Clarified butter
Coconut Soy Sauce (Recipe appears on page 324.)
1 tablespoon butter

Combine lobster meat, 4 finely chopped scallions, crème of coconut, and ginger. Place a dollop of lobster filling in center of each dumpling wrapper. Brush with beaten egg, fold, and seal.

Sauté dumplings in clarified butter for about 2 minutes on each side until golden brown.

Deglaze pan with coconut soy sauce. Add butter and 1 tablespoon chopped scallion. Heat until sauce is hot and butter melted. Serve immediately.

Yields 8 servings

Laura Kaplan, Chef/Owner
Emerald Fish, Cherry Hill, NJ

Scallop and Shrimp Dumplings

Whisk Wisdom

Napa cabbage is a common ingredient in Asian stir-fries. It is from the same family as the green cabbage but has a more sweet and mild flavor. A head of Napa cabbage somewhat resembles a head of romaine, except that it is more compact and has slightly curly edges. Its long, flat, wide leaves make it well-suited to stuffing or for wrapping fish to be steamed. It's also wonderful when cut into strips and sautéed in a wok with garlic and ginger.

Refrigerate in a bag for up to 5 days. To cook, cut out the core and wash under running water. Blanch for a few minutes and discard the blanching water. Cook the lower part first, and add the leaves halfway through the cooking time.

1 cup coarsely chopped raw scallops

1 cup shelled, deveined, and coarsely chopped medium raw shrimp

1 cup finely chopped Napa cabbage

½ cup finely chopped leeks

½ cup finely chopped fresh water chestnuts

1 cup finely chopped scallions

1 teaspoon finely chopped ginger root

1 teaspoon white pepper

1 teaspoon salt

1 teaspoon soy sauce

1 teaspoon sesame oil

2 teaspoons rice wine

1 16-ounce package round dumpling wrappers

Soy Basil Dipping Sauce (Recipe appears on page 325.)

Combine all ingredients, except wrappers and dipping sauce, in a large bowl. Mix with hands or a large spoon until all ingredients are thoroughly blended.

Place 1 tablepoon filling in the center of 1 wrapper. Fold wrapper in half to form a semicircle. Use fingers to form 5 or 6 pleats on one side of the opening at each end of the arc to gather the wrapper around the filling. Pinch all along the top of dumpling to seal pleats and smooth edges together. Cover filled dumpling with a towel. Continue stuffing process with remaining wrappers and filling, placing each completed dumpling under the towel.

Line the bottom of a steamer with a small damp cloth. Arrange dumplings, without crowding, on cloth. Cover and steam over boiling water for about 8 minutes. Serve with dipping sauce.

Yields 4 dozen dumplings, about 6 servings

Michael M. Wei, Executive Chef/Owner
Yangming, Bryn Mawr, PA

Shau Mai Dim Sum

10 ounces pork loin, diced small
8 ounces 50-60 count shrimp
1 ounce pork fat, diced small
4 Chinese black mushrooms, cut small
1 tablespoon corn starch
1 teaspoon salt
½ teaspoon sugar
¼ teaspoon white pepper
½ teaspoon sesame oil
20 1-inch-round Cantonese wonton wrappers
2 shrimp, ground
Few drops red food coloring

Combine first nine ingredients. Place 2 teaspoons filling in the center of 1 wrapper. Wrap like a small cup. Repeat with remaining wrappers and filling.

Combine ground shrimp and coloring. Reserve.

Line the bottom of a steamer with a small damp cloth. Arrange dumplings, without crowding, on cloth. Place 1 drop of ground shrimp on each dim sum. Cover and steam over boiling water for about 7 to 8 minutes.

Yields 20 pieces

Joseph Poon, Chef/Nutritionist
Joseph Poon Asian Fusion Restaurant, Philadelphia

Crab and Lobster Roll

Chef's Notes

— Egg roll sheets and sweet chili sauce can be found in an Oriental cooking store.

— Robert Mondavi Cabernet is an excellent complementary wine for this dish.

2 yellow peppers, chopped
2 yellow squash, chopped
2 zucchini, chopped
1 onion, chopped
Salt and pepper to taste
1 pound cooked lobster meat
1 pound cooked crabmeat
8 ounces sweet chili sauce
8 egg roll sheets
2 egg whites, beaten
½ cup vegetable oil
1 bunch leeks
½ cup flour

Sauté peppers, squash, zucchini, and onion until soft. Season with salt and pepper to taste. Dip lobster meat and crabmeat in sweet chili sauce.

Brush egg roll sheets with egg whites. Layer with vegetables, lobster meat, and crabmeat. Roll each sheet into a cylinder. Seal with egg whites.

Heat oil to 350°. Fry rolls until golden and crispy. Dip leeks in flour, then fry. Place rolls on a serving plate and garnish with leeks.

Yields 4 servings

Biagio Scotto, Chef
Lamberti's Cucina, Wilmington, DE

Seared Ahi Tuna Summer Rolls

1 pack dried rice noodles

1 pound ahi tuna loin

1 teaspoon salt

1 teaspoon pepper

2 tablespoons blended olive oil

1 pint water, room temperature

1 pack dried rice paper (Papers are 8-inches round, 25 to 30 pieces in each pack. You'll need 10 papers.)

10 pieces red leaf lettuce or romaine lettuce, washed, dried, and cut into strips

1 2- or 4-ounce tube wasabi paste

1 teaspoon black and white sesame seeds, toasted

1 small bundle fresh mint, washed and dried

6 ounces soy sauce

Bring 1 quart cold water to a boil. Add noodles, using chopsticks to toss noodles. Strain noodles and cool for 30 to 60 minutes.

Season tuna on all sides with salt and pepper. Heat oil in an 8-inch nonstick pan on high heat. Sear tuna on each side for 30 seconds. Remove from pan. Cut into 10 1½-ounce pieces measuring about 3½ x ½-inch in size. Reserve.

Place 1 pint room temperature water in a glass soup bowl. Wet rice paper by moving it around in water on both sides until moist. Lay 1 wet paper in front of you and add (layered) to bottom edge one-tenth of lettuce, rice noodles, tuna, wasabi paste, and sesame seeds. Fold left and right sides of paper towards the center and roll tightly up from the bottom. Cut roll in half. Continue process with remaining papers and ingredients. Garnish with fresh mint and soy sauce for dipping.

Yields 10 servings

Kiong Banh, Executive Chef
Twenty Manning, Philadelphia, PA

Tuna Tartare with Sesame Chips and Soy Wasabi Drizzle

Rouge

Known for:
outside seating on
Rittenhouse Square

Year opened:
1998

Most requested table:
the window table

Menu:
French bistro

Chef:
Michael Yeamans

Chef's training:
Johnson & Wales University

**Chef's hobbies/
accomplishments:**
playing with Andrew Yeamans

Chef's favorite food:
pastrami Reubans

15 wonton skins, cut in half diagonally
¼ cup sesame oil
Salt and pepper
4 teaspoons wasabi powder
2 teaspoons water
2 teaspoons soy sauce
1 teaspoon honey
1 pound sushi-grade tuna, top inside loin, diced into ¼-inch cubes
3 teaspoons minced shallot
3 teaspoons chopped chives
2 teaspoons chopped parsley
3 tablespoons Soy Chili Vinaigrette (Recipe appears on page 84.)
2 tablespoons extra virgin olive oil
Wakame (seaweed salad)

Preheat oven to 350°.

Brush wonton skins with oil. Place skins on a sesame oiled sheet pan. Season with salt and pepper. Bake until golden. Reserve chips.

Mix together wasabi powder, water, soy sauce, and honey. (The drizzle should be at a consistency that can be poured. Add extra water if needed.) Reserve.

In a separate bowl bowl, combine remaining ingredients except wakame. Mix well.

Place tuna mixture on a serving platter. Drizzle with soy wasabi drizzle and top with wakame. Serve with sesame chips.

Yields 6 servings

**Michael Yeamans, Executive Chef
Rouge, Philadelphia, PA**

Big Eye Tuna Tartare

Yardley Inn

Known for:
service and warm decor

Year opened:
established in 1832,
with current owner since 1990

Most requested table:
porch seating (offering an indoor
view of the river)

Menu:
Continental

Chef:
Dominick Zirilli

Chef's training:
The Restaurant School,
Philadelphia

**Chef's hobbies/
accomplishments:**
spending time off with family/
continued guest satisfaction

Chef's favorite ingredient:
specialty vinegars (I use them to
finish almost all sauces.)

Chef's favorite food:
artisanal cheeses (I love the
small cheese farms of the
world.)

12 ounces big eye tuna
½ ounce sesame seeds
1 tablespoon chopped shallots
1 tablespoon chopped chives
1 tablespoon olive oil
1 teaspoon soy sauce
½ teaspoon cumin powder

Dice tuna into small cubes about the size of a pea. Place in a metal mixing bowl.

Toast sesame seeds. Add seeds and remaining ingredients to tuna and toss like a salad until tuna is well coated.

Present on crostinis as an hors d'oeuvre or eat by the spoonful.

Yields about 12 to 24 servings

**Dominick Zirilli, Executive Chef
Yardley Inn, Yardley, PA**

Hazelnut Crusted Calamari and Rock Shrimp

Recommended Wine

2001 Raymond Estates Chardonnay, Monterey, CA
The combination of nutty breading and smoky aïoli in this recipe are a natural for a crisp, mid-weight white wine with oak accented flavors. Barrel aging adds a distinctive toasty, spicy richness to wines like this Central Coast Chardonnay. Here, bright tropical fruit flavors, like pineapple and mango, are intensified with a modest touch of oak, adding a layer of caramelized vanilla and spice. Approximately $12

— Marnie Old
Old Wines LLC, Philadelphia

10 ounces calamari (8 ounces of tubes and 2 ounces of skirts)
4 ounces small broken shrimp
4 tablespoons hazelnut flour
4 tablespoons cornmeal
4 tablespoons all-purpose flour
4 tablespoons garlic powder
4 tablespoons onion powder
1 teaspoon ground cayenne pepper
2 quarts oil (vegetable or blended)
Chipolte Aïoli (Recipe appears on page 332.)

Cut calamari and shrimp into bite-size pieces. In a deep mixing bowl, blend all dry ingredients well. Add calamari and shrimp and mix until well coated.

In a deep-fryer or pan, heat oil to 375°. Add coated calamari and shrimp and deep-fry until golden and crispy, approximately 90 seconds. Remove pieces from oil and drain well.

Place on a serving plate with a ramekin of chipotle aïoli and serve immediately.

Yields 2 servings

David Grear, Executive Chef
La Terrasse, Philadelphia, PA

Bourbon Grilled Shrimp Skewers

Company's Coming Catering

Known for:
personalized service and affordability

Year opened:
1980

Menu:
foods of the world

Chef:
Joshua J. Hunter

Chef's training:
The Restaurant School;
Philadelphia Country Club

Chef's hobbies/ accomplishments:
back packing, camping,
Eagle Scout

Chef's favorite ingredient:
creativity and seafood

Chef's favorite food:
duck a l'orange

1 cup Jim Beam bourbon
1 cup brown sugar, packed
½ cup light corn syrup
1 tablespoon cracked black pepper
¾ cup chopped shallots
24 U-12 shrimp, peeled and deveined
24 slices bacon

Soak 24 bamboo skewers in water.

Combine bourbon, brown sugar, corn syrup, and black pepper in a large sauté pan and simmer. (Be CAREFUL: bourbon will flambé.) Simmer sauce until thick enough to coat the back of a spoon. Set aside.

Wrap 1 slice bacon around 1 shrimp. Pierce with skewer. Continue with remaining bacon and shrimp. Grill over medium heat until bacon is crisp and shrimp is cooked through, about 15 minutes. Serve with sauce for dipping.

Yields 8 servings

**Joshua J. Hunter, Chef/Owner
Company's Coming Catering, Philadelphia, PA**

Riverboat Shrimp

Whisk Wisdom

Creole mustard is a hot, spicy wholegrain mustard, made from vinegar-marinated brown mustard seeds with a hint of horseradish. The ingredients may vary from producer to producer; however, they all have the same basic flavor, and the seeds are usually slightly crushed instead of being ground or whole. True to Louisiana's "melting pot" history, this mustard originated in France, but the distinguishing technique — marinating the mustard seeds in vinegar —came to New Orleans with the Germans. Creole mustard is available in gourmet markets or the gourmet section of some supermarkets or through on-line retailers.

1 cup Creole mustard
1 cup honey
2 ounces Triple Sec
8 jumbo shrimp, U15 size, peeled and deveined
½ cup Cajun seasoning (I recommend Chef Paul
    Prudhomme's Blackened Redfish Magic Seasoning.)
2 lemon wedges

Combine Creole mustard, honey, and Triple Sec. Reserve.
    Coat shrimp with Cajun seasoning. Blacken shrimp on a hot grill or in a cast-iron skillet for approximately 3 minutes per side.
    Serve shrimp with mustard-honey sauce for dipping and a lemon wedge.

Yields 2 servings

**Thommy Geneviva, Executive Chef
Thommy G's, Burlington, NJ**

Classic Baked Clams Oregano

Culinary Quote

"We found some large clams...which the storm had torn up from the bottom, and cast ashore. I selected one of the largest, about six inches in length, and carried it along.....We took our nooning under a sand-hill, covered with beach grass...I kindled a fire with a match and some paper, and cooked my clam on the embers for my dinner.....Though it was very tough, I found it sweet and savory, and ate the whole with a relish. Indeed, with the addition of a cracker or two, it would have been a bountiful dinner."

Henry David Thoreau
in *"Cape Cod"*

24 fresh clams in shells
2 tablespoons fresh lemon juice
¼ cup fresh grated Parmesan
¼ cup seasoned breadcrumbs
¼ cup chopped fresh parsley
2 cloves garlic, crushed
1 teaspoon oregano
½ teaspoon fine sea salt
Fresh ground pepper to taste
Olive oil
Lemon wedges

Preheat oven to 425°.

Open clams, discard top shell, and loosen meat from bottom shell. Arrange clams on a cookie sheet. Sprinkle with lemon juice. Combine cheese, breadcrumbs, parsley, garlic, oregano, salt, and pepper. Cover each clam with about 1 teaspoon of mixture. Sprinkle a few drops of olive oil on top and bake for 15 minutes. Serve with lemon wedges.

Yields 8 servings

Kristin Albertson, Assistant Director
Albertson's Cooking School, Wynnewood, PA

Chilled Monk's Mussels

Chef's Note

— You can't be a Belgian restaurant without serving lots and lots of mussels. Monk's Café serves between two and three tons of mussels each month. That's a lot of mussels! We offer half a dozen hot mussel dishes, but this chilled dish is a big hit in the summer months. We use New Zealand Green Lip mussels for this dish, although we have used Maine cultivated mussels on occasion. Many grocers carry both styles. I use the New Zealand grocer pack when I make this dish for guests at home.

— Serve with a crisp, white wine or a Victory HopDevil, Nodding Head IPA, Duvel or any full-flavored pale ale.

1 2.2-pound bag precooked frozen New Zealand Green Lip mussels
½ cup finely diced red onion
2 cloves garlic, finely diced
1 teaspoon finely diced shallots
1 cup peeled, seeded, and diced plum tomatoes
1 teaspoon black pepper
¼ teaspoon salt
¼ cup Boon Gueuze (Belgian beer)
1 teaspoon finely chopped fresh parsley
2 teaspoons finely chopped fresh chervil
1 teaspoon finely chopped fresh chives
1 teaspoon finely chopped fresh basil
Parsley, optional

Remove mussels from package and thaw overnight in refrigerator.

Lightly sauté onion, garlic, shallots, tomatoes, pepper, salt, and beer for about 1 minute in a hot sauté pan. (Do not overcook — mixture should be slightly crunchy.) Add chopped herbs. Refrigerate until cool.

Arrange cold thawed mussels on a serving plate. Stir to recombine marinade and spoon over each mussel. Sprinkle with parsley or other herb, if desired.

Yields 4 servings

Tom Peters, Chef/Owner
Monk's Café, Philadelphia, PA

Puffed Asparagus Spears

Culinary Quote

"You needn't tell me that a man who doesn't love oysters and asparagus and good wines has got a soul, or a stomach either. He's simply got the instinct for being unhappy."

"Saki"
pen name of Scottish writer
Hector Hugh Munro

1 sheet puff pastry
1 egg, beaten
1 cup grated Parmesan cheese
18 medium to large asparagus spears, blanched

Preheat oven to 400°. Lightly grease a baking sheet.

Lay puff pastry sheet on work surface to thaw. Brush lightly with beaten egg and sprinkle with Parmesan cheese. Cut into 18 ½-inch-wide strips. (You can use a pizza cutter for this.) Place 1 end of pastry to the end of 1 asparagus spear. Secure and wrap dough around spear to the top like a candy cane. Place on prepared sheet. Repeat with remaining spears and dough.

Bake for 7 to 10 minutes or until golden.

Chef's note … You can find puff pastry in the freezer section of your local supermarket. This dish has been a great hit at many of our functions and will add an elegant and unqiue touch to yours.

Yields 6 servings

Joseph Condrone, Chef/Owner
Creative Cuisine Catering, Philadelphia, PA

Grape Tomato and Goat Cheese Bruschetta

Maggiano's Little Italy

Year opened:
2001

Most requested table:
booth number 6 or 7

Menu:
Southern Italian, family style

Chef:
Steve Olson

Chef's training:
Kendall Culinary School, Chicago, IL

Chef's hobbies/ accomplishments:
hunting, fishing, spending time with my family

Chef's favorite ingredient:
all fresh herbs

Chef's favorite food:
If care is put into it, I love anything homemade.

1 pint grape tomatoes
1 tablespoon plus ½ teaspoon olive oil
Salt and pepper to taste
½ cup sliced red onion
4 ounces goat cheese
1 teaspoon finely chopped parsley
1 teaspoon finely chopped basil
1 clove garlic, finely chopped
½ cup shredded spinach leaves
2 tablespoons Maggiano's house dressing or your favorite Italian dressing
10 slices Italian bread

Preheat oven to 300º. Cut tomatoes in half. Mix with 1 tablespoon olive oil and salt and pepper to taste. Place, cut side up, on a baking sheet. Do not crowd tomatoes. Roast for 1 hour until tomatoes are half-dried. Cool completely and reserve.

Increase oven to 350°. Toss together onion, remaining ½ teaspoon olive oil, and salt and pepper to taste. Spread on a sheet pan and bake until golden brown, stirring often. Cool and reserve.

When ready to serve, preheat oven to 450°. Combine goat cheese, parsley, basil, and garlic in a mixing bowl. Toss dried tomatoes, onion, and spinach with dressing. Toast bread. Spread each slice with approximately 1 tablespoon goat cheese. Top with tomato mixture.

Yields 10 pieces

Steve Olson, Executive Chef
Maggiano's Little Italy, Philadelphia, PA

The Love Note

1¼ tablespoons raspberry vinegar
1¾ teaspoons red wine vinegar
1¾ teaspoons balsamic vinegar
1¼ tablespoons honey
5 shallots, peeled and diced
4 ounces Asian pear, peeled and diced
1½ ounces goat cheese
1¼ ounces calvados
Pinch EACH of kosher salt and black pepper
4 sheets phyllo dough
3 tablespoons sweet butter, melted

Combine vinegars and honey in a saucepan and cook until liquid is reduced by half.

Remove mixture from pan but do not rinse pan. Put pan back on medium heat and let glaze for 1 minute. Add shallots and sauté until soft, broken down, and brown from the vinegar glaze. Add vinegar honey mixture back to pan and cook until liquid is almost completely gone. (It should be dark, syrupy, and caramelized. Be careful not to cook it too much, or it will be like candy.) Remove mixture from pan and cool to room temperature.

Add pears to the same unwashed pan and sauté for 3 to 5 minutes. Deglaze and flambé with calvados. Add a pinch of salt and pepper. Allow pears to cool.

Combine shallot mixture, pears, and goat cheese in a bowl and mix well to combine.

Preheat oven to 400°. Lay out 1 sheet phyllo dough and brush with some butter. Cover with another sheet of phyllo. Cut into 4 equal strips. Repeat with remaining two sheets. Place mixture onto the bottom of each strip. Fold up to form triangles. Place on a sprayed baking sheet and brush with butter. Bake for 7 to 9 minutes.

Yields 8 servings

Anthony G. Lucas, Executive Chef
Jeffrey Miller Catering, Lansdowne, PA

Appetizers

Tomato, Melon, and Stoli Crab Cocktail 30

Seafood Cocktail 31

Blue Crab Jumbo Lump "Tamale" 32

Salmon Tartare with Fried Sesame Wontons 33

Citrus Marinated Salmon Carpaccio 34

Smoked Salmon and Goat Cheese Carpaccio 35

Octopus Carpaccio with Fennel and Tomato 36

Jumbo Sea Scallop with Radish and Brioche Crouton 37

Pan Seared Diver Scallops with Herbed Goat Cheese 38

Seared Scallops with Basil-Dijon Vinaigrette 39

Tequila Shrimp with Spicy Polenta 40

Santa Barbara Spot Shrimp Ceviche 41

Oyster Rockefeller 42

Blue Corn Fried Oysters with Poblano Crema 43

Tuna Nuta 44

Lenguado Handroll 45

Japanese Smoked Eel and Pineapple Ceviche 46

Steamed Crawfish 47

Mussels in Tomato Saffron Broth 48

"The Captain's" Drunken Clams 49

Balsamic Grilled Calves Liver with Sun-dried Apricot Vinaigrette 50

Grilled Mozzarella with Spiced Tomato Chutney 51

Sautéed Mozzarella di Bufala 52

Criniti Appetizer 53

Deep Fried Spinachi Fritti with Red Capers 54

Marinated Stuffed Portobello Mushrooms 55

Tomato, Melon, and Stoli Crab Cocktail

La Terrasse

Year opened:
originally opened in 1966;
reopened in 1998

Most requested table:
by the windows
in the lower terrace

Menu:
French/American

Chef:
David Grear

Chef's training:
self taught, learned "in the field"

**Chef's hobbies/
accomplishments:**
weight lifting, sports, recipe
development/my son!

Chef's favorite food:
anything I don't have
cook myself!

¼ pint EACH red and yellow cherry tomatoes
½ ripe honeydew melon
½ ripe cantaloupe
8 leaves fresh mint, chiffonade
1 375-milliliter bottle Stolichnaya vodka (any flavor)
6 ounces jumbo lump crabmeat
6 sprigs fresh mint

Make a small "X" cut in the bottom of each tomato. Bring 1 quart of water to a boil in a medium saucepan. Add tomatoes and boil for 30 seconds. Remove tomatoes and immediately plunge them into a bowl of ice water. Within 1 minute, skins should loosen. Peel by hand from the bottom where cuts were made. Place peeled tomatoes in a mixing bowl.

Using a melon-baller, scoop both melons into small balls. Add melon balls and mint leaves to mixing bowl and cover with vodka. Marinate for 24 hours.

Fill 6 martini glasses with tomato/melon mixture. Cover with vodka marinade. Top each with crabmeat and garnish with a sprig of fresh mint.

Chef's note ... Use as an appetizer or salad (or even a dessert!)—*perfect* for a summer picnic!!

Yields 6 "cocktails"

**David Grear, Executive Chef
La Terrasse, Philadelphia, PA**

Seafood Cocktail

Culinary Quote?

"Fish is held out to be one of the greatest luxuries of the table and not only necessary, but even indispensable at all dinners where there is any pretence of excellence or fashion."

Isabella Beeton
Cookbook writer
"The Book of Household Management," 1859

1 pound jumbo lump crabmeat, picked over for shells
3 hard-cooked eggs, chopped fine
½ cup finely chopped red onion
1 red bell pepper, seeded and diced
1 large tomato, seeded and diced
2 tablespoons chopped fresh tarragon
2 tablespoons brandy
¼ cup mayonnaise
1 teaspoon Tabasco sauce
¼ pound smoked salmon
4 cherry tomatoes
4 black olives

Place crabmeat and chopped egg in a large mixing bowl. Gently mix in onion, pepper, and tomato. Add tarragon, brandy, and mayonnaise and lightly toss as to not break up the jumbo lump.

Line 4 martini glasses with salmon. Fill with crab salad. Garnish each with a cherry tomato and olive skewered with a sword pick.

Yields 4 servings

Joseph Stewart, Executive Chef
GG's Restaurant at the Doubletree Hotel, Mt. Laurel, NJ

Blue Crab Jumbo Lump "Tamale"

Iron Hill Brewery and Restaurant

Known for:
creative, casual menu and handcrafted beers

Year opened:
1996

Most requested table:
booths in dining room

Menu:
new American

Chef:
Daniel D. Bethard

Chef's training:
self taught, restaurant trained

Chef's hobbies/accomplishments:
strength training, sports, and what else ... cooking!

Chef's favorite ingredient:
chiles

Chef's favorite food:
authentic Mexican, seafood

3 avocados, skin and stone removed
1 tablespoon chopped cilantro
1 tablespoon sour cream
2 limes
Kosher salt
1 mango, peeled and chopped
1 chipolte pepper in adobo
2 tablespoons canola oil
20 dried corn husks, soaked in water
1 pound jumbo lump blue crabmeat, picked through
    for shells
Tomato-Habañero Salsa (Recipe appears on page 337.)
1 bunch watercress

Combine avocados, cilantro, sour cream, juice of 1 lime, and kosher salt to taste in a bowl. Mash together. Add more lime juice, if desired.

Combine mango, chipolte, juice of 1 lime, and a tiny pinch of salt in a blender or food processor. Puree. With machine still running, drizzle in oil until combined.

Remove husks from water. Make ties by slicing a few husks into ¼-inch strips along the grain of the husk. Take 2 husks and lay them next to each other. Tie both ends together with husk ties to create a vessel. Repeat with remaining husks until you have 6 vessels.

Fold crabmeat into tomato-haberñero salsa. Divide mixture between corn husk vessels. Divide mango coulis between 6 plates. Place husks on coulis. Place a dollop of avocado-cilantro crème next to corn husks. Garnish with sprigs of watercress.

Yields 6 servings

Daniel Bethard, Executive Chef/Operating Partner
Iron Hill Brewery and Restaurant, West Chester, PA

Salmon Tartare with Fried Sesame Wontons

Chef's Note

— Sambal chili is a Thai red chili paste that can be found in specialty supermarkets or any Asian grocery store.

— In order to find high quality fresh salmon, visit your local fish market and inquire about sushi grade salmon. They should have it or help you find it. I use Norwegian salmon in my restaurant.

— While whisking the vinaigrette, prevent the mixing bowl from sliding by placing the bowl on a damp tea towel.

3 tablespoons sesame oil
2 tablespoons Sambal chili
2 tablespoons soy sauce
2 tablespoons rice wine vinegar
Juice of 2 lemons
1 piece ginger root, finely diced
½ cup olive oil
Salt and pepper
1 pound Norwegian salmon or other sushi grade salmon,
    diced with skin and blood line removed
2 shallots, finely diced
¼ cup finely chopped chives
Vegetable oil for frying
3 eggs
2 tablespoons black sesame seeds
4 small wontons
1 English cucumber, sliced into thin rounds
Osetra caviar, optional
Chervil sprigs

Combine sesame oil, Sambal chili, soy sauce, rice wine vinegar, lemon juice, and ginger in a large mixing bowl and whisk vigorously for 1 to 2 minutes. Continue whisking and slowly add olive oil. Season with salt and pepper.

Place salmon in a mixing bowl with shallots and chives. Add Sambal vinaigrette and toss to coat. (You do not need to use all the vinaigrette.) Season with salt to taste. Reserve.

Pour some vegetable oil into a pot and bring to 325°. Beat eggs and sesame seeds together in a small bowl. Dredge wontons in egg mixture and place in hot oil. Fry until golden brown on both sides. Place on paper towels to drain.

Place approximately 8 to 10 cucumber rounds in the middle of each of 4 plates. Place 1 wonton on cucumbers. Spoon 4 ounces of tartar atop wonton. Garnish with a dollop of caviar and chervil sprigs.

Yields 4 servings

Jason P. McHugh, Executive Chef
Chadd's Ford Inn, Chadd's Ford, PA

Citrus Marinated Salmon Carpaccio

Did You Know?

Carpaccio, named after the 15th century painter Vittore Carpaccio, was invented at Harry's Bar in Venice, Italy. Originally, carpaccio consisted of paper-thin, almost translucent slices of raw beef drizzled with a creamy dressing. Today, carpaccio can be almost anything sliced tissue thin — tuna, mushrooms, even fruit.

When you purchase the salmon for this recipe, have your fish monger portion it into six 4-ounce portions and have them either slice it thin or pound it gently for you.

2 tablespoons lemon juice

¼ cup orange juice

¼ teaspoon dried dill weed

1½ tablespoons minced red onion

1½ pounds salmon fillet, sliced or pounded thin

Salt (sea salt preferred) to taste

1 bulb fennel, core removed and sliced paper thin

2 tablespoons capers

2 cups watercress, washed and large stems trimmed

2 tablespoons extra virgin olive oil

Fresh ground black pepper to taste

2 oranges, peeled and cut into 12 slices

1 lemon, peeled, cut in half, and sliced into 12 half-moon slices

Combine lemon juice, orange juice, dill, and red onion.

Place salmon in a shallow glass dish and pour citrus mixture over it. Sprinkle with salt and marinate for at least 4 hours or overnight.

Right before serving, combine fennel, capers, watercress, and olive oil. Toss and add salt and pepper to taste.

To serve, place 4 ounces salmon in the center of each plate. Arrange 2 slices each orange and lemon in a pinwheel design on top of salmon. Divide fennel salad into 6 portions and place on top of citrus slices and salmon. Serve immediately and offer additional fresh ground pepper.

Yields 6 servings

Trish Morrissey, Chef/Partner
The Chef Did It, Personal Chef and Catering Service, Philadelphia, PA

Smoked Salmon and Goat Cheese Carpaccio

Le Castagne

Year opened:
2001

Most requested table:
table 40 by the window with its view of Chestnut Street

Menu:
Italian

Chef:
Brian Wilson

Chef's training:
Johnson & Wales University

Chef's hobbies/ accomplishments:
snowmobiling

Chef's favorite ingredient:
porcini mushroom

Chef's favorite food:
pasta

2 pounds smoked salmon
1 8-ounce log goat cheese
6 sprigs chives, chopped
Salt and pepper to taste
2 tablespoons honey
2 tablespoons red wine vinegar
1 tablespoon chopped fresh parsley
1 bunch scallions, tops and bottoms removed
Dash of red pepper flakes
½ cup extra virgin olive oil

On a piece of plastic wrap, overlap slices of salmon to create a rectangle about 8 inches long by 5 inches wide. Cover salmon with another piece of plastic wrap and lightly flatten with a kitchen mallet. (Be careful not to make any holes in the plastic.) Remove top piece of plastic.

Place goat cheese in a mixing bowl. Add chives and mix on low speed until smooth. Add salt and pepper to taste. Spread cheese evenly over entire salmon, leaving a 1-inch boarder across long sides. Grasp plastic underneath salmon and tightly roll like a cigarette. Wrap in another piece of plastic and tie each end with string or rubber band to make roll tighter. Refrigerate for at least 1 hour.

Place remaining ingredients, except olive oil in a blender and finely chop. Slowly drizzle olive oil into blender and emulsify. Reserve until ready to serve.

Remove salmon from plastic and slice salmon with a hot, sharp knife into rounds about ¼-inch thick. Drizzle with vinaigrette and serve.

Yields 8 servings

Brian Wilson, Executive Chef
Le Castagne, Philadelphia, PA

Octopus Carpaccio with Fennel and Tomato

Mixto

Known for:
Latin fusion

Year opened:
2002

Most requested table:
those adjacent to front window

Menu:
Cuban, Columbian, and more!

Chef:
Migula Leonardo León León

Chef's training:
Centro Venezoiano
Capacitation Gastronomica

Chef's hobbies/ accomplishments:
working out and eating out!

Chef's favorite ingredient:
garlic and sweet pepper

Chef's favorite food:
"pabellon criollo"

4 1-ounce pieces octopus
Court-bouillon (see Chef's note)
¼ cup vegetable oil
2 tablespoons lemon juice
2 tablespoons white wine vinegar
1 teaspoon Dijon mustard
2 ounces fennel, sliced as thinly as possible
2 ounce tomatoes
3 tablespoons olive oil
Pinch of salt
½ ounce scallions, chopped

Attach 2 pieces octopus together using cotton string, with tentacles crossed together. Boil in court-bouillon for 90 minutes. Remove strings and freeze octopus.

Slice frozen octopus very thin and arrange evenly around a serving plate.

Whisk together vegetable oil, lemon juice, vinegar, and mustard. Season sliced fennel with vinaigrette. Julienne tomato and season with olive oil and salt. Top octopus with seasoned fennel and garnish with tomato and scallion.

Chef's note ..."Court-bouillon" is made by cooking various vegetables and herbs in water for about 30 minutes. Typical items used are small onions pierced with a few whole cloves, celery, carrots, and a bouquet garni (grouped herbs). Wine, lemon juice, or vinegar may be added to increase tartness. The broth should be allowed to cool before removing the vegetables.

Yields 2 servings

Migula Leonardo León León, Executive Chef
Mixto Restaurant, Philadelphia, PA

Jumbo Sea Scallop with Radish and Brioche Crouton

Recommended Wine

2000 Landmark Courtyard Chardonnay
Crisp apple notes with a spicy vanilla edge make this an excellent match for the spice of the radishes and the buttery texture of the scallops and sauce. $17

2001 Ligenfelder Riesling
This is not a "sweet" Riesling. Made from fruit of the Pfalz region, it has more body and alcohol than its counterparts from the Mosel. The wine features apple and pear flavors with a lush finish.

— John McNulty
Corkscrewed, Cherry Hill, NJ

3 leeks, white and light green parts diced
1 cup chicken stock
2 cups heavy cream
Salt and pepper to taste
2 tablespoons olive oil
6 large jumbo sea scallops
½ loaf brioche, cut into circles
¼ pound butter, softened
6 large radishes, thinly sliced
3 ounces osetra caviar

Cover a medium sauté pan with a film of olive oil. Add leeks and sweat. Add chicken stock and cook until translucent. Add cream. Season with salt and pepper to taste. Remove from heat and keep warm.

In another pan, heat 2 tablespoons olive oil over medium heat. Season scallops with salt and pepper. When pan starts to smoke, place scallops in pan and sauté on both sides until golden, approximately 3 minutes per side.

Smear brioche with butter. Arrange radish slices on bread. Top with a dollop of caviar. Spoon creamed leeks onto 6 plates. Place scallop on top of leeks and lean crouton against scallop.

Yields 6 servings

Martin Hamann, Executive Chef
Fountain Restaurant, Philadelphia, PA

Pan Seared Diver Scallops with Herbed Goat Cheese

Upstares at Varalli

Known for:
pasta, pre-theater, and view

Open since:
1989

Most requested table:
#35

Menu:
Northern Italian with American and French influences

Chef:
William Carroll

Chef's training:
Culinary Institute of America

Chef's hobbies/ accomplishments:
fishing, family, wine

Chef's favorite ingredient:
fresh herbs, wild mushrooms, sea salt

Chef's favorite food:
French with Asian influence

2 cups balsamic vinegar
1 cup white wine
1 cup goat cheese
1 teaspoon EACH thyme, tarragon, chives
½ teaspoon black pepper
1 tablespoon water
Vegetable oil
8 diver scallops
1 cup baby arugula
1 large tomato, peeled, seeded, and diced

Combine balsamic vinegar and wine in a small saucepan. Cook over medium heat until liquid is reduced by half. Reserve.

Combine goat cheese, herbs, pepper, and water in a separate saucepan. Heat just until cheese is melted. Add more water if necessary to achieve a sauce-like consistency. Reserve.

Place a small amount of oil in a sauté pan over medium-high heat. Heat until oil is just smoking. Add scallops. Cook until each side is golden brown, about 1½ to 2 minutes per side.

Place a small amount of creamy goat cheese on each plate. Top with 2 scallops. Cover with arugula and tomatoes. Drizzle with balsamic reduction.

Yields 4 servings

William Carroll, Executive Chef
Upstares at Varalli, Philadelphia, PA

Seared Scallops with Basil-Dijon Vinaigrette

Dome Restaurant & Bar

Known for:
city sexy urban restaurant in a suburban setting

Year opened:
2000

Most requested table:
corner banquette overlooking outside terrace

Menu:
urban American cuisine

Chef:
Jeffrey Thiemann

Chef's training:
self taught chef with 20 years of experience

Chef's hobbies:
scuba diving and sky diving

Chef's favorite ingredient:
root vegetables

Chef's favorite food:
rack of lamb

1 bunch basil
¼ cup fresh stemmed spinach
3 medium cloves garlic
2 medium shallots
4 tablespoons Dijon mustard
3 tablespoons red wine vinegar
½ cup plus 2 tablespoons olive oil
Kosher salt and fresh ground pepper to taste
16 large (21/25) sea scallops
4 small Roma tomatoes, peeled, seeded, and diced

Combine first six ingredients in a blender or food processor and puree for 1 minute. Very slowly add ½ cup olive oil and puree for 1 minute more. Season with salt and pepper to taste. Hold at room temperature.

Heat a large sauté pan over medium-high heat. Add 2 tablespoons olive oil. When slightly smoking, add scallops and sear on each side to golden brown.

Place a small pool of vinaigrette in center of plates. Arrange scallops around the outer edge of vinaigrette. Garnish plates with diced tomatoes.

Yields 4 servings

Jeffrey Thiemann, Executive Chef
Dome Restaurant & Bar, Hockessin, DE

Tequila Shrimp with Spicy Polenta

GG's

Known for:
fresh seafood,
outstanding service

Year opened:
1993

Most requested table:
all window tables

Menu:
creative American

Chef:
Joseph Stewart

Chef's training:
The Restaurant School,
Philadelphia

**Chef's hobbies/
accomplishments:**
just celebrated 25 years of
marriage to Jane; three children
— Jamie (24), Joe Jr.
(12), and Jessica
(2)

Chef's favorite ingredient:
fresh seafood, game

Chef's favorite food:
any meal that is created
from the love of cooking

24 large shrimp, peeled and deveined
2 tablespoons olive oil
½ cup tequila
Juice and zest of 2 limes
1 tablespoon chopped garlic
1 tablespoon chopped fresh cilantro
½ cup chicken stock
2 tablespoons butter
Spicy Polenta (Recipe appears on page 236.)
Fresh greens
4 slices lime

Sauté shrimp in olive oil until just pink. Take pan away from flame and deglaze with tequila. Add lime juice, lime zest, garlic, and cilantro. Add chicken stock and reduce until shrimp are completely cooked. Add butter and swirl to incorporate.

   Place polenta on serving plates and top with shrimp and sauce. Garnish each plate with mixed greens and a fresh lime slice.

Yields 4 servings

**Joseph Stewart, Executive Chef
GG's Restaurant at the Doubletree Hotel
Mt. Laurel, NJ**

Santa Barbara Spot Shrimp Ceviche

Chef's Note

The Santa Barbara spot shrimp, *Pandalus platyceros*, also called California spot prawn, is named for the four bright white spots on its body located on both sides of the first and fifth shell segments. It is called *tarabaebi* in Japan, where it is a highly prized sushi bar item. Spot shrimp have pink to red shells with spots and sweet, firm flesh. Commonly found from Alaska to San Diego, spot prawns inhabit rocky areas. In Monterey, California, fishermen trap spot prawns all year. In southern California, trawlers fish for spot prawns during summer. If you find spot shrimp, look for the delicious roe under their belly shells. Use the roe as a garnish for the ceviche.

5 pounds whole Santa Barbara spot shrimp (substitute pink or white shrimp, not tiger shrimp)

1 cup fresh lime juice

4 teaspoons kosher salt

5 tablespoons rocoto puree

3 tablespoons Slow-Roasted Garlic Oil (Recipe appears on page 347.)

2 tablespoons water

½ red onion, peeled and shaved into paper-thin rings

½ cup fresh cilantro leaves

½ teaspoon finely chopped garlic

2 tablespoons extra virgin olive oil

2 tablespoons fresh lime juice

1 teaspoon kosher salt

¼ teaspoon freshly ground black pepper

Peel the shells from the bodies of the shrimp, leaving their heads and the last segment of tail shells attached. In a large bowl, combine the lime juice with 1 tablespoon of salt. Add the shrimp and toss to combine. Cover and refrigerate for 30 minutes.

In a small bowl, whisk together the rocoto puree, Slow-Roasted Garlic Oil, water, and remaining teaspoon of salt to obtain a thick but pourable sauce.

In a medium nonreactive (stainless steel or enameled) bowl, combine all remaining ingredients and lightly toss.

Drain the shrimp and arrange on a large platter in concentric circles with their heads facing inward. Drizzle the rocoto puree across the shrimp and serve. Serve the salad in a separate bowl to accompany the shrimp. Each guest takes a portion of shrimp and tops it with a little of the salad.

Yields 8 to 10 servings

Guillermo Pernot, Executive Chef/Owner
¡Pasión!, Philadelphia, PA

Oyster Rockefeller

Sansom Street Oyster House

Known for:
oysters and fresh seafood

Year opened:
1947

Menu:
fresh seafood

Chef:
Cary Neff

Chef's favorite ingredient:
seafood!

Chef's favorite food:
seafood!

1 pound fresh spinach, stems removed
8 tablespoons salted butter
½ cup chopped parsley
2 anchovy fillets
1 tablespoon Pernod
1½ teaspoons Worcestershire sauce
½ cup fresh breadcrumbs
3 drops Tabasco sauce
Salt and pepper
24 oysters, shucked with deep shell
1 cup fresh grated Parmesan cheese

Blanch spinach in boiling water for 2 to 3 minutes. Drain and chop. Heat butter in a sauté pan. Add spinach, parsley, and anchovies. Add Pernod, Worcestershire sauce, and breadcrumbs. Transfer mixture to a food processor and puree. Season to taste with Tabasco and salt and pepper.

Preheat oven to 450°. Arrange oysters in shells on a baking tray. Top oysters with spinach mixture. Top spinach with Parmesan cheese. Bake for 5 to 10 minutes until cheese melts and lightly browns.

Yields 6 servings

Cary Neff, Executive Chef
Sansom Street Oyster House, Philadelphia, PA

Blue Corn Fried Oysters with Poblano Crema

Culinary Quote

"Before I was born, my mother was in great agony of spirit and in a tragic situation. She could take no food except iced oysters and champagne. If people ask me when I began to dance, I reply, 'In my mother's womb, probably as a result of the oysters and champagne - the food of Aphrodite.'"

Isadora Duncan
American dancer

½ cup olive oil
5 EACH poblano peppers, red bell peppers, yellow bell peppers
Juice of 3 limes
10 cloves garlic, roasted
Salt
2 quarts mayonnaise
1 tablespoon malt vinegar
2 teaspoons sugar
2 tablespoons plus 1 gallon canola oil
36 36-count-size oysters
6 eggs
1 cup milk
2 cups flour
10 cups blue cornmeal

Smear olive oil over peppers and roast in oven until skins are blistered. Remove and place in a bowl. Cover with plastic wrap for a few minutes while cooling. Peel and deseed. Reserve.

Combine poblano peppers, lime juice, 3 cloves garlic, and a pinch of salt in a food processor and puree. Add 4 cups mayonnaise and pulse until combined. Reserve.

Combine red bell peppers, 7 cloves garlic, 1 teaspoon sugar, and a pinch of salt in food processor and puree. Add 4 cups mayonnaise and pulse until combined. Reserve.

Combine yellow bell peppers, malt vinegar, 1 teaspoon sugar, and a pinch of salt in food processor or a blender. With motor running, drizzle in 2 tablespoons canola oil.

Drain oysters. Combine eggs and milk and whip. Bread oysters by dredging in flour, then egg mixture, and then into cornmeal. (Keep one hand wet and one hand dry.)

Heat 1 gallon oil to 350°. Fry oysters, in batches if necessary, until golden brown, approximately 1½ minutes.

Serve oysters accompanied by poblano crema, roasted red pepper aïoli, and sweet yellow pepper coulis.

Yields 6 servings

Daniel Bethard, Executive Chef/Operating Partner
Iron Hill Brewery and Restaurant, West Chester, PA

Tuna Nuta

Anjou

Known for:
sushi

Year opened:
2002

Most requested table:
sushi bar

Menu:
French Asian cuisine

Chef:
Dung Nguyen

Chef's training:
11 years

**Chef's hobbies/
accomplishments:**
food competitions at Hyatt Hotel

Chef's favorite ingredient:
ponzu sauce

Chef's favorite food:
sushi and sashimi

1 tablespoon miso powder base
2 tablespoons Merin Mitsukan (sweet cooking wine)
1 egg yolk
2 teaspoons sugar
2 tablespoons sushi vinegar
1 tablespoon bonito soup base
1 teaspoon soy sauce
6 pieces fresh tuna, sliced sashimi-style
1 cucumber, thinly sliced, salted, and drained
Diced scallion
Sesame seeds
Fish roe, optional

Combine miso powder, Merin, egg yolk, and 1 teaspoon sugar. Reserve.

Combine remaining sugar, vinegar, soup base, and soy sauce. Dip tuna in vinegar dressing and arrange on a serving plate. Dip cucumber slices in vinegar dressing and place in a small pile next to tuna. Spread miso sauce on plate for dipping. Sprinkle with scallions and sesame seeds. Garnish with fish roe, if desired.

Yields 2 servings

**Dung Nguyen, Executive Chef
Anjou Restaurant, Philadelphia, PA**

Lenguado Handroll

4 thin, skinless flounder fillets, about ½ pound
¼ cup fresh lime juice
2 teaspoons kosher salt
2 tablespoons fresh cilantro leaves
1 firm but ripe Hass or Pinkerton avocado, peeled, trimmed to flatten edges, and cut into sticks
½ English cucumber, lightly peeled and cut into sticks
2 ripe plum tomatoes, seeded and cut into fillets
½ bunch fresh chives, cut into 3-inch lengths, plus 8 whole chives for tying
2 tablespoons wasabi powder
½ small habañero chile, seeded and finely chopped
½ cup Green Mango Escabeche (Recipe appears on page 229.)
¼ cup soy sauce, for dipping

Arrange the flounder fillets on a clean work surface. Cover with plastic wrap and pound lightly, using the side of a heavy chef's knife. Combine the lime juice and salt. Transfer flounder to a nonreactive (stainless steel or enameled) tray and sprinkle with the lime-and-salt mixture. Cover and refrigerate for about 30 minutes, or until the fillets are nearly opaque.

Remove the flounder from the marinade and place on a clean work surface, with the outer side of the fish down. Cut each flounder fillet into a 4-inch length, discarding the trimmings.

Cover the exposed inner side of the fish with a layer of cilantro leaves. Over the cilantro, on one short end of each of the flounder pieces, place one-quarter of the avocado, cucumber, tomato, and chives. Roll the fish up as tightly as possible around the vegetables, and repeat with remaining ingredients. Cover and refrigerate briefly to firm the rolls. Using a sharp knife, cut each roll crosswise into 2 pieces, and tie to secure with a chive. Place the rolls on a tray covered with plastic wrap or waxed paper, cover with a dampened paper towel, and refrigerate until ready to serve, up to 6 hours ahead.

In a small bowl, mix the wasabi and chile with enough water to make a thick, stiff paste. Form the paste into 4 marble-size balls and reserve. To serve the handrolls, place 2 pieces on each of 4 small serving plates. Garnish with a portion of the wasabi paste and a small mound of Green Mango Escabeche, and serve with a small dipping bowl of soy sauce.

Yields 4 servings

Reprinted with permission from *¡Ceviche!* Copyright © 2001 by Guillermo Pernot and Aliza Green, Photographs © 2001 by Steve Legato, published by Running Press Book Publishers, Philadelphia and London, http://www.runningpress.com.

Guillermo Pernot, Executive Chef/Owner
¡Pasión!, Philadelphia, PA

Japanese Smoked Eel and Pineapple Ceviche

Did you know?

Ceviche is a centuries old South and Central American cooking method. Fish and seafood are marinated in citrus, herbs, and spices; and the chemical process that happens when the citrus acid comes in contact with the fish is similar to what happens when the fish is cooked — the flesh becomes opaque and firm. It can be eaten as a first course or main dish.

2 9-ounce packages unagi
1 large golden pineapple
Pineapple-Chile Pequin Salsa (Recipe appears on page 338.)
8 skewers fresh sugar cane

Remove the unagi from the packages. Remove the skin and reserve both skin and meat. Preheat the oven to 300°. Arrange the unagi skin pieces in a single layer on a parchment-lined baking pan. Bake for 30 minutes or until browned and crispy. Remove from oven, drain on paper towels, and reserve.

Preheat a grill (preferably using hardwood charcoal) or a broiler. Cut a 1-inch slice off the top and bottom of the pineapple and stand it upright. Using a sharp knife, cut down the sides of the pineapple in long strips to remove the skin. Continue cutting until all the skin has been removed. Cut away any remaining "eyes," using the tip of a paring knife. Cut the pineapple lengthwise into ⅜-inch slabs. Discard the hard core.

Brush the pineapple with a little of the Pineapple-Chile Pequin Salsa and grill or broil until well browned, with crusty edges.

Cut the grilled pineapple into rectangles 2 inches long by 3 inches wide. Cut the unagi into pieces the same size as the pineapple. Make 2 stacks by layering 1 piece of pineapple on the bottom, topping with a layer of unagi, and then with a piece of pineapple. Repeat for a total of 4 layers of pineapple and 3 layers of unagi in each stack.

Secure the layers by piercing with 4 sugar cane spears, one in the center of each quadrant of the stack. Using a serrated knife, slice down the center of each stack to make 2 smaller rectangular stacks, each secured with 2 sugar cane skewers.

Place a stack on each of 4 serving plates. Drizzle with the remaining salsa, garnish each plate with a portion of the grilled unagi skin, and serve immediately.

Yields 4 servings

Guillermo Pernot, Executive Chef/Owner
¡Pasión!, Philadelphia, PA

Steamed Crawfish

Did you know?

— Crawfish are one of the staples of the Cajun diet. They are one of the most tasty, healthy, and inexpensive forms of seafood you can get.

— About 50,000 tons of crawfish are produced in the United States each year, with more than 50% cultured in ponds.

— Breaux Bridge, Louisiana, is known as the "Crawfish Capital of the World."

48 whole fresh crawfish (Frozen may be substituted.)
1 bottle (12 ounces) dark beer
4 cups water or fish stock
2 tablespoons chopped fresh garlic
2 tablespoons Old Bay Seasoning
1 teaspoon cayenne pepper
2 teaspoons kosher or sea salt
½ teaspoon black pepper

Clean crawfish and reserve.

Combine remaining ingredients in a large stockpot and bring to a boil. Add crawfish and cover. Boil for 6 to 10 minutes or until crawfish shells are bright red. Remove crawfish. Arrange on a serving platter and reserve.

Strain broth. Measure out 3 cups and return to stockpot. Reheat over medium heat. Taste and adjust seasonings. Pour broth over crawfish and serve.

Yields 4 servings

**Joe Brown, Chef/Owner
Melange Cafe, Cherry Hill, NJ**

Mussels in Tomato Saffron Broth

2 tablespoons olive oil

1 tablespoon chopped garlic

48 whitewater mussels, cleaned and debearded

¼ cup white wine

¼ cup clam juice

Pinch of red pepper flakes

1½ cups tomato sauce

½ cup chicken stock

Pinch of saffron

Heat olive oil in a large saucepan. Add garlic and cook until almost brown. Add mussels, white wine, clam juice, and pepper flakes. Cover and steam just until mussels open, about 3 minutes.

Add tomato sauce, chicken stock, and saffron. Cover and cook for an additional 2 minutes. Serve mussels in shallow bowls with tomato broth.

Yields 4 servings

Joseph Stewart, Executive Chef
GG's Restaurant at the Doubletree Hotel
Mt. Laurel, NJ

"The Captain's" Drunken Clams

Terrace at Greenhill

Known for:
al fresco dining

Year opened:
1970

Most requested table:
#24 or any table overlooking the golf course

Menu:
American comfort

Executive chef:
Daniel J. Dogan

Chef's training:
The Restaurant School; working abroad

Chef's hobbies/ accomplishments:
extreme sports, music, riding my Harley Davidson/father to Joseph David

Chef's favorite ingredient:
T.L.C.

Chef's favorite food:
M&M's

1½ cups Captain Morgan's Spiced Rum
2 cloves garlic, minced
2 pounds 1-inch hard-shell clams, well scrubbed
3 Roma tomatoes, diced
½ small red onion, diced
2 tablespoons minced fresh basil
3 tablespoons unsalted butter
2 teaspoons fresh lemon juice

In a large saucepan, combine rum and garlic and bring to a boil. Simmer for 1 to 2 minutes. Add clams. Cover and steam for 3 to 5 minutes or until they have all opened. Transfer clams with a slotted spoon to a large bowl and keep warm.

Strain cooking liquid into a bowl through a sieve lined with cheesecloth and return liquid to pan. Add tomatoes, onion, and basil and bring to a boil. Stir in butter and lemon juice. Divide clams among 4 bowls and pour sauce over. Enjoy!

Yields 4 servings

**Daniel Dogan, Executive Chef
Terrace at Greenhill, Wilmington, DE**

Balsamic Grilled Calves Liver with Sun-dried Apricot Vinaigrette

Rembrandt's

Known for:
being quaint and romantic

Year opened:
1983

Most requested table:
#30

Menu:
French and Italian

Chef:
Peter McAndrews

Chef's training:
Penn State University and Italian Culinary Institute

Chef's hobbies/accomplishments:
baking breads, wine

Chef's favorite ingredient:
fresh rosemary and extra virgin olive oils

Chef's favorite food:
artisan-made cheeses

2 tablespoons plus 1 cup balsamic vinegar
2 tablespoons plus 2 cups olive oil
1 teaspoon minced garlic
½ teaspoon salt
6 portions calves liver, 6 ounces each
¼ cup diced pancetta
1 cup sun-dried apricots
¼ cup Dijon mustard
1 tablespoon fresh thyme

Combine 2 tablespoons vinegar, 2 tablespoons oil, garlic, and salt. Cover livers with mixture and marinate in the refrigerator for 2 hours.

Brown pancetta in a skillet. Add apricots and remaining 1 cup of vinegar. Cook for 10 minutes. Gently stir in remaining ingredients and continue stirring until mixture reaches a dressing consistency.

Grill livers to desired doneness. Serve with apricot vinaigrette.

Chef's notes ... Fresh and light — good for summer.

Yields 6 servings

Peter McAndrews, Executive Chef
Rembrandt's, Philadelphia, PA

Grilled Mozzarella with Spiced Tomato Chutney

Paradigm

Known for:
peek-a-boo bathrooms

Year opened:
1998

Menu:
new American

Chef:
Chase Gerstenbacker

Chef's training:
graduated in 1995 from The Restaurant School in Philadelphia

Chef's hobbies/ accomplishments:
winner "Best Appetizer" in Philly Cooks competition

Chef's favorite ingredient:
changes daily

Chef's favorite food:
changes daily

½ cup diced red onion
1 cup diced yellow tomato
¾ cup diced red tomato
1 cup dark brown sugar, packed
1 tablespoon minced roasted garlic
1 tablespoon chopped ginger
¾ cup red wine vinegar
1 stick cinnamon
1 tablespoon red pepper flakes
1 teaspoon cumin
3 tablespoons cornstarch
6 lobes fresh Oveline mozzarella, cut in half lengthwise
½ pound prosciutto di Parma, thinly sliced
Baby lettuce
Herb-infused extra virgin olive oil to taste
Pinch of salt

Sauté onion until translucent. Add next nine ingredients and bring to a boil. Reduce heat and simmer for 5 minutes. Remove cinnamon stick. Dissolve cornstarch in some cool water to form a slurry. Add slurry to chutney and stir to thicken. Cool to room temperature.

Wrap each mozzarella half with 1 piece of prosciutto. Toss baby lettuce in herb oil with a pinch of salt and place in center of a serving plate. Grill mozzarella on a hot grill until cheese begins to ooze out. Place cheese around greens and top each cheese with a dollop of chutney.

Yields 6 servings

Chase Gerstenbacher, Executive Chef
Paradigm, Philadelphia, PA

Sautéed Mozzarella di Bufala

Stella Notte

Known for:
sparkling starry ceiling

Year opened:
2001

Most requested table:
table 5 in the alcove
by the window

Menu:
Italian seasonal cuisine with
many wood-oven specialties

Chef:
Aliza Green

Chef's training:
self taught

**Chef's hobbies/
accomplishments:**
author of three — soon to be
four — cookbooks

Chef's favorite ingredient:
fresh cranberry beans

Chef's favorite food:
wood-oven pizza Margherita

8 eggs
1½ cups flour
8 ounces grated Parmigiano-Reggiano cheese
½ cup chopped Italian parsley
¼ cup thinly sliced chives
Olive oil
1 large round mozzarella di bufala, cut into 6 ½-inch slices
  (Fresh mozzarella can be substituted.)
Fresh tomato basil sauce (Use your own favorite recipe.)

Preheat oven to 400°.

Whisk together eggs, flour, grated cheese, parsley, and chives to form a thick batter. Let rest at least 30 minutes.

Heat olive oil in a nonstick sauté pan over moderate heat. Dip mozzarella slices into batter, making sure to coat completely. Sauté cheese until browned on both sides.

Transfer to an ovenproof pan and bake for 5 minutes or until cheese is melted. Serve with tomato basil sauce.

Chef's note ...Mozzarella di bufala is made from the milk of water buffalos in southern Italy. Its tangy flavor and rich melt-in-you-mouth texture make this an exquisite appetizer.

Yields 6 servings

**Aliza Green, Chef/Partner
Stella Notte, Philadelphia, PA**

Criniti Appetizer

Criniti Ristorante Italiano

Known for:
feels like you are in Italy; consistency

Year opened:
1985

Menu:
Southern Italian

Chef:
Massimo Criniti

Chef's training:
family/Widener University

Chef's hobbies/ accomplishments:
motorcycling, cooking/ #1 South Philly restaurant

Chef's favorite ingredient:
basil — a must!!

Chef's favorite food:
pizza

1 clove garlic, chopped
¼ cup extra virgin olive oil
¼ teaspoon EACH salt and black pepper
½ cup chopped roasted peppers
8 to10 fresh mozzarella ciliegini balls
6 whole canned marinated artichokes, halved
6 kalamata olives (or any olive of your choice)
6 whole basil leaves

Combine garlic, oil, and salt and pepper in a bowl and mix. Add peppers and mozzarella. Mix and marinate for at least 1 hour.

Place artichokes around outside of a serving plate. Place an olive in the center of each artichoke. Place pepper and cheese mix in center of plate and drizzle remaining olive oil mixture around entire plate. Place a basil leaf on each artichoke. Refrigerate for 30 minutes. Serve cool and enjoy!!!!

Yields 2 servings

Massimo Criniti, Chef/Owner
Criniti Ristorante Italiano, South Philadelphia, PA

Deep Fried Spinachi Fritti with Red Capers

Joseph Poon Asian Fusion Restaurant

Known for:
Joe Poon!

Menu:
Asian fusion

Chef:
Joseph K.K. Poon

Chef's training:
B.S. in Nutrition; continuing education at CIA

Chef's hobbies/ accomplishments:
ping pong, testing recipes/ teaching and sharing

Chef's favorite food:
dim sum, pasta, Asian noodles

10 cups oil
1 bag spinach, cleaned and dried
½ teaspoon five-spice salt
½ teaspoon Indian spicy herb mix (spicy cumin and garlic)
1 tablespoon powdered Asiago cheese
1 tablespoon red capers
1 tablespoon chopped scallion
1 tablespoon sliced banana yellow pepper
Chinese parsley

Heat oil to 350° in a deep fryer or large pot. Add spinach leaves and fry for about 30 seconds until leaves turn transparent. Remove from oil and drain well on paper towel.

Spread leaves on serving plate. Sprinkle leaves with five-spice and Indian spicy herbs. Top with Asiago cheese, red capers, scallion, and banana pepper rings. Garnish with a piece of parsley.

Yields 2 servings

Joseph Poon, Chef/Nutritionist
Joseph Poon Asian Fusion Restaurant, Philadelphia, PA

Marinated Stuffed Portobello Mushrooms

Did you know?

Kennett Square, Pennsylvania, is considered the mushroom capital of world. Mushroom cultivation in the United States began in Kennett Square in 1896 when two local florists wanted to make more efficient use of their greenhouses by utilizing the area underneath the shelves used to grow ornamental plants. The town of Kennett Square celebrates their famous fungus in a big way. Since 1985, the Mushroom Festival has been an annual event. State Street, the main artery through the town, closes down for two days and festival goers enjoy a huge block party complete with food, music, antique cars, and family fun.

16 portobello mushroom caps, about 4½ to 6 inches in
   diameter, stems and gills removed
9 tablespoons soybean oil
3 tablespoons balsamic vinegar
Kosher salt and pepper to taste
1½ cups diced peeled carrots
1½ cups diced green squash
1½ cups diced yellow squash
5 ounces Truffle Oil Vinaigrette (Recipe appears on page 83.)
8 ounces goat cheese, cut into 16 slices

Place mushrooms in a bowl and gently toss with oil and balsamic vinegar. Lay mushrooms on a sheet pan, top sides down. Lightly season with salt and pepper. Grill for 1 minute on each side. Reserve.

Sauté carrots in a large skillet. Add squashes. Season with salt and pepper. Remove from heat and toss with truffle vinaigrette.

Preheat oven to 375°. Fill each cap with some squash mixture. Cover with 1 slice goat cheese. Place on a baking sheet and bake until hot. (Do not overcook as this will shrink the mushrooms and dry out the vegetables.) Serve immediately.

Yields 8 servings

Anthony G. Lucas, Executive Chef
Jeffrey Miller Catering, Lansdowne, PA

Salads

Field Greens with Goat Cheese and Walnut Vinaigrette 58

Roasted Peanut, Green Papaya, and Baby Green Salad 59

Romaine and Endive Salad with Blue Cheese Buttermilk Dressing 60

Red and Yellow Tomato Carpaccio 61

Solaris Chopped Vegetable Salad 62

Avocado Salad 63

White Salad with Blood Orange Champagne Vinaigrette 64

Portobello Napoleon 65

Roasted Mushroom and Golden Apple Salad 66

Grilled Asparagus, Amaranth, and Wild Watercress Salad 67

Potato Salad 68

Purple Potato Salad with Crispy Bacon 69

Spicy Texas Slaw 70

Pan Seared Swordfish with Heirloom Tomato Panzanella 71

Smoked Trout, Potatoes, and Pecans with Dill Dressing 72

Insalata di Tonno con Arugula 73

Pan Seared Foie Gras with Fingerling Potato Salad 74

Lamb Salad With Brown's Balsamic Dressing 75

Blue Crab-Petites Herbes Salad with Lobster Vinaigrette 76

Crab and Avocado Salad 77

Maine Lobster Asparagus Salad 78

Grilled Shrimp with Mango and Avocado Salads 79

Fried Oyster Salad with Oven Dried Tomatoes 80

Roasted Five-spice Duck Caesar Salad 81

Balsamic Vinaigrette 82 · Truffle Oil Vinaigrette 83

Soy Chili Vinaigrette 84 · Horseradish Dressing 85

Field Greens with Goat Cheese and Walnut Vinaigrette

Restaurant Passerelle

Known for:
Venetian chandeliers, beautiful gardens, and floating swans

Year opened:
1987

Most requested table:
any table in the restaurant

Menu:
New American with French influences

Chef:
Allan Vanesko

Chef's training:
graduated first in class at The Restaurant School, Philadelphia

Chef's hobbies/ accomplishments:
working!!

Chef's favorite ingredient:
salt

Chef's favorite food:
pizza

2 tablespoons plus 1 teaspoon red wine vinegar
2 tablespoons Dijon mustard
2 tablespoons honey
1 tablespoon chopped shallots
1 teaspoon chopped thyme
1 cup walnut oil
2 ounces olive oil
Salt and pepper to taste
1 pound mesclun greens (spring mix)
4 ounces goat cheese, crumbled
4 ounces walnut pieces
2 ounces dried cranberries

Process vinegar, mustard, honey, shallots, and thyme in a food processor or blender. While machine is running, slowly add walnut oil and olive oil. Season with salt and pepper.

Toss greens with vinaigrette. Garnish each salad with equal portions of goat cheese, walnuts, and dried cranberries.

Yields 8 to 12 servings

Allan Vanesko, Executive Chef
Restaurant Passerelle, Radnor, PA

Roasted Peanut, Green Papaya, and Baby Green Salad

Whisk Wisdom

The papaya is an exotic tropical fruit native to Central America and cultivated in semitropical zones around the world. Papaya trees grow from seed to a 20-foot, fruit-bearing tree in less than 18 months. It has a sweet-tart, musky flavor similar to apricots and ginger. The bright orange-pink flesh is soft, smooth, and juicy. Silvery-black papaya seeds are edible and add a peppery flavor to salad dressings and can be used as a substitute for capers. Unripe, green papaya is well-suited for slaws or cooked as a vegetable. Mature papayas are much more sweet and perfect for desserts. An enzyme in unripe papayas can be used as a tenderizer for meats. Historically, papaya tree leaves have been used to wrap and tenderize tough cuts of meat. Look for fruit that is bruise-free with smooth, unwrinkled skin. A ripe papaya will give slightly to palm pressure and have a sweet aroma. Avoid very soft fruit that smells fermented.

½ pound green papaya, shredded
⅙ pound carrots, shredded
4 ounces simple syrup
2 ounces fish sauce
2 ounces fresh lime juice
1 ounce tamarind juice
Juice of 2 tangerines
¼ cup chopped fresh Thai basil
⅛ head pineapple, shredded
¼ pound mixed baby greens (baby arugula, baby frisee,
    baby red oak leaf lettuce)
1 tablespoon crushed roasted peanuts

Place papaya and carrots in ice water for 5 minutes. Drain. Toss together with pineapple.

Whisk together simple syrup, fish sauce, lime juice, tamarind juice, tangerine juice, and chopped basil. Toss with papaya mixture.

Divide greens among 4 plates. Top with papaya mixture. Garnish with peanuts.

Yields 4 servings

Kiong Banh, Executive Chef
Twenty Manning, Philadelphia, PA

Romaine and Endive Salad with Blue Cheese Buttermilk Dressing

Manayunk Restaurant & Brewery

Known for:
on-premise brewery, ribs

Year opened:
1996

Most requested table:
outside deck

Menu:
eclectic American fare

Chef:
David Wiederholt

Chef's training:
Culinary Institute of America

Chef's hobbies/ accomplishments:
woodworking, fishing, playing with son

Chef's favorite ingredient:
salt

Chef's favorite food:
duck confit

2 cloves garlic
2 anchovy fillets
2 egg yolks
2 tablespoons whole grain mustard
2 lemons
1 cup extra virgin olive oil
1 cup blended oil
1 cup Stilton blue cheese
½ cup buttermilk
Salt and pepper
2 tablespoons good red wine vinegar
2 hearts romaine, washed and torn into pieces
2 heads Belgian endive, washed and torn into pieces
1 ripe Bartlett pear, sliced into bite-size pieces

Place garlic in a food processor and chop. Add anchovy and mix into a paste. Add egg yolks and whole grain mustard and process until a pale paste forms. Add juice of half of 1 lemon. Turn machine on and slowly begin to drizzle in extra virgin olive oil, then blended oil. Dressing will reach a mayonnaise consistency. (If dressing gets extremely thick, add some cold water to adjust.)

Crumble in ¾ cup blue cheese and process until very creamy. Thin dressing with buttermilk to the desired consistency. Season with salt and pepper and adjust acidity levels with remaining juice of lemons and red wine vinegar as desired. (Dressing should be a bit tart to cut through the creamy texture.)

Toss dressing with romaine, endive, and pears. Top with remaining ¼ cup crumbled blue cheese. Serve immediately.

Yields 4 servings

David Wiederholt, Executive Chef
Manayunk Restaurant & Brewery, Philadelphia, PA

Red and Yellow Tomato Carpaccio

D'Angelo's Summit Caterers

Known for:
Sunday brunch

Year opened:
1960

Menu:
banquet catering and weddings,
Sunday brunch

Chef:
Dan D'Angelo CEC AAC

Chef's training:
Culinary Institute of America

**Chef's hobbies/
accomplishments:**
music/member of the America
Academy of Chefs and
American Culinary Federation

Chef's favorite ingredient:
sweet basil and garlic

Chef's favorite food:
homemade pasta

1 ripe yellow tomato
1 ripe red tomato
4 ounces spring mix salad
¼ cup extra virgin olive oil
Kosher salt to taste
Cracked black pepper to taste
3 ounces sharp provolone cheese, shaved with a peeler
8 fresh basil leaves, stacked, rolled, and cut into thin
    ribbons
1 baguette, sliced

Slice tomatoes paper-thin. Overlap tomatoes on a serving plate, alternating colors, to form a circle.

Toss spring mix with some oil, salt, and pepper. Set in the middle of the circle of tomatoes. Drizzle tomatoes with remaining oil. Add shaved provolone, salt, and pepper. Top with basil.

Toast and season bread and serve with tomatoes.

Yields 4 servings

**Dan D'Angelo CEC AAC, Chef/Owner
D'Angelo's Summit Caterers, Roxborough, PA**

Solaris Chopped Vegetable Salad

Solaris Grille

Known for:
outdoor dining

Year opened:
1999

Most requested table:
table 50 outside

Menu:
American Grille

Chef:
John Anderson

Chef's training:
Culinary Institute of America;
training with Daniel Boulud
and Edward Brown

**Chef's hobbies/
accomplishments:**
launching rockets with my
son Danny and daughter Josie

Chef's favorite ingredient:
viagra — just kidding —
mushrooms

Chef's favorite food:
foie gras

1 cup chopped blanched asparagus
1 cup chopped cucumber
1 cup chopped sugar snap peas
1 avocado, peeled, seeded, and chopped
¼ cup chopped roasted red pepper
¼ cup chopped cooked bacon
¼ cup crumbled blue cheese
4 tablespoons olive oil
2 tablespoons balsamic vinegar
Salt and pepper to taste

Simply mix all ingredients together. Season to taste with salt and pepper. Portion evenly on 4 chilled plates and serve.

Chef's note ... This salad, one of our signature dishes, looks great when it is molded with a spoon in the center of the plate with mixed greens around it as garnish. It is also great with grilled chicken and/or shrimp.

Yields 4 servings

**John Anderson, Executive Chef
Solaris Grille, Chestnut Hill, PA**

Avocado Salad

Trust

Known for:
"blue eyes" — just kidding;
Circle of Trust bar

Year opened:
2002

Menu:
American bistro

Chef:
Matthew Spector

Chef's training:
work, work, work!

Chef's favorite ingredient:
heart and soul

Chef's favorite food:
Italian hoagie

2 avocados, skins removed, pitted, and diced
1 small jícama, diced
¼ bunch cilantro, chopped
Juice of 4 limes
Salt and pepper to taste

Combine first four ingredients together. Season to taste with salt and pepper. Serve alone or with Grilled Shrimp with Mango and Avocado Salads (Recipe appears on page 79.).

Yields 4 servings

Matthew Spector, Executive Chef
Trust, Philadelphia, PA

White Salad with Blood Orange Champagne Vinaigrette

Toto

Known for:
wonderfully painted French Impressionist murals on walls of the "Rotunda"

Year opened:
1985

Most requested table:
in the 16-seat "Cantina" room (wine cellar)

Menu:
contemporary Italian cuisine, presented elegantly

Chef:
Toto Schiavone

Chef's training:
3 decades of experience in the PA restaurant field

Chef's hobbies/ accomplishments:
beautiful gardening at home/the restaurant has won the high "DiRoNa" award many times

Chef's favorite ingredient:
basil

Chef's favorite food:
polenta or pasta & fagioli

1 large celeriac (celery root)
1 medium bulb fennel
1 medium parsnip
3 medium blood oranges
3 tablespoons extra virgin olive oil
1 tablespoon champagne vinegar
1 tablespoon chopped fresh chives
Salt and pepper to taste
1 bunch peppercress
Cracked black pepper, optional

Shave and julienne celeriac, fennel, and parsnip and place in a large mixing bowl. Juice 2 oranges (to yield approximately ¼ cup liquid) into a small saucepan. Cook over medium heat until liquid is reduced by half. Add oil, vinegar, chives, and salt and pepper to taste and blend well. Pour vinaigrette into mixing bowl and toss with vegetables until coated.

Mound salad onto 6 small plates or shape with a round mold on plates. Top loosely with peppercress and cracked black pepper, if desired. Section remaining orange and use as a garnish. Serve chilled.

Yields 6 servings

**Toto Schiavone, Chef/Owner
Toto, Philadelphia, PA**

Portobello Napoleon

Recommended Wine

2000 Pinot Noir Brancott "Reserve," Marlborough, New Zealand
A tangy, earthy, light-bodied red wine will perfectly echo the mushrooms and roasted peppers that dominate this dish. This New Zealand bottling is a rare red wine from a cool district famous for its white wines. It displays Pinot Noir's classic sour raspberry flavors and its haunting, woodsy perfume. Approximately $14

— Marnie Old
Old Wines LLC, Philadelphia

8 large portobello mushrooms, stems removed
¼ cup extra virgin olive oil
½ teaspoon salt
¼ teaspoon fresh ground black pepper
8 ounces cream cheese, softened
1 clove garlic, minced
1 shallot, finely chopped
1 tablespoon chopped fresh parsley
Salt and pepper to taste
2 red bell peppers
¾ cup balsamic vinegar
3 cups mixed baby greens
Balsamic Vinaigrette (Recipe appears on page 82.)

Preheat oven to 350°.

Place portobellos on a baking sheet, gill sides down. Brush with olive oil. Sprinkle with salt and pepper. Roast in oven for 10 minutes or until tender. Let cool.

In a medium bowl, combine cream cheese, garlic, shallot, and parsley and blend until smooth. Season to taste with salt and pepper. Reserve.

Under a broiler or over an open flame, char red peppers until blackened on all sides. Place in a paper bag and steam for 10 minutes. Peel off skin and discard seeds and stem. Cut peppers into strips.

In a small saucepan over medium-high heat, reduce balsamic vinegar by two-thirds or to a syrup consistency. Cool.

Place 4 mushrooms, gill sides up, on baking sheet. Spread each with one-quarter of cheese mixture. Divide roasted red peppers evenly over cheese mixture. Top each with a remaining mushroom, gill sides down. Warm in a 350° oven for approximately 6 minutes or until heated through.

Toss greens with balsamic vinaigrette and divide equally among 4 plates. Top each with a portobello napoleon and drizzle with balsamic syrup.

Chef's note … Can be made one day ahead. Keep covered in refrigerator.

Yields 4 servings

Robert Mansfield, Executive Chef
Porterhouse Steaks and Seafood, Cherry Hill, NJ

Roasted Mushroom and Golden Apple Salad

8 ounces grapeseed oil

1½ tablespoons sesame oil

4 tablespoons rice wine vinegar

1 clove garlic, minced

1 tablespoon grated fresh ginger

10 large shiitake mushroom caps, stems removed

2 bunches watercress, large stems removed

2 Golden Delicious apples, julienned

1 bunch chives, cut into 2-inch pieces

Preheat grill or oven to 350°.

Combine oils, vinegar, garlic, and ginger. Coat mushrooms with dressing. Reserve remaining dressing. Grill or roast mushrooms until tender. Slice mushrooms while warm as thinly as possible and add to dressing.

Toss watercress and apples with dressing. Garnish with chives.

Yields 4 to 6 servings

Bruce Cooper, Owner
Novelty, Philadelphia, PA

Grilled Asparagus, Amaranth, and Wild Watercress Salad

Chef's Notes

— This salad is a celebration of the arrival of our spring season. Lollo rosso or baby arugula can be substituted for the red amaranth or red orach.

— Banyuls vinegar is a slightly sweet style of sherry vinegar, aged for a minimum of 6 years in oak barrels from the south of France.

— Red amaranth has a hearty, tangy flavor and is even more nutritious than spinach or beet greens. This vegetable is very popular in Southern Asia where it is used in stir-frys and soups.

6 tablespoons canola oil
2 ounces spring onions, chopped
½ teaspoon minced garlic
3 tablespoons banyuls vinegar
½ tablespoon honey
½ teaspoon Dijon mustard
3 tablespoons extra virgin olive oil
½ cup wild watercress, washed and dried
15 jumbo asparagus, peeled and grilled
½ cup red amaranth, washed and dried
¼ ounce Parmigiano cheese, shaved
Kosher salt to taste
Fresh ground pepper to taste

Heat canola oil in sauté pan over medium heat. Add spring onions and sauté until tender. Add garlic and cook for 30 seconds. Remove from heat and cool.

Combine vinegar, honey, mustard, and spring onion mixture in a blender. Process until smooth. Add extra virgin olive oil in a steady stream to emulsify. Reserve.

Place watercress in center of a serving plate. Stack asparagus over watercress. Season red amaranth with some vinaigrette and place in center of asparagus. Garnish with cheese. Season with salt and pepper. Drizzle remaining vinaigrette around plate.

Yields 5 servings

Vince Alberici, Executive Chef
Marker Restaurant at Adam's Mark Hotel, Philadelphia, PA

Potato Salad

Chef's Note

— By using the new season crop, you have a thinner skinned potato; and by making this salad with the skin on, not only do you get a more colorful salad, you also preserve the nutritional value.

— Other herbs, such as mint, tarragon, and parsley, may be used in place of the basil.

— As well as being a traditional accompaniment at a cookout, it also works perfectly with hoagies, hamburgers, grilled meats and fish, as well as an addition to any buffet. I highly recommend making extra as it keeps well under refrigeration, and once made, it will be that much less heat and humidity in the house throughout the summer.

3 pounds red potatoes, well scrubbed
½ cup mayonnaise
½ cup milk
2 tablespoons cider vinegar
½ cup chopped fresh basil
Salt and pepper to taste

Cut potatoes into your favorite size dice. Put into a saucepan and cover with cold water. Add salt, bring to a rolling boil, and cook until fork tender.

While potatoes are cooking, place mayonnaise and milk into a nonreactive bowl and mix thoroughly. Add vinegar, herbs, and pepper and mix again. (This will allow the acid in the vinegar to acidulate the milk, causing it to thicken.)

As soon as potatoes are ready, drain off liquid, quickly rinse under cold water, and drain again. (The potatoes should still be warm.) Mix into dressing and adjust seasoning.

Yields 10 servings

**Philip Pinkney CEC, CCE, Director of Culinary Arts
The Restaurant School at Walnut Hill College
Philadelphia, PA**

Purple Potato Salad with Crispy Bacon

Albertson's Cooking School

Known for:
Philadelphia's longest standing cooking school for home cooks

Year opened:
1973

Menu:
easy multi-cultural recipes for home cooks

Chef:
Ann-Michelle Albertson

Chef's training:
La Varenne; Johnson & Wales University

Chef's hobbies/ accomplishments:
biking

Chef's favorite ingredient:
tomatoes

Chef's favorite food:
pizza

1½ pounds new potatoes
1½ pounds purple fingerling potatoes (If you cannot find, use an additional 1½ pounds new potatoes.)
6 to 8 slices bacon, cut into short slices crosswise (may use turkey bacon)
1 large Vidalia onion, minced
⅔ cup whole grain mustard
3 tablespoons cider vinegar
2 tablespoons sugar
Pinch of fine sea salt
Pepper to taste

Scrub potatoes and cook in boiling water until tender, about 15 to 20 minutes. Drain and peel while warm.

Meanwhile, fry bacon pieces until crisp and drain on paper towel. Mix together bacon, onion, mustard, vinegar, sugar, salt, and pepper. Slice or quarter potatoes. Add to bacon mixture.

Keep covered at room temperature several hours for flavors to develop.

Yields 8 servings

Ann-Michelle Albertson, Assistant Director
Albertson's Cooking School, Wynnewood, PA

Spicy Texas Slaw

Trax Restaurant & Cafe

Known for:
personalized service, BYOB

Year opened:
1998

Most requested table:
7 for two; #1 for larger parties

Menu:
tastefully American

Chef:
Steven Waxman

Chef's training:
extensive training beginning 1977

Chef's hobbies/ accomplishments:
working with youth and training, wine collection

Chef's favorite ingredient:
local produce and herbs in season

Chef's favorite food:
changes day to day

2 carrots
1 daikon
1 jicama
1 head cabbage
1 red onion
2 red bell peppers
1 small bunch scallions
3 jalapeños, seeded and chopped
1 bunch parsley, chopped
1 cup mayonnaise
¾ cup sirachi
½ cup rice vinegar
6 tablespoons honey
2 teaspoons Old Bay Seasoning
2 teaspoons salt

Using a mandolin, slice carrots, daikon, and jicama into strips. Place in a large mixing bowl.

On a Japanese mandolin, shred cabbage, onion, red peppers, and scallions and add to bowl. Toss in chopped jalapeños and parsley and combine well.

In a separate bowl, combine remaining ingredients, stirring until well blended. Add to vegetable mixture and toss until well coated.

Yields 8 servings

Steven Waxman, Chef/Owner
Trax Restaurant and Cafe, Ambler, PA

Pan Seared Swordfish with Heirloom Tomato Panzanella

Wild Tuna

Known for:
warm neighborhood feeling

Year opened:
2003

Menu:
fish/seafood

Chef:
Anthony Bonett

Chef's training:
The Restaurant School, Philadelphia; Four Seasons Hotel, Philadelphia

Chef's hobbies/ accomplishments:
wife and 5-year-old son Bruno

Chef's favorite ingredient:
shallot, avocado, butter, salt

Chef's favorite food:
good food

½ pound butter, softened
2 tablespoons Tabasco hot sauce
1 tablespoon minced chives
1 tablespoon minced parsley
1 tablespoon clarified butter
4 8-ounce pieces swordfish steaks, about 1-inch thick or more
Kosher salt and fresh ground pepper
2 teaspoons whole butter
½ lemon
3 medium heirloom tomatoes, cored and diced medium
½ loaf stale Italian long bread, diced
3 tablespoons good quality olive oil
2 tablespoons thinly sliced Thai basil
1 tablespoon red wine vinegar
1 small shallot, minced
¼ pound fresh spinach
1 small clove garlic, minced

Mix butter, Tabasco, chives, and parsley together. Roll into a log and chill well.

Preheat oven to 350°. Heat clarified butter in a heavy ovenproof pan over medium-high heat. Season swordfish on both sides with salt and pepper. Sauté fish on one side until browned, about 1 minute. Flip and add 2 teaspoons whole butter and a squeeze of lemon. Place pan in oven and cook for 4 to 6 minutes.

Meanwhile, mix tomatoes, bread, 2 tablespoons olive oil, basil, vinegar, shallot, salt, and pepper.

Lightly sauté spinach in remaining 1 tablespoon oil with garlic, salt, and pepper.

Divide tomato salad among 4 plates. Place fish on salad, then cover with spinach.

Cut Tabasco butter into 4 discs and top each plate with a disc.

Yields 4 servings

Anthony Bonett, Executive Chef
Wild Tuna, Wayne, PA

Smoked Trout, Potatoes, and Pecans with Dill Dressing

The Inn at Twin Linden

Known for:
elegant accommodations and superb breakfasts

Year opened:
1990

Most requested table:
near the fireplace

Menu:
American — fresh, seasonal dishes

Chef:
Donna Leahy

Chef's training:
self taught; former video producer, Temple University

Chef's hobbies/ accomplishments:
has written two cookbooks — *Morning Glories* (Rizzoli 1996) and *Recipe for a Country Inn* (Harper Collins 2002)

Chef's favorite ingredient:
mascarpone

Chef's favorite food:
French toast

6 large fingerling potatoes, ends trimmed

1 large egg

1 cup corn oil

3 tablespoons white wine vinegar

¼ cup sour cream

¼ cup chopped dill

4 ounces smoked trout (about 1 fillet), skin removed

2 heads Boston lettuce, leaves separated

½ cup pecans, toasted

Slice potatoes crosswise into ⅛-inch-thick pieces. Bring lightly salted water to a boil in a medium skillet. Add potatoes and simmer until just tender, about 3 to 4 minutes. Immediately drain and cool. Refrigerate until thoroughly chilled.

Process egg in a food processor until light in color. Gradually drizzle in corn oil, processing until well emulsified. Add vinegar, sour cream, and dill and process just to combine.

Crumble trout into a small bowl. Add potatoes. Toss with about half the dressing and set aside. In another bowl, toss lettuce with remaining dressing. Arrange half the lettuce in the centers of 6 chilled plates and top with half the trout mixture. Repeat to form another layer. Sprinkle with pecans and serve.

Chef's note ... The combination of flavors and textures and ease of preparation make this salad perfect for any occasion.

Yields 6 servings

Donna Leahy, Chef/Owner
The Inn at Twin Linden, Churchtown, PA

Insalata di Tonno con Arugula

Caffe Aldo Lamberti

Known for:
highest quality seafood/
progressive Italian cuisine

Year opened:
1987

Menu:
contemporary Italian using
prime ingredients

Chef:
William W. Fischer, C.E.C.

Chef's training:
graduated from Academy of
Culinary Arts in 1994 with high
honors; continued education at
Culinary Institute of America;
retired commercial fisherman

**Chef's hobbies/
accomplishments:**
striper fishing in Absecon/
awards, competitions, certified
Coast Guard caption for 100-ton
vessel

Chef's favorite food:
anything, as long as it's fresh

2 ounces extra virgin olive oil
1½ ounces lemon juice (or juice from 1 or 2 fresh lemons)
¾ teaspoon sea salt
⅛ teaspoon black pepper
10 ounces cooked and sliced potato wedges
8 to 10 ounces imported Italian tuna fish in olive oil,
    drained and flaked
3 vine ripe tomatoes, cut in eighths
1¼ cups French green beans, blanched
1 cup large pieces arugula, packed
¾ cup pitted olives (kalamata, Gaeta, or fleshy green Sicilian)
½ cup chopped iceberg lettuce
⅓ cup chopped red onions

Whisk together oil, lemon juice, salt, and pepper. Combine
remaining ingredients and toss together with dressing. Taste
and adjust seasoning as needed. Divide onto 8 plates for
appetizers or 4 plates as main course. Served with grilled
olive loaf or foccacia.

Yields 8 servings

**William W. Fischer, C.E.C., Executive Chef
Caffe Aldo Lamberti, Cherry Hill, NJ**

Pan Seared Foie Gras with Fingerling Potato Salad

Whisk Wisdom

Foie gras is the fattened liver of either duck or goose. Its rich meaty flavor and velvety texture has made it a sought-after delicacy for over 4,500 years. The Egyptians sort of invented foie gras when they discovered that ducks and geese have beautifully fattened livers just before they migrate. The Romans perfected the art of "gavage" or force-feeding geese. They force-fed their geese figs to obtain their foie gras, but today corn is more widely used. Traditionally, it can be cooked in a terrine and served cold. Over the last few decades, it has become popular to sear and serve foie gras hot.

½ pound fingerling potatoes
1 bunch thin asparagus
1½ cups sherry vinegar
2 tablespoons sugar
4 ounces foie gras, cut into 1-ounce pieces
Salt and pepper
2 tablespoons chopped chives
Horseradish Dressing (Recipe appears on page 85.)

Boil potatoes in salted water for 20 minutes or until tender. Let stand until cool. Slice to desired thickness. Reserve.

Blanch asparagus in salted water until al dente. Shock in ice water. Chop to desired size. Reserve.

Cook vinegar and sugar in a small saucepan over low heat until reduced to a syrup consistency. Reserve.

Season both sides of foie gras pieces with salt and pepper. Heat a sauté pan until very hot. Add foie gras and sear on both sides until dark brown and crispy. Place on a towel to absorb excess fat. Toss potatoes, asparagus, and chives with horseradish dressing. Add salt and pepper to taste.

Place salad in center of plates. Top with foie gras. Drizzle with sherry vinegar reduction.

Yields 4 servings

Alex Capasso, Executive Chef
Max's Fine Dining, Cinnaminson, NJ

Lamb Salad With Brown's Balsamic Dressing

Whisk Wisdom

It's important to select the right lamb chops. Look for a loin, rib, or sirloin chop. They should have light red, finely textured meat with smooth, white fat. Marbling is not too important, but the fat should be evenly distributed. Lamb chops should be grilled on a covered grill over a medium-high heat. Grill them to medium rare or medium or until they reach an internal temperature of 140˚. Let the meat rest a few minutes before you serve it.

¼ cup balsamic vinegar

1 teaspoon chopped fresh garlic

1 teaspoon fresh or ½ teaspoon dried oregano

½ cup extra virgin olive oil

Salt and pepper

16 baby lamb chops, about 2 to 3 ounces each

4 Idaho potatoes, cut into shoestrings

4 cups soy oil

Salt and pepper

1 pound mesclun or mixed greens, washed and dried

2 tomatoes, cut into eighths

1 cucumber, cut into 16 slices

Whisk together vinegar, garlic, and oregano. Gradually add oil, whisking until mixture emulsifies. Season to taste with salt and pepper. Refrigerate until ready to serve and up to 10 days.

Heat grill or grill pan to medium-high heat. Grill lamb chops approximately 2 minutes per side or until desired doneness. Reserve.

Heat oil in a deep fryer or heavy-bottomed pan to 350°. Add potatoes and fry to golden brown, about 4 minutes. Drain on paper towel. Season with salt and pepper and reserve.

Toss green with dressing. Divide among 4 plates. Cover greens with chops and shoestring fries. Garnish with tomatoes and cucumbers.

Yields 4 servings

Joe Brown, Chef/Owner
Melange Cafe, Cherry Hill, NJ

Blue Crab-Petites Herbes Salad with Lobster Vinaigrette

Recommended Wine

2001 Vouvray, Chateau de Montfort, Loire Valley, France
A tart, off-dry white wine will best suit both the fresh herb salad and the natural sweetness of the crabmeat. Made from Chenin Blanc grapes from France's Loire Valley, Vouvray will fit those needs perfectly. This wine's suggestion of sweetness, sharp acidity, and its vibrant Asian pear and pea shoot flavors will showcase the fresh ingredients without overpowering them. Approximately $12

— Marnie Old
Old Wines LLC, Philadelphia

¼ ounce Thai basil leaves

¼ ounce Israeli basil leaves, torn

¼ ounce mint leaves

¼ ounce chives, snipped

¼ ounce cilantro

¼ ounce chervil

¼ ounce Italian parsley, chiffonade

1 small leek, white part only, blanched, cut into ¼-inch strips

3 Jersey tomatoes (Heirlooms preferred), peeled, seeded, and diced

1 small cucumber, peeled, seeded, and diced

4 tablespoons extra virgin olive oil

Juice of 1 lemon plus 1 teaspoon lemon juice

8 ounces blue crab meat, picked for cartilage

Sea salt and fresh cracked pepper to taste

2 cups lobster stock

2 tablespoons canola oil

4 6-ounce portions wild rockfish fillets (also known as wild striped bass)

Combine first seven ingredients and refrigerate herb salad.

Combine leek, tomatoes, cucumber, 2 tablespoons olive oil, juice of 1 lemon, and 4 ounces crab meat. Season to taste with sea salt and cracked pepper. Mold into 12 quenelles (ovals) and refrigerate until ready to serve.

Heat lobster stock until reduced to 1 tablespoon. Combine with remaining 1 teaspoon lemon juice and 2 tablespoons olive oil. Season to taste with salt and pepper. Toss herb salad with remaining 4 ounces crabmeat. Coat with lobster vinaigrette.

Heat canola oil in a nonstick pan over medium heat. Score skin of fish. Season with sea salt and cracked pepper. Cook, flesh side down, for 2 minutes. Flip, weigh down fish, and cook for 2 more minutes.

Place 3 quenelles in the center of each plate. Top with 1 fillet, skin side up. Drizzle vinaigrette around plates. Top with crab-herb salad.

Yields 4 servings

Greg Salisbury, Owner
Rx, Philadelphia, PA

Crab and Avocado Salad

Whisk Wisdom

Avocados are extremely versatile. Taiwanese eat avocados with milk and sugar; Indonesians mix them with milk, coffee, and rum for a cold libation; and the Filipinos puree them with sugar and milk to make a dessert drink. Go beyond guacamole: avocados can be an important addition to breads, desserts, and entrees.

— Add avocado slices to fruit or salad plates.

— Serve avocado dip or guacamole with crudite instead of traditional ranch dressing.

— Spice up sandwiches with avocado wedges.

— Add diced avocados to omelets or frittatas.

— Make a creamy smoothie by adding an avocado.

— Spread mashed avocado instead of butter on wheat toast.

— Top soups and stews with diced avocados rather than sour cream.

3 ripe avocados, peeled and diced
3 plum tomatoes, skin and flesh only, diced
½ medium red onion, peeled and diced
4 ounces celery root, peeled and diced
¼ cup extra virgin olive oil
Juice of 1 lemon, fresh squeezed
2 tablespoons minced chives
1 tablespoon minced parsley
10 ounces jumbo lump crabmeat
Salt to taste
Coarse pepper to taste

Combine all ingredients except crab and salt and pepper. Stir until well mixed. Fold in crabmeat, taking care not to break up lumps. Season to taste with salt and pepper.
Serve with your favorite green salad and toast points.

Yields 4 to 6 servings

**Tracey A. Hopkins, Sr., Executive Chef
Museum Restaurant at the Philadelphia Museum of
Art, Philadelphia, PA**

Maine Lobster Asparagus Salad

3 quarts fish bouillon

2 fresh live Maine lobsters, 1¼ pounds each

2 heads Belgium endive, bottoms chopped, 12 leaves reserved

1 bunch arugula, cleaned, 12 leaves reserved

1 heaping tablespoon finely chopped red onion

½ cup extra virgin olive oil, divided

Juice of 1 lemon

Salt and pepper

6 stalks jumbo asparagus, peeled, blanched, and sliced on bias

1 seedless orange, segmented, juice reserved

Bring bouillon to a boil in a pot large enough to hold both lobsters. Add lobster and boil for 12 to 15 minutes. Remove meat from shells. Slice tail meat. Keep claw meat intact. Remove claw bone. Reserve halves of tails.

Toss lobster meat, arugula, a "pinch" of onion, 4 tablespoons olive oil, and half the lemon juice. Season with salt and pepper. Reserve.

Toss 1 tablespoon onion, chopped endive, asparagus, and orange segments with remaining olive oil and lemon and orange juices. Season with salt and pepper.

Center endive mix on plates. Fan 3 endive leaves across mix. Place tail side of shell against endive. Top with seasoned arugula mixture. Place lobster meat on tail, top with claw meat. Garnish with reserved arugula leaves and orange segments. Drizzle with remaining oil mixtures.

Yields 4 servings

William W. Fischer, C.E.C., Executive Chef
Caffe Aldo Lamberti, Cherry Hill, NJ

Grilled Shrimp with Mango and Avocado Salads

Chef's Notes

These simple salads require no cooking: great separately for a dramatic presentation or mix them together and scoop with tortilla chips. As with any recipe, feel free to experiment and have fun.

12 jumbo shrimp, peeled and deveined
Juice of 2 limes
Olive oil
2 ripe mangoes, peeled and diced
1 jalapeño pepper, minced
½ red bell pepper, diced
Juice of 1 orange
Splash of tequila
Salt and pepper to taste
Avocado Salad (Recipe appears on page 63.)

Marinate shrimp in lime juice and olive oil and reserve.

Combine next five ingredients and season to taste with salt and pepper.

Grill shrimp over medium heat.

Place a ring mold in center of one serving plate. Fill mold half way with one-quarter avocado salad. Top with one-quarter mango salad. Remove ring. Repeat with remaining plates and salads. Surround each salad with 3 shrimp.

Yields 4 servings

Matthew Spector, Executive Chef
Trust, Philadelphia, PA

Fried Oyster Salad with Oven Dried Tomatoes

Culinary Quote

"I never was much of an oyster eater, nor can I relish them 'in naturalibus' as some do, but require a quantity of sauces, lemons, cayenne peppers, bread and butter, and so forth, to render them palatable."

William Makepeace Thackeray
(1811-1863)

1 pint grape tomatoes
3 teaspoons olive oil
2 teaspoons chopped thyme leaves
Salt and pepper to taste
2 cups all-purpose flour
4 cups finely ground Metropolitan Bakery breadcrumbs
5 eggs
½ cup whole milk
24 freshly shucked oysters
3 cups vegetable oil
2 bunches watercress
Lemon Aïoli (Recipe appears on page 331.)
6 lemon wedges

Preheat oven to 180°. Place tomatoes on a parchment-lined sheet tray. Spray tomatoes with olive oil to coat. Season with thyme leaves and salt and pepper to taste. Place in oven until dry, about 1½ hours.

Place flour and breadcrumbs into two separate bowls. Place eggs and milk into a third bowl and whisk. Lightly season oysters with salt and pepper on both sides. Dredge oysters in flour, shaking off excess. Dip in egg mixture and then roll in breadcrumbs, pressing so oysters are well coated. Lay oysters on a wax paper-lined sheet tray and chill for 1 hour.

Heat oil in a heavy skillet. Fry oysters, a few at a time, until golden on both sides. Drain on paper towel.

Divide watercress between 6 plates. Arrange oysters evenly over watercress. Sprinkle several tomatoes on each plate. Drizzle lemon aïoli over salad and garnish with a lemon wedge.

Yields 6 servings

Daniel Grimes, Co-Chef/Co-Owner
Chlöe, Philadelphia, PA

Roasted Five-spice Duck Caesar Salad

Twenty Manning

Most requested table:
front window tables

Menu:
new American with an Asian flare

Chef:
Kiong Banh

Chef's training:
self taught

Chef's hobbies/ accomplishments:
cooking, shopping at the food markets in Chinatown

Chef's favorite food:
light, simple foods

1 Long Island duck, 4 pounds
6 ounces hoisin sauce
3 ounces lemon juice
2 tablespoons minced ginger
1 tablespoon oyster sauce
1 teaspoon five-spice powder
1 teaspoon sesame oil
8 tablespoons fresh lime juice
1 tablespoon honey
4 tablespoons water
4 tablespoons sugar
4 tablespoons fish sauce
1 clove garlic, chopped
½ pound napa cabbage leaves
⅓ cup Asian Thai basil
2 leaves red radicchio
Toasted sesame seeds

Remove duck innards and clean very well. Poke duck skin all over with a fork. Bring 1 quart of water to a boil. Pour boiling water over duck. (This allows duck to tighten up and shrink.) Combine next six ingredients. Use hands to coat duck with three-quarters of mixture. Reserve remaining seasoning mixture. Let duck dry on a cooling rack for about 2 hours.

Preheat oven to 400°. Roast duck for 45 minutes. Remove from oven. Combine 2 tablespoons lime juice and honey and brush onto breast with a pastry brush. Return duck to oven and roast for 20 more minutes. Remove from oven and let sit for 30 minutes. Debone and julienne duck meat. Combine with remaining seasoning mixture and mix well.

Whisk together remaining lime juice, water, sugar, fish sauce, and garlic. Toss cabbage, basil, and radicchio with dressing. Place on plates. Top with duck. Garnish with toasted sesame seeds.

Yields 4 to 6 servings

Kiong Banh, Executive Chef
Twenty Manning, Philadelphia, PA

Balsamic Vinaigrette

Porterhouse Steaks and Seafood

Known for:
prime steaks and seafood

Year opened:
2002

Most requested table:
any in front room

Menu:
fine dining steakhouse

Chef:
Robert Mansfield

Chef's training:
graduated with honors from The Restaurant School, Philadelphia

Chef's hobbies/ accomplishments:
collecting cookbooks, running/ prepared meals for Julia Child and President Carter and President Clinton

Chef's favorite ingredient:
truffles

Chef's favorite food:
Thai/Vietnamese

1 cup extra virgin olive oil
3 tablespoons balsamic vinegar
1 tablespoon Dijon mustard
½ teaspoon salt
⅛ teaspoon pepper

Whisk all ingredients together in a small bowl. Serve with Portobello Napoleon (Recipe appears on page 65.) or your favorite salad.

Yields approximately 1 cup

Robert Mansfield, Executive Chef
Porterhouse Steaks and Seafood, Cherry Hill, NJ

Truffle Oil Vinaigrette

7½ tablespoons truffle vinegar
2 tablespoons Dijon mustard
2 tablespoons minced shallots
¼ cup truffle oil
3 tablespoons soybean oil
Kosher salt and pepper to taste

Whisk together vinegar, mustard, and shallots. While whipping vigorously, drizzle in a steady stream of oil until all are combined and emulsified. Season to taste with salt and pepper.

Yields approximately 1 cup

Anthony G. Lucas, Executive Chef
Jeffrey Miller Catering, Lansdowne, PA

Soy Chili Vinaigrette

Whisk Wisdom

Sambals are to Indonesian cuisine what salsas are to Mexican cooking. These multi-purpose condiments — basically relishes made from chilis — are served at almost every meal throughout Indonesia, Malaysia, and southern India. There are many varieties of sambals. Oelek, the most common sambal, is made by chopping up fresh, red, very HOT chilis and grinding them to a paste. Use this to heat up your everyday cooking .

2 tablespoons soy sauce
2 tablespoons water
2 tablespoons rice wine vinegar
1 tablespoon sambal oelek chili paste
1 tablespoon sesame oil

Combine all ingredients and whisk until well blended.

Yields approximately ½ cup

Michael Yeamans, Executive Chef
Rouge, Philadelphia, PA

Horseradish Dressing

Did you know?

Horseradish, a member of the mustard family, is native to eastern Europe, and it may have originated in Asia, Germany, or the Mediterranean area. It has been used for so long that no one knows for sure when and where it originated. The ancient Greeks used it, so did the Jews in their exodus from Egypt in 1500 BC. It is one of the five bitter herbs of the Jewish Passover. It was originally used for medicinal purposes.

www.foodreference.com

1 shallot, chopped
1 clove garlic, chopped
1½ tablespoons Dijon mustard
3 tablespoons white wine vinegar
½ cup horseradish
2 egg yolks
4 sprigs fresh thyme
2½ cups blended oil
Salt and pepper

Place all ingredients in a blender except oil and salt and pepper. Puree. Continue to puree and slowly drizzle in oil. Add salt and pepper to taste. Pass through a fine strainer.

Yields approximately 3 cups

Alex Capasso, Executive Chef
Max's Fine Dining, Cinnaminson, NJ

Soups

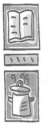

Artichoke and Crab Bisque

Bravo Bistro

Year opened:
1987

Most requested table:
outside al fresco

Menu:
upscale bistro

Chef:
Allan Vanesko

Chef's training:
graduated first in class at
The Restaurant School,
Philadelphia

**Chef's hobbies/
accomplishments:**
working!!

Chef's favorite ingredient:
salt

Chef's favorite food:
pizza

½ cup chopped onion
½ cup chopped fennel
½ cup chopped carrots
½ cup chopped celery
1 pound butter
2 cups flour
1 quart canned clam juice
1 cup canned artichoke hearts
½ cup sherry
½ cup heavy cream
1 pound backfin crabmeat
Salt and pepper

Sauté onion, fennel, carrot, and celery in butter until tender. Add flour and cook for 3 to 4 minutes, stirring occasionally. Whisk in clam juice. Simmer until slightly thickened. Add artichokes, sherry, and cream and simmer for 15 to 20 minutes.

Add half the crabmeat. Puree (in small batches to avoid burns) until smooth and strain back into pot.

Add remaining crabmeat and cook until heated through. Season with salt and pepper to taste.

Yields 8 to 12 servings

Allan Vanesko, Executive Chef
Bravo Bistro, Radnor, PA

Tomato and Roasted Garlic Bisque

Culinary Quote

"Do you have a kinder, more adaptable friend in the food world than soup? Who soothes you when you are ill? Who refuses to leave you when you are impoverished and stretches its resources to give a hearty sustenance and cheer? Who warms you in the winter and cools you in the summer? Yet who also is capable of doing honor to your richest table and impressing your most demanding guests? Soup does its loyal best, no matter what undignified conditions are imposed upon it. You don't catch steak hanging around when you're poor and sick, do you?"

Judith Martin
(Miss Manners)

1 cup diced onion
⅓ cup peeled, diced carrot
1 clove raw garlic, minced
2 28-ounce cans peeled whole plum tomatoes and juice
1¼ cups peeled, diced potato
4 cloves roasted garlic
1 cup heavy cream
½ cup half-and-half
Salt and fresh cracked black pepper

Sauté onions, carrots, and raw garlic over medium heat until soft. Add tomatoes, potatoes, and roasted garlic. Cook until potatoes are soft. Add heavy cream and half-and-half and allow to boil.

Remove from heat. Carefully puree with a hand blender. Season with salt and pepper to taste.

Yields 8 servings

Ryan McCauley, Head Chef
Christopher's, A Neighborhood Place, Wayne, PA

Butternut Squash Soup with Cinnamon Cream

Chef's Note

— I like to bypass roasting the squash, and instead, cook it all at once in the stockpot. The squash and potato will thicken the soup with their natural starch.

½ cup unsalted butter
1 small onion, minced
½ teaspoon grated nutmeg
3 2-pound butternut squash, peeled, seeded, and cubed
2 large potatoes, peeled and cubed
6 to 8 cups chicken stock
1 cup plus ¼ cup heavy cream
Salt and pepper to taste
2 teaspoons sour cream
½ teaspoon cinnamon

Melt butter in a stockpot. Sauté onion with nutmeg. Add squash and potato and sauté over high heat for 10 minutes. Add chicken stock and bring to a boil. Turn heat to medium and cook for 45 minutes.

Process soup in a blender, working in batches, or use a hand blender in pot until smooth. Bring soup back to a boil. Add 1 cup heavy cream and season with salt and pepper.

Combine remaining ¼ cup heavy cream, sour cream, and cinnamon.

Ladle soup into bowls. Spoon on cinnamon cream and serve.

Yields 8 servings

John Caiola, Chef/Owner
What's for Dinner ... It's a Mystery, Mount Laurel, NJ

Roasted Eggplant and Walnut Soup

Cresheim Cottage Cafe

Known for:
8th oldest building in Philadelphia

Year opened:
1997

Most requested table:
104 — in front of the large colonial fireplace

Menu:
seasonal American cuisine

Chef:
Craig Stewart

Chef's training:
Culinary Institute of America

2 medium eggplants
2 tablespoons olive oil
3 cloves garlic, minced
1 Spanish onion, diced
1 tablespoon chopped fresh rosemary
1 quart vegetable stock (Chicken stock can be substituted.)
1 cup walnuts
3 tablespoons butter
3 tablespoons all-purpose flour
Salt and pepper to taste

Preheat oven to 350°. Grease a baking sheet.

Cut stem end off eggplants and split lengthwise down the middle. Place eggplants, flesh sides down, on baking sheet and bake for approximately 15 to 30 minutes. Remove from oven and let cool to touch. Scrape out pulp from skins. Discard skins. Coarsely chop pulp and reserve.

Heat oil in a large stockpot over medium heat. Add garlic to hot oil and fry for approximately 30 seconds. Add onion and fry approximately 3 to 4 minutes until onions become transparent. Add rosemary and cook for 1 minute. Add eggplant and cook for 5 minutes. Add stock. Bring to a boil, reduce to a simmer, and cook for 20 minutes.

While stock is simmering, place walnuts in a food processor and pulse to a course grind. Remove and set aside.

Remove soup from heat. Strain vegetables through a fine strainer. Pour stock back into pot. Puree eggplant mixture in food processor and return to pot.

Melt butter in a small pot over low heat. When melted, add flour. Turn up heat and stir with a wooden spoon for 4 to 5 minutes. Remove from heat and let stand for about 5 minutes to cool. Whisk flour mixture into soup quickly to ensure no lumps. Turn heat to high under pot and bring back to a boil. Reduce to simmer and cook for 15 to 20 minutes. Add salt and pepper to taste. Stir in walnuts and your soup is done. Enjoy!

Yields 4 servings

Craig Stewart, Executive Chef
Cresheim Cottage Cafe, Philadelphia, PA

Cream of Portobello Soup

Anthony's Creative Italian Cuisine

Known for:
fresh fish

Year opened:
2000

Most requested table:
window seat

Menu:
Italian with creative flair

Chef:
John Pilarz

Chef's training:
Academy of Culinary Arts at Atlantic Community College

Chef's hobbies/ accomplishments:
wine tasting, playing golf

Chef's favorite ingredient:
roasted garlic, fresh oregano

Chef's favorite food:
fresh halibut or any fish

3 to 4 portobello mushrooms, stems removed
16 ounces chicken stock (Beef could also be used.)
16 ounces heavy cream
1 tablespoon chopped cilantro
½ cup butter
½ cup flour
Salt and pepper

Cut each cap into 1-inch-wide strips. Cut strips into thin pieces. Bring stock to a simmer in a stockpot. Add mushrooms and simmer for 20 minutes. Add heavy cream and cilantro and simmer for 20 more minutes.

Meanwhile, melt butter in a sauté pan. Gradually incorporate flour, whisking until a fully blended roux is formed. Slowly whisk roux into soup and simmer for 20 minutes.

Pour soup through a sieve, whisking to remove lumps. Add mushrooms back into soup. Season with salt and pepper to taste.

Yields 4 servings

John Pilarz, Chef/Owner
Anthony's Creative Italian Cuisine, Haddon Heights, NJ

Champagne Mushroom Soup

Whisk Wisdom

Country Gentleman is an heirloom corn. In the South it's known as shoe peg because of its peglike shape.

It has an irregular pattern of creamy white, slender kernels and a sweet, old fashioned corn flavor. Many consider it to be one of the finest roasting varieties available.

Master fishermen find it makes a superior corn bait.

If you can't find it fresh, it is available frozen.

2 tablespoons olive oil

2 onions, diced

1 parsnip, diced

2 carrots, diced

1 tablespoon kosher salt

½ tablespoon freshly ground black bepper

1 tablespoon finely minced garlic

1 red bell pepper, diced

1 tablespoon chopped fresh parsley

2 tablespoons chopped fresh basil

1 teaspoon chopped fresh thyme

1 cup sliced shiitake mushrooms

1 cup sliced oyster mushrooms

1 cup quartered button mushrooms

1 cup quartered crimini mushrooms

6 plum tomatoes, seeded and chopped

3 cups champagne

½ cup champagne vinegar

6 cups chicken stock

1 cup shoe peg corn

In a heavy bottom stockpot, heat olive oil over medium heat. Add onions, parsnip, and carrots and sweat for about 10 minutes. Season with salt and pepper, a little at a time, as you continue adding ingredients to the pot. Add garlic, bell pepper, and herbs and cook for 5 minutes. Add mushrooms and cook until they release juices, about 15 minutes. Add tomatoes, champagne, vinegar, and chicken stock. Bring to a boil. Reduce to a simmer and cook for 30 minutes.

Add corn just before serving so that it still has crunch. Taste and adjust seasoning with salt and pepper.

Yields 10 servings

Meg Votta, Executive Chef
Joseph Ambler Inn, North Wales, PA

Ulana's Mushroom Soup

Ulana's

Known for:
romantic wine cellar restaurant

Year opened:
1976

Most requested table:
by the fireplace

Menu:
romantic Continetal

Chef:
Ulana Mazurkevich

Chef's training:
self taught

4 dried wild mushrooms, optional

4 tablespoons butter

1 medium onion, diced

3 cups sliced cultivated mushrooms

1 cup chopped carrots

1 cup chopped celery

2 tablespoons flour

5 cups chicken stock or water

1 egg

1 tablespoon water

⅛ teaspoon salt

¼ cup sour cream

If using wild mushrooms, soak in water to cover overnight.

Drain soaking water, then simmer wild mushrooms in fresh water for 20 minutes. Chop and reserve mushrooms and soaking water.

Melt 2 tablespoons butter in a skillet. Add onion and sauté until limp and golden in color. Add cultivated mushrooms and sauté until dark. Remove mushrooms from skillet and reserve. Melt remaining butter in skillet. Add carrots and celery. Cook until celery is translucent but still firm. Sprinkle 1 tablespoon flour over carrots and celery. Stir to blend well.

Bring stock to boil in a soup pot. Add sautéed mushrooms (includes optional wild mushrooms and their liquid) and vegetables. Bring soup to a boil, then reduce to a simmer.

Meanwhile, combine remaining tablespoon flour, egg, water, and salt. Stir until ingredients are smooth and mixture is elastic but still fairly liquid. Drop slowly from the end of a spoon into soup. (Batter will form thin dumplings when cooked in soup.) Cook for 2 or 3 minutes. Stir in sour cream.

Chef's note … This soup was named the "Critic's Choice" by *The Philadelphia Inquirer*.

Yields 4 to 6 servings

Ulana Baluch Mazurkevich, Chef/Owner
Ulana's, Philadelphia, PA

Vegetable Chowder

Jack Kramer's Catering

Known for:
creative menus
with impeccable service

Year opened:
1970

Menu:
eclectic

Chef:
Jasper Reid

Chef's training:
self taught

Chef's hobbies/ accomplishments:
collector of music and movies

Chef's favorite ingredient:
garlic

Chef's favorite food:
Asian

1 small Spanish onion, chopped
3 ounces clarified butter or extra virgin olive oil
2 cloves garlic, minced
1 large zucchini, diced
1 large carrot, diced
1 medium celery stalk, diced
4 ounces mushrooms, sliced
¼ cup chopped fresh basil
1 tablespoon chopped fresh parsley
Salt and pepper
1 quart heavy cream
2 cups vegetable stock
½ cup shredded cheese

Sauté onion in butter or oil over medium heat until translucent. Add garlic and sauté for about 15 minutes. Add zucchini, carrot, celery, mushrooms, basil, parsley, and a pinch each of salt and pepper. Cook for approximately 30 minutes.

Add heavy cream and vegetable stock. Bring to a boil and simmer for 15 minutes. Add cheese and salt and pepper to taste.

Yields 8 servings

Jasper Reid, Executive Chef
Jack Kramer's Catering, Philadelphia, PA

Chicken Corn Soup

Amish Barn Restaurant

Known for:
courtyard patio, kitchen garden

Year opened:
1968

Most requested table:
window seats overlooking our garden and nearby farms

Menu:
Pennsylvania Dutch, American fare

Chef:
Pete Skiadas

Chef's training:
self taught

Chef's hobbies/ accomplishments:
gardening

Chef's favorite food:
crab cakes

1 pound chicken breast
4 chicken bouillon cubes
1 quart water
½ cup diced celery
½ cup diced onions
2 16-ounce cans creamed corn
1 16-ounce can whole kernel corn
1 10¾-ounce can cream of celery soup
1 teaspoon salt
½ teaspoon white pepper
½ teaspoon celery seed

Dough balls
1 cup flour
1 egg
½ teaspoon salt
¼ teaspoon baking powder

Place chicken breast, bouillon cubes, and water in a large pot. Bring to a boil and simmer for 1 hour or until chicken is done.

Remove chicken from pot, pick chicken from the bone, and discard bones and skins. Dice meat and return it to pot. Add remaining soup ingredients and simmer for approximately 15 minutes until celery and onions are tender.

Combine dough ball ingredients in a bowl and mix thoroughly. Sift mixture through your hand into the soup and continue to stir. Simmer for 15 minutes, stirring occasionally.

Yields approximately 3 quarts

Pete Skiadas, Chef/Owner
Amish Barn Restaurant, Bird-in-Hand, PA

Italian Wedding Soup

The Spaghetti Warehouse Restaurant

Known for:
More than $1 million in decorations and antiques added to our early 1900's warehouse, including an authentic trolley car, stained-glass windows, and original 19th and 20th century advertisements

Year opened:
1991

Most requested table:
our canopy brass bed that seats up to 10 people

Menu:
Italian, children friendly, and great for large groups

1 gallon water
1 ounce chicken base or bouillon
1 cup diced celery
1 cup shredded carrots
1 cup diced yellow onions
1 cup frozen chopped spinach
1 teaspoon chopped sweet basil
1 teaspoon chopped garlic
1 teaspoon black pepper
1 pound chicken breast meat, cooked and diced
1 pound tiny meatballs
1 cup angel hair pasta, broken long and cooked

Bring water to a boil in a large pot. Add chicken base and stir to dissolve. Add celery, carrots, onions, spinach, basil, garlic, and pepper. Simmer for 10 minutes. Add chicken, meatballs, and cooked pasta. Simmer until heated through.

Chef's notes ... If you can't find tiny meatballs at the grocery store, you can use larger meatballs cut into quarters. If you make your own meatball mix, bake in oven and drain ahead of time.

Yields 1 gallon

Christopher Beers, Manager
The Spaghetti Warehouse Restaurant, Philadelphia, PA

West Indian Pepper Pot Soup

Chef's Note

— To salt-cure pork and beef shoulder, choose meat that appears well-marbled. Then rub with coarse (kosher) salt and refrigerate for at least three days. Wash the salt off the meat before cooking as directed.

— Always wear rubber gloves when handling the fiery hot Scotch bonnet pepper, which is a close relative of the *habañero* pepper.

— The allspice *must* be freshly ground, or the flavor will be compromised.

— The only substitution you can make in this recipe and still achieve the intended flavor is to use collard greens instead of callaloo, the leafy top of the taro root. You can find both the taro root and callaloo at most Asian and West Indian markets.

¾ pound salt-cured pork shoulder, chopped
¾ pound salt-cured beef shoulder, chopped
2 tablespoons vegetable oil
1 medium white onion, chopped
4 garlic cloves, chopped
¼ Scotch bonnet pepper, seeded and chopped
1 bunch scallions, chopped, about 1 cup
1 pound taro root, peeled and cut into 2-inch by ¼-inch strips
4 quarts Chicken Stock (Recipe appears on page 316.)
2 bay leaves
1 teaspoon fresh chopped thyme
1 tablespoon freshly ground allspice
1 tablespoon freshly ground black pepper
1 pound callaloo or collard greens, rinsed and chopped
Salt

In a large stockpot, sauté the pork and beef in the oil over high heat for 10 minutes, until brown.

Add the onion, garlic, and Scotch bonnet pepper; sauté for 3 to 5 minutes, until the onion is translucent. Add the scallions and sauté for 3 minutes. Add the taro root and sauté for 3 to 5 minutes more, until translucent.

Add the Chicken Stock, bay leaves, thyme, allspice, and ground pepper. Bring to a boil over high heat. Reduce the heat to a medium and cook about 30 minutes, until the meat and taro root are tender.

Stir in the callaloo. Reduce the heat and simmer about 5 minutes, until wilted. Season with salt and pepper to taste. Serve in a tureen or divide among individual soup bowls.

Yields 10 servings

Walter Staib, Executive Chef/Proprietor
City Tavern, Philadelphia, PA

From the *City Tavern Cookbook*, ©1999 by Walter Staib
Running Press Book Publishers, Philadelphia and London, http://www.runningpress.com

Celeriac Soup with Smoked Salmon and Scallions

Whisk Wisdom

Celeriac, a variety of celery, is a knobby, brown root vegetable with an ivory-white interior. It tastes like parsley crossed with celery. Choose celeriac that are smallish and pale with no visible wrinkling or soft spots. Store in a plastic bag in the refrigerator for up to a week. Trim and peel just before using. A sprinkle of lemon juice will prevent discoloration. Celeriac can be boiled, braised, sautéed, baked, or cooked in soups. Raw celeriac can also be grated or shredded and used in salads.

4 large celery roots (celeriac), peeled and sliced
½ medium onion, peeled and sliced
½ cup white wine
½ quart heavy cream
Salt and pepper
½ cup thinly sliced smoked salmon
3 scallions, white and light green parts sliced

Coat a large pan with a film of olive oil. Add celery root and onion and sweat until soft. Add white wine and simmer until reduced by half. Add heavy cream and simmer for an additional 5 minutes. Puree soup. Season to taste with salt and pepper.

Divide salmon and scallions among 4 bowls. Pour soup on top and serve.

Yields 4 servings

Martin Hamann, Executive Chef
Fountain Restaurant, Philadelphia, PA

Summer Pepper Clam Chowder

Albertson's Cooking School

Known for:
Philadelphia's longest standing cooking school for home cooks

Year opened:
1973

Menu:
easy multi-cultural recipes for home cooks

Chef:
Charlottte-Ann Albertson

Chef's training:
La Varenne; Culinary Institute of America; American Embassy Kitchen in Switzerland

Chef's hobbies/ accomplishments:
swimming, hiking

Chef's favorite ingredient:
onion

Chef's favorite food:
calamari

1 tablespoon canola oil

1 large yellow onion, diced

1 red bell pepper, diced

1 green or purple bell pepper, diced

1 yellow or orange bell pepper, diced

4 large potatoes, diced

1 jalapeño chili, finely chopped

1 tablespoon chopped fresh thyme

½ tablespoon chopped garlic

½ teaspoon dried oregano

1 teaspoon ground black pepper

10 ounces canned diced tomatoes in juice

1 tablespoon tomato paste

2 quarts fish stock or bottled clam juice

1 cup dry sherry

3 pounds clams, chopped (or if small, left whole)

Salt

Hot sauce, optional

Heat canola oil in a heavy-bottomed saucepot. Add onion, bell peppers, potatoes, and chili and sauté until translucent. Add thyme, garlic, oregano, and black pepper and continue to cook until seasonings become aromatic.

Add diced tomatoes and tomato paste and cook until liquid is reduced by about half. Add stock or clam juice, sherry, and clams. Simmer for about 30 minutes. Season to taste with salt and a little hot sauce, if desired.

Yields 6 to 8 servings

Charlotte Ann Albertson, Owner/Director
Albertson's Cooking School, Wynnewood, PA

Smoked Sea Scallop Chowder

Whisk Wisdom

Smoked scallops are available at speciality stores. Surf the Web and you'll find lots of retailers who specialize in smoked seafood.

6 tablespoons butter
1 tablespoon minced garlic
1 tablespoon minced shallot
4 strips bacon, diced
3 potatoes, diced
1 onion, diced
2 carrots, peeled and diced
2 stalks celery, diced
¼ pound button mushrooms, sliced
3 ounces flour
1 quart heavy cream
2 cups clam or fish stock
½ pound smoked sea scallops
Salt and pepper to taste

Melt butter in a stockpot over medium-high heat. Add next eight ingredients and sauté for 4 to 5 minutes. Sift flour over ingredients and combine well. Add cream and stock and bring to a boil. Add scallops and reduce heat. Simmer for at least 10 minutes. Season with salt and pepper to taste.

Yields 4 servings

Chris Difilippo, Sous Chef
Mixmaster Café, Malvern, PA

Louisiana Creole Bouillabaisse

Chef's Notes

— Bouillabaisse is a fish soup, more like a whole meal by itself because of the variety of seafood in the dish. Bouillabaisse is a favorite in Marseilles, France. Marseilles is the seafood capital of Provence, France.

The soup was created by fisherman who wanted to make an inexpensive dish using their catch. Chefs and home cooks have created dramatically different variations by using different domestic ingredients to give the soup a new taste.

— Andouille sausage is a Cajun smoked sausage made from pork butt, shank, and a small amount of pork fat. The Cajuns usually season it with salt, pepper, and garlic and then slowly smoke it for 7 or 8 hours. Andouille sausage can be found in specialty markets, online stores, and butcher shops.

13 large ripe tomatoes, stems removed
Kosher salt
Olive oil
1 pound andouille sausage links
15 large raw shrimp, cleaned and butterflied, tails reserved
6 rock lobster tails, 3 ounces each, shells reserved
1 large bulb fennel, chopped
1 leek, well washed and chopped
1 red bell pepper, chopped
1 large onion, chopped
3 large cloves garlic, chopped
6 bay leaves
3 cups dry white wine
1 tablespoon EACH dried oregano and dried basil
2 tablespoons EACH red pepper flakes and cayenne pepper
1 teaspoon saffron threads
1½ cups boiling water
1 6-ounce can tomato paste
1 pound red snapper, skin and bones removed and cut into 1½-inch cubes
22 large scallops, muscle removed
12 little neck clams, well scrubbed
15 mussels, well cleaned and beards removed
1 day-old baguette, sliced ¼-inch thick
5 cloves garlic
1 red bell pepper, roasted, core and seeds removed
½ cup olive oil
Classic Rouille (Recipe appears on page 335.)
Chopped parsley

A day in advance, chop tomatoes and place tomatoes and their juices in a plastic container. Sprinkle with kosher salt. Cover and refrigerate for 24 hours. Then squeeze tomatoes with hands to break up tomatoes and squeeze out additional liquid. Reserve.
    Coat the bottom of a 5-gallon pot with olive oil and heat over medium-high heat

until gently smoking. Add sausage links and brown on all sides until firm to the touch. Remove from pan and reserve. Retain cooking fat in pot.

Add shrimp tails and lobster shells (reserve meat) and cook until they turn red in color. Add fennel, leek, red bell pepper, onion, garlic, and bay leaves. Stir. Fill pot with wine and bring to a gentle simmer. Stir in oregano, basil, and 1 tablespoon EACH red pepper flakes and cayenne pepper. Remove pot from heat. In a separate pan, dissolve saffron threads in boiling water and add to large pot along with 6½ cups water. Simmer for about 1½ hours until stock is lightly colored and flavors of the shrimp and lobster shells have been released. Strain through a fine sieve into a clean pot and discard solids.

Stir in chopped tomatoes and juice, tomato paste, remaining 1 tablespoon EACH red pepper flakes and cayenne pepper, and salt. Slice sausage links at an angle and add to pot. Add reserved shrimp and lobster meat and remaining seafood. Bring to a simmer. Cook for 10 to 15 minutes.

Meanwhile, preheat oven to 400°. Place bread slices on a lightly oiled baking sheet. Combine garlic and roasted pepper in a food processor and chop until small. While machine is running, drizzle in olive oil and blend until smooth. Spread mixture on bread slices and bake until golden.

Place 1 teaspoon rouille in each soup bowl. Ladle in some soup broth and stir to combine. Divide seafood and sausage among bowls. Garnish with chopped parsley and serve with croutons.

Yields 6 servings

Justin Sanders, Chef/Culinary Student

Soupe de Crabe Marseillaise

La Bonne Auberge

Year opened:
1972

Most requested table:
bay #1

Menu:
French cuisine

Chef:
G. Caronello

Chef's training:
French classic training

Chef's hobbies/ accomplishments:
flying, skiing

Chef's favorite ingredient:
fresh from the farm

Chef's favorite food:
simple food

1 head garlic, halved, skin on
½ cup olive oil
½ teaspoon dried thyme
1 bay leaf
12 jumbo soft-shell crabs (frozen during the winter, fresh and dressed during the season)
2 large onions, cut into small pieces
5 stalks celery, cut into small pieces
4 leeks (whites only), cut small
3 large ripe tomatoes, cut into small pieces
4 tablespoons tomato puree
½ cup Pernod
1 ounce saffron
5 leaves fresh basil
1 teaspoon fennel seeds
3 quarts water
1 orange, cut into 4 pieces
Salt and pepper to taste

Crush half of garlic head (skin on). In a very large pot, put garlic, olive oil, thyme, and bay leaf on high heat. Once oil is sizzling, add crabs. Stir until nice and brown. Add onion, celery, and leeks. Cook for 10 to 15 minutes.

Add tomatoes and tomato puree. Cook for 5 more minutes. Add Pernod, saffron, basil, and fennel. Remove remaining garlic from skins and chop. Add garlic, water, orange, and salt and pepper. Cook for 25 to 30 minutes.

Grind soup or puree in a food processor. Serve with garlic croutons and grated Parmesan cheese.

Yields 8 servings

G. Caronello, Chef/Owner
La Bonne Auberge, New Hope, PA

Carolyn's Crab Chile

Buffalo Bill's BBQ Restaurant

Known for:
unusual specialty platters and wings

Year opened:
1995

Menu:
BBQ

Chef:
J. Scott Jemison, aka Many Lives

Chef's training:
self taught

Chef's hobbies/ accomplishments:
martial arts/surviving death many times

Chef's favorite ingredient:
garlic, herbs, spices

Chef's favorite food:
filet mignon

4 large tomatoes, cored and diced
1 large onion, diced
1 small red bell pepper, diced
1 large yellow or orange bell pepper, diced
1 chili pepper, diced
½ cup The Greatest Grub Ever Garlic Parmesan Sauce
1 tablespoon chili powder
1 teaspoon dried red pepper flakes
1 teaspoon dried oregano
1 teaspoon salt
½ teaspoon dried cayenne pepper
½ teaspoon ground cumin
½ cup flour
2 cups strong chicken or fish stock
2 cups cooked black beans
1 pound crabmeat
Sour cream, optional

In a large pot, sauté tomatoes, onion, and all diced peppers in garlic parmesan sauce for 10 minutes. Stir vegetables often to avoid sticking. Stir in spices and continue to sauté for 5 minutes. Mix in flour. Slowly stir in chicken stock and simmer for 10 minutes, stirring often. Add beans and crabmeat. Serve with a garnish of sour cream, if desired.

Yields 6 to 8 servings

J. Scott Jemison, Chef/Owner
Buffalo Bill's BBQ Restaurant, Williamstown, NJ

Creative's Award-winning Black Bean Chile

Creative Cuisine Catering

Known for:
corporate catering and personalized service

Year opened:
1999

Chef:
Joseph Condrone

Chef's training:
The Restaurant School, Philadelphia

Chef's accomplishments:
married to a wonderful woman and have four wonderful children

Chef's favorite ingredient:
garlic (Isn't it everyone's?)

Chef's favorite foods:
pizza, a good steak

1 pound black beans
1 cup diced onions
1 cup diced green bell peppers
1 whole carrot
1 tablespoon EACH salt and black pepper
1 16-ounce can chili sauce
3 stalks celery, chopped
2 tablespoons chopped chipolte chili pepper
2 tablespoons chopped ancho chili pepper
¼ cup diced red bell pepper
¼ cup diced tomatoes
1 bunch cilantro, chopped
2 tablespoons garlic powder
3 tablespoons chili powder
2 tablespoons cumin
2 tablespoons fresh lime juice

Boil black beans in 1 quart water with onion, green pepper, carrot, salt, and black pepper. Cook until beans are slightly tender.

Add remaining ingredients and simmer for about 1 hour. Add more water, if needed. Remove carrot before serving.

Serve with your favorite toppings: sour cream, grated cheese, chopped green onions, minced cilantro, chopped jalapeños, diced avocado.

Yields 4 to 6 servings

Joseph Condrone, Chef/Owner
Creative Cuisine Catering, Philadelphia, PA

Lamb Stew with Lentils

Culinary Quote

"The smell and taste of things remain poised a long time, like souls, ready to remind us....."

Marcel Proust
French writer

3 pounds lamb, cut into cubes
Flour
2 tablespoons olive oil
2 cups chopped onion
2 cloves garlic, chopped
1 cup lentils
1 carrot, peeled and diced
1 cup crushed tomatoes
2 cups chicken stock
1 tablespoon minced lemon zest
Pinch of dried thyme
1 bay leaf

Dredge lamb in flour. Heat oil in a large stockpot over medium-high heat. Add lamb and brown on all sides.

Add onion and garlic and cook until transparent.

Add remaining ingredients and simmer until lentils and lamb are tender, about 1 hour or so.

Yields 4 to 6 servings

Joe Brown, Chef/Owner
Melange Cafe, Cherry Hill, NJ

Chilled Cucumber and Mint Soup

Culinary Quote

"It [soup] is to a dinner what a portico or a peristyle is to a building; that is to say, it is not only the first part of it, but it must be devised in such a manner as to set the tone of the whole banquet, in the same way as the overture of an opera announces the subject of the work."

Grimod de la Reynière
Considered the first great gastronomical critique and author of "l'Amanach Gourmand"

2 cups plain lowfat yogurt
1 European seedless cucumber, peeled
2 teaspoons cider vinegar
1 teaspoon extra virgin olive oil
2 tablespoons finely minced fresh mint leaves
½ teaspoon finely minced fresh dill
Salt and pepper to taste

Place a coffee filter inside a sieve and place that over a bowl. Scoop yogurt into filter, cover, and allow to drain in the refrigerator for at least 1 hour.

Roughly chop cucumber and place in a food processor. Pulse until cucumber is a smooth puree. Add drained yogurt curd (reserve the whey), vinegar, olive oil, mint, and dill and pulse until thoroughly blended. Adjust consistency with reserved whey. Season with salt and pepper. Refrigerate for at least 2 hours.

Serve in a chilled soup terrine or individual chilled soup bowls. Garnish with sprigs of mint and herbed croutons.

Chef's note … If fresh herbs are not available, dried herbs may be substituted.

Yields 4 servings

Philip Pinkney CEC, CCE, Director of Culinary Arts
The Restaurant School at Walnut Hill College, Philadelphia, PA

Crab Gazpacho

15 ripe Roma tomatoes
3 cloves garlic
½ medium red onion
1 medium cucumber
1 medium red pepper
1 celery stalk
2 jalapeño peppers, seeded
2 tablespoons chopped cilantro
2 cups tomato juice
¼ cup lime juice
¼ cup coarse breadcrumbs
2 tablespoons extra virgin olive oil
Salt and pepper
6 ounces jumbo lump crabmeat

Rough chop all vegetables and puree in a blender or food processor. (You may have to do this in batches.) Strain through a medium strainer or food mill. Add tomato juice, lime juice, and breadcrumbs. Puree with an immersion blender. Slowly drizzle in olive oil and blend in with immersion blender. Add salt and pepper to taste.

Garnish with crabmeat. (Cooked shrimp or lobster meat is an optional garnish.)

Yields 6 servings

Dominick Zirilli
Yardley Inn, Yardley, PA

Pastas and Risottos

Cavatelli Pasta

Max's

Known for:
romantic atmosphere

Year opened:
2002

Most requested table:
any table by the fireplace or in an
intimate room upstairs

Menu:
Italian/French

Chef:
Alex Capasso

Chef's training:
classically French trained/
Italian heritage

**Chef's hobbies/
accomplishments:**
spending time with family/
candidate for James Beard Rising
Star Chef Award

Chef's favorite food:
anything I don't have to cook
myself

3 pounds ricotta cheese
1 pound durum flour
1 tablespoon salt
1 teaspoon pepper
¼ cup extra virgin olive oil
4 to 5 eggs
⅓ pound mascarpone cheese
All-purpose flour, approximately ½ pound

Place 2 large spoonfuls ricotta cheese, durum flour, salt, and pepper in a 5-quart tabletop mixer with a dough hook attachment. Mix on lowest speed. Add olive oil and eggs. Spoon in remaining ricotta cheese and mascarpone a little at a time. (The dough will be sticky.) Divide into 6 pieces and wrap in plastic. Let rest for 30 minutes.

Cover work surface with some all-purpose flour. Work one-third of dough at a time. Divide and roll into 6 lengthwise pieces. Roll each piece into ropes ⅓-inch in diameter. Flour well and cut with knife into ⅓-inch pieces. Toss with flour. With a butter knife, form pasta by rolling knife edge across dough's surface; this will curl edges of dough. Place finished pasta on a floured tray. Continue with remaining dough.

Bring a pot of salted water to boil. Cook pasta 2 servings at a time. Pasta will be finished cooking when it floats to the top of pot. Keep cooked pasta warm until all pasta is cooked.

Serve alone, with sauce of choice, or with Rabbit Bolongnese (Recipe appears on page 215.).

Yields 6 servings

Alex Capasso, Executive Chef
Max's Fine Dining, Cinnaminson, NJ

Ricotta Gnocchi

Valentes

Known for:
homemade pasta and specialty ravioli, catering

Year opened:
2000

Most requested table:
take out

Menu:
Italian specialties available for takeout and catering

Chef:
Jason McMullen

Chef's training:
Academy Culinary Arts

Chef's hobbies/ accomplishments:
hockey, dining out/ opening my own pasta/catering company at age 24; winning Best of South Jersey in 2002 and 2003 for Pasta and Catering

Chef's favorite ingredient:
fresh herbs, roasted garlic

Chef's favorite food:
veal

2 cups sifted durum flour
1 pound ricotta cheese
3 eggs
½ cup grated locatelli cheese
1 tablespoon melted butter

Combine all ingredients and knead until dough is formed. (If too soft, add a little more flour.) Cover with a bowl and let stand for 1 hour.

Sprinkle flour on a work surface. Roll a ball of dough (about the size of a tennis ball) with both hands into a long rope about 1-inch thick. Repeat process until all dough is used. Cut ropes into 1-inch pieces and place on a cloth towel to dry.

Cook gnocchi in a large pot of boiling salted water. After they rise to top of pot, gently boil for 2 to 3 minutes. Remove from pot and drain. Toss gnocchi in your favorite sauce and serve.

Yields 4 to 6 servings

Jason McMullen, Chef/Owner
Valentes, Mt. Laurel, NJ

Shrimp Scampi

8 ounces pasta of your choice (Chef Carlo recommends capellini or another fast cooking, delicate pasta.)
4 tablespoons olive oil
10 large shrimp, peeled and deveined
4 ounces baby shrimp
Flour
2 tablespoons chopped garlic
½ cup diced tomatoes
½ cup white wine
½ cup clam juice
2 tablespoons chopped fresh basil
2 tablespoons chopped fresh parsley
2 tablespoons lemon juice
4 tablespoons butter
Salt and pepper to taste

Prepare pasta according to package instructions and reserve.

Meanwhile, heat a medium sauté pan and add olive oil. Dust shrimp in flour and sauté in olive oil. Add garlic and sauté until golden brown. Add tomatoes and all remaining ingredients, except butter and salt and pepper, and cook until liquid is reduced by one-third. Add butter and simmer until thickened. Season to taste with salt and pepper. Serve over pasta.

Yields 2 servings

**Carlo D'Alesio, Chef
Lamberti's Cucina, Wilmington, DE**

Garlic Shrimp and Pasta

Melange Cafe

Known for:
unique cuisine,
friendly atmosphere,
crabmeat cheese cake!

Year opened:
1995

Most requested table:
#17

Menu:
Italian and Louisiana fusion

Chef:
Joe Brown

Chef's training:
The Restaurant School;
cooking with mom

**Chef's hobbies/
accomplishments:**
playing basketball, boating,
coaching son's football team

Chef's favorite ingredient:
garlic

Chef's favorite food:
pasta

1 pound capellini (angel hair) pasta, fresh or dried
¼ cup extra virgin olive oil
24 large shrimp, peeled and deveined
½ cup chopped scallions
2 tablespoons chopped fresh garlic
2 tablespoons chopped fresh basil
2 tablespoons Joe's Cajun Seasoning (Recipe appears on page 348.) or your favorite Creole seasoning
¼ cup white wine
3 cups fish or chicken stock
4 tablespoons cold butter, cubed

Cook pasta according to package directions until al dente (or till it sticks on the wall). Strain and reserve.

Meanwhile, heat oil in a large skillet over medium-high heat. Add shrimp and sauté for 2 minutes per side. Add scallions, garlic, basil, and Joe's Cajun Seasoning. Stir to combine. Splash with wine and cook for about 2 minutes. Add stock and cook until liquid is reduced by half.

Whisk butter into skillet until sauce is thickened and glossy. Serve immediately over hot pasta.

Yields 4 servings

Joe Brown, Chef/Owner
Melange Cafe, Cherry Hill, NJ

Orecchiette alla Panorama

Recommended Wine

Verdicchio dei Castelli di Jesi Classico Brunori 2002
From the same family that has produced elegant Verdicchios and supple and juicy red wines for three generations, comes this clean and ripe white wine, endowed with good structure, nice acidity, and dry, slightly bitter finish. Mostly Verdicchio with only a splash of Trebbiano for acidity and body, this is a fruity and delicate wine whose nutty flavors and aromatic complexity will ideally complement risotto, pasta, and fish dishes.

— Moore Brothers Wine Company
Pennsauken, NJ, and
Wilmington, DE

2 tablespoons extra virgin olive oil
1 tablespoon chopped parsley
½ tablespoon chopped garlic
Pinch of red pepper flakes
1 cup 1-inch pieces calamari
1 cup rock shrimp, peeled and deveined
Salt and fresh black pepper
1½ quarts water
1 pound orecchiette pasta
½ cup grated Parmigiano cheese

Heat olive oil in a heavy-bottomed saucepot over medium heat. Add parsley, garlic, and pepper flakes and cook slightly. Add calamari, lower heat to a simmer, and cook for 5 minutes. Add rock shrimp and cook for 5 more minutes. Season with salt and black pepper to taste.

In a separate pot, bring water to a rolling boil. Add salt, then pasta, and boil for 7 to 8 minutes. Drain pasta and toss with sauce. Add Parmigiano cheese and serve.

Che's note … Simmering the calamari and rock shrimp will create a sauce.

Yields 6 servings

Rosario T. Romano Jr., Executive Chef
Ristorante Panorama, Philadelphia, PA

Seafood Marinara

Jack Kramer's Catering

Chef:
Jerome C. Seeney

Chef's training:
kitchen management and chef training with two national restaurant groups

Chef's hobbies/ accomplishments:
creative writing, video games, herb gardening

Chef's favorite ingredient:
garlic

Chef's favorite food:
sometimes Italian, sometimes Mexican, sometimes Thai

¼ cup olive oil
1 tablespoon chopped garlic
6 tablespoons canned chopped tomato
2 ounces white wine
6 tablespoons tomato sauce
½ tablespoon oregano
½ tablespoon crushed red pepper
1 teaspoon Old Bay Seasoning
½ teaspoon sugar
16 ounces mixed cooked seafood (can use frozen blend from supermarket)
1 pound pasta, cooked and drained

Heat oil in a medium sauté pan over medium heat. Add garlic and sauté until garlic starts to sizzle. Add chopped tomatoes and simmer. Deglaze pan with wine and cook until liquid is reduced by one-quarter. Add tomato sauce, oregano, crushed pepper, Old Bay, and sugar. Continue to simmer. Toss in seafood medley and heat thoroughly. Serve over pasta.

Yields 4 servings

Jerome C. Seeney, Chef
Jack Kramer's Catering, Philadelphia, PA

Ocean Sake Pasta

2 teaspoons canola oil
1 clove garlic, minced
8 ounces jumbo lump crabmeat, cleaned
8 ounces crayfish or lobster meat, cleaned, or smoked trout, or cooked shrimp
8 ounces bay scallops
¼ cup sake (any good brand)
2 tablespoons minced fresh ginger
6 ounces clam juice
2 cups chopped plum tomatoes, skin-on
¾ pound dry pasta (Penne is good.)
Salt and pepper to taste
½ cup chopped fresh cilantro

Heat oil in a medium sauté pan over medium heat. Add garlic and sauté for 30 seconds. Add seafood and sauté for 2 to 3 minutes longer. Add sake and let liquid reduce by half. Add ginger, then clam juice and tomatoes. Bring to a slight boil, reduce heat, and let simmer for 5 minutes.

Have pasta water boiling with a little olive oil and salt; cook pasta to desired doneness while making the sauce.

Season sauce with salt and pepper and add cilantro.

Drain pasta. Toss with seafood sauce. Serve immediately.

Yields 4 to 6 servings

Kevin Meeker, Chef/Owner
Philadelphia Fish & Company, Philadelphia, PA

Salmone Positano

¼ cup fresh basil

¼ cup Italian flat leaf parsley

8 ounces dry fettuccine

2 ounces plus 1 tablespoon extra virgin olive oil

2 cloves garlic, thinly sliced

1 shallot, finely diced, optional

2 cups diced fresh tomatoes

3 ounces white wine

1 cup clam broth

Juice of 1 lemon

Pepper to taste

7 ounces salmon fillet

Salt to taste

6 ounces jumbo lump crabmeat, shells removed

Wash basil and parsley thoroughly and dry in a small salad spinner or on a lint free towel. Roughly chop and reserve.

Cook pasta according to package instructions. Reserve.

Preheat grill. Meanwhile, place 2 ounces olive oil, garlic, and shallot in a pan and heat lightly, infusing the flavor into the oil but making sure oil does not smoke and garlic does not turn brown. Add tomatoes and cook slightly. Add wine and clam broth. Cook until liquid is reduced by half. Add lemon juice and pepper. Cook for 3 to 5 minutes. Add basil and parsley. Reserve and keep warm.

Coat salmon with remaining oil and season with salt and pepper. For each inch of thickness, grill salmon for 10 minutes (as a general rule). To be sure salmon is cooked through, slice open a piece. You should see only light pink flesh and no rawness.

Add crabmeat to sauce and heat lightly. Place cooked fettuccine on the side of each plate. Add grilled salmon. Cover pasta with sauce and Bon Appetite!

Yields 4 servings

**Leonardo Coppola, Chef
Lamberti's Cucina, Lawrenceville, NJ**

Pasta Papa Luke

Tony Luke's

Known for:
roast pork, chicken cutlets, and
steak sandwiches

Year opened:
1992

Most requested table:
any one you can get

Menu:
old-style Italian sandwiches

Co-owner:
Tony Luke, Jr.

Chef's training:
my father who was self taught

**Chef's hobbies/
accomplishments:**
acting, songwriting,
motorcyling, boxing

Chef's favorite ingredient:
garlic!

Chef's favorite food:
cheese steaks

4 tablespoons butter, softened
2 teaspoons canola or vegetable oil
4 small cloves garlic, chopped
8 ounces boneless, skinless chicken breasts, cut into bite-size
    cubes
½ cup fresh mushrooms
2 roasted red peppers, cut into strips (Jarred is fine.)
Salt and pepper to taste
½ cup white wine
½ cup heavy cream
2 handfuls grated Parmesan cheese
8 ounces penne pasta, cooked
Chopped fresh parsley

Heat butter and oil in a sauté pan over medium heat. Add
garlic and gently sauté. Add cubed chicken, mushrooms,
and roasted peppers. Season to taste with salt and pepper
and stir to combine. Sauté for 2 to 3 minutes or until
chicken is almost cooked through.

Pour in wine and simmer for 1 to 2 minutes. Stir in
heavy cream and simmer until hot. Add Parmesan cheese
and stir to combine. Remove from heat.

Serve over cooked penne pasta. Garnish with chopped
parsley.

Chef's note … I created this dish for my father, and it's
now his favorite.

Yields 2 servings

Tony Luke, Jr., Co-Owner
Tony Luke's Old Philly Style Sandwiches
Philadelphia, PA

Creole Chicken Alfredo

Recommended Wine

2001 Colosi Sicilia Rosso
A fruit bomb of a wine, but not a lightweight. The Nero d'Avola grape is well expressed here in this Sicilian wine that works well with the Creole sauce of this chicken dish. $9

2001 St Urbans-Hof Riesling
Here's another terrific wine from the lauded 2001 vintage. Crisp and fresh with minimal residual sugar and a lemony finish makes it a wine that can put out the heat and cool the palate. $12

— John McNulty
Corkscrewed, Cherry Hill, NJ

½ cup cooking oil
1 tablespoon oregano
1 tablespoon basil
½ tablespoon minced garlic
½ teaspoon salt
½ teaspoon pepper
½ pound boneless chicken breasts
½ red bell pepper, julienned
¼ Vidalia onion, julienned
3 shiitake mushrooms, julienned
½ teaspoon minced garlic
¼ cup white wine
2 cups cream
2 tablespoons chili sauce (siracha)
2 tablespoons butter
½ cup Cajun seasoning
¼ teaspoon salt
¼ teaspoon pepper
½ cup grated Parmesan cheese
½ pound linguini, cooked al dente

Mix first six ingredients together in a mixing bowl. Add chicken and marinate in refrigerator for 1 hour.

Grill on preheated grill until cooked through. Slice on an angle and reserve. (Keep warm.)

Sauté bell pepper, onion, mushrooms, and garlic until tender. Add white wine and deglaze pan. Add cream, chili sauce, butter, and Cajun seasoning. Bring to a simmer and cook until somewhat reduced and thickened. Season with salt and pepper. Add Parmesan cheese. Toss with linguini. Add chicken and combine.

Yields 4 servings

Brian Watson, Sous Chef
Bourbon Blue, Philadelphia, PA

Cavatappi Stir-Fry

Culinary Quote

"One of the very nicest things about life is the way we must regularly stop whatever it is we are doing and devote our attention to eating."

Luciano Pavarotti
"My Own Story"

1 pound cavatappi or penne pasta
2 tablespoons olive oil
1 pound boneless, skinless chicken breasts, sliced and cubed
1 pound London broil, sliced and cubed
½ cup sliced red onions
2 cups sliced roasted red peppers
½ cup crumbled Gorgonzola cheese
1 cup freshly grated Pecorino Romano cheese
1 quart heavy cream
½ cup unsalted butter
2 tablespoons chopped fresh parsley
Salt and pepper

Cook pasta in boiling salted water according to package directions.

Heat oil in a skillet. Add chicken and beef and sauté until browned. Add red onions and sauté until transparent. Add roasted peppers, cheeses, and heavy cream. Simmer for 5 minutes. Add butter and parsley. Season to taste with salt and pepper. Toss with pasta and serve.

Yields 4 servings

Thommy Geneviva, Executive Chef
Thommy G's Restaurant, Burlington, NJ

Penne Italiano

Recommended Wine

1996 Pandofelli Castel del Monte Special Reserve
Made from the obscure Uva di Troia grape, this wine has some bottle age and exhibits plenty of ripe berry flavors and firm tannins that work sublimely with the sausage and broccoli rabe in this dish. $12

— John McNulty
Corkscrewed, Cherry Hill, NJ

4 ounces penne pasta

2 ounces olive oil

4 ounces ground fresh sausage

1 cup chicken stock (I like College Inn.)

4 tablespoons butter

8 sun-dried tomatoes, halved

1 bunch broccoli rabe, cut into 2-inch pieces

Salt and pepper to taste

Grated Parmesan cheese, optional

Cook penne al dente according to package instructions. Drain and reserve.

Heat oil in a large sauté pan. Add ground sausage and cook until no pink is left in meat. Drain off excess fat. Add chicken stock, butter, and sun-dried tomatoes. When butter is melted, add broccoli rabe. Cover and cook for approximately 3 minutes until rabe is wilted. Fold in penne pasta. Toss until well blended. Season with salt and pepper. Serve with grated cheese, if desired.

Yields 2 servings

John Pilarz, Chef/Owner
Anthony's Creative Italian Cuisine, Haddon Heights, NJ

Pappardelle Trastevere

Chef's Notes

This dish, made with a red meat sauce, dried porcini mushrooms, and wide, flat pasta called pappardelle, was inspired by the Trastevere district within Rome, Italy. During the ancient Roman period, Trastevere was a green neighborhood belonging to noble families, including that of Julius Caesar. Cleopatra is thought to have lived here. Today, the area is well known for its spirited inhabitants, culinary specialities, and the stunning Piazza di Santa Maria.

¼ cup olive oil

1 pound ground beef

6 ounces salt pork, chopped

¼ cup chopped onions

Salt and pepper to taste

8 ounces white wine

2 28-ounce cans peeled tomatoes

1 small whole carrot

1 stalk celery

¾ cup dry porcini mushrooms, soaked in 1 cup warm water

½ cup butter

½ cup light cream

1½ pounds Serverino's fresh pappardelle pasta

3 ounces grated Parmesan cheese

Heat oil in a medium saucepan over medium heat. Add beef, salt pork, and onions. Cook slowly. Season with salt and pepper. Add white wine and cook until liquid evaporates. Add tomatoes, carrot, and celery. Cook covered for 1½ hours.

Add porcini mushrooms and ¼ cup of soaking water. Cook for 30 minutes more. Remove carrot and celery. Add butter and light cream and heat through.

Boil pasta in salted water for 6 minutes. Drain and toss with sauce. Garnish with Parmesan cheese.

Yields 4 to 6 servings

Anna Maria Severino, Co-Owner
Severino Pasta Manufacturing Company, Westmont, NJ

Rotelli With Curried Mushroom Ragoût

Recommended Wine

Red or white works here.

1999 Rene Lequin Colin Santenay Vielles Vignes
An earthy yet full flavored mouthful of Pinot Noir. This wine sings with anything containing mushrooms. $17

2000 Domaine Daniel Pollier, Sain Veran
The rich earthiness of this Chardonnay captures both the flavors of the curry and the mushrooms. $10

— John McNulty
Corkscrewed, Cherry Hill, NJ

3 tablespoons clarified butter
1 tablespoon finely chopped garlic
1 yellow onion, chopped
1 pound fresh portobello mushrooms, stems removed, cut into fourths
½ pound oyster mushrooms, sliced in half
2 tablespoons curry powder
1 cup heavy cream
½ cup half-and-half
⅓ cup Riesling wine
2 tablespoons sliced into thin ribbons fresh basil
¼ cup chopped cashews
¼ cup golden raisins
Salt and white pepper to taste
1 pound rotelli pasta, cooked al dente

Place clarified butter in a large saucepan over medium heat. Add garlic and onion and sauté for 2 to 3 minutes. Add mushrooms and curry powder and sauté for 7 to 10 minutes more. Stir in cream and half-and-half. Add all remaining ingredients, except pasta, and cook for about 5 minutes.

Add pasta to saucepan and cook until heated through. Adjust seasonings with salt and pepper. Divide pasta and sauce among individual bowls.

Yields 4 to 6 servings

Jim Coleman, Executive Chef
Normandy Farm, Blue Bell, PA

Macaroni and Cheese with Lobster and Sage

Chef's Notes

To make lobster stock, place lobster in a pot not much bigger than the lobster. Add enough water to just cover the lobster. Cook and remove lobster. Save cooking water. Let lobster cool, then remove meat from shells. Wash meat and cut into cubes. Add shells back to cooking water and cook to reduce liquid. Add celery, carrots, cracked pepper, bay leaf, and parsley and make like you would any other stock. Allow to cook for 2 hours. Strain the liquid and return to pot. Cook until liquid reduces to 1 cup. Use this to flavor the cheese sauce.

1 lobster, 1¼ pounds

1 pound elbow macaroni

1¼ pounds orange Cooper sharp Cheddar cheese, cubed

1 cup half-and-half

¼ teaspoon nutmeg

¼ teaspoon cayenne pepper

1 cup diced celery

1 cup diced onion

½ cup white wine

2 tablespoons fresh chopped sage

Salt and pepper to taste

½ cup chopped scallion

Steam or boil lobster. Allow to cool. Remove all meat from shell plus the coral and eggs. Cut lobster meat into good-size cubes. (If you want to make a lobster stock, see sidebar for optional stock recipe.)

Cook macaroni in salted water.

Heat cheese and half-and-half in a double boiler. Add nutmeg and cayenne pepper. Let cheese melt. In a separate pan, sweat celery and onion in white wine. (The celery should stay a little crunchy.) Add celery and onion to cheese mixture. If needed, thin sauce with a little additional half-and-half or optional concentrated lobster stock.

Add macaroni and lobster to cheese sauce. Add sage and warm through. Add salt and pepper to taste. Top with scallion.

Yields 4 to 6 servings

Steven Poses, Owner/Chef
Frog Commissary Catering, Philadelphia, PA

Risotto Bianco E Nero

Chef's Notes

— An excellent red wine that may be paired with this dish is Merlot.

— Parmigiano cheese is recommended for this dish, but any other grated cheese can be substituted.

4 tablespoons butter
1 small onion, finely chopped
4 ounces Italian pancetta or bacon
5 ounces sun-dried prunes and apricots
½ cup red wine
12 ounces Arborio Italian rice
3 cups chicken or vegetable stock
Salt and pepper to taste
Parmigiano grated cheese

Preheat oven to 450°.

Melt butter in an ovenproof sauté pan over medium-high heat. Add onion and pancetta and cook for 1 minute. Add prunes and apricots and stir once. Add wine and reduce heat. Add rice and stir for 1 minute. Add stock and salt and pepper. Place in oven and bake for 30 minutes. Sprinkle with Parmigiano cheese and serve hot.

Yields 4 servings

Franco Parmisciano, Chef
Lamberti's Cucina, Philadelphia, PA

Seafood Saffron Risotto

Whisk Wisdom

Saffron is the yellow-orange stigmas from purple crocus flowers. Each flower produces three stigmas, which are hand-picked from the blossom, dried, and permitted to ferment slightly. It takes an experienced picker about 12 days to harvest the stigmas from 80,000 flowers that make up a pound of saffron. This labor-intensive process makes it the world's most expensive spice. By the time saffron gets to retail stores, its cost is $600 to $2000 per pound. Happily, a little bit goes a long way, and $10 worth of saffron can contribute to a number of dishes.

2 ounces garlic, chopped
2 ounces shallots, chopped
1 cup Arborio rice
1 quart seafood stock (Clam juice can be substituted, if necessary.)
Pinch of saffron
¼ cup heavy cream

Sauté garlic and shallots in a large sauté pan until translucent. Do not overcook. Stir in Arborio rice and bring it up to temperature. Add saffron, then slowly add stock, stirring constantly. When desired consistency is almost achieved, add heavy cream and stir until combined and heated through.

Yields 2 servings

Manlon Randolph, Chef
Pinziminio Trattoria, Cherry Hill, NJ

Shellfish Risotto

Recommended Wine

Collio Ronco Della Chiesa Borgo del Tiglio 2000

Nicola Manferrari is a bio-dynamic farmer in Collio in Northeast Italy. With about 20 acres of vines, he vinifies each plot separately to preserve each vineyard's individual character. This is old vine Tocai, the classic grape of Friuli. Very rich, with a plush mouthfeel balanced by vibrant acidity.

Condrieu Les Terrasses de l'Empire Domaine Georges Vernay 2001

Georges Vernay's unrelenting efforts in the Northern Rhône appellation of Condrieu is legendary. Almost single-handedly, he resuscitated this ancient town, brought the world's attention to the local grape, Viognier, and inspired wine-makers around the world with his vision. In 1997 he passed the baton to his daughter Christine and her husband Paul Amsellem. The subtle mineral scents in the wine come from the hard granite soil of the appellation–the structure of the wine from impeccable farming, low yields in the vineyard, and careful winemaking.

— Moore Brothers Wine Company Pennsauken, NJ, and Wilmington, DE

¼ cup olive oil

2 tablespoons minced garlic

3 cups Arborio rice

5 cups fumet (fish stock)

Salt and pepper to taste

½ cup butter

½ cup mascarpone cheese

2 lobster tails, cooked and meat removed

1 pound jumbo lump crabmeat

2 tablespoons grated Parmesan cheese

Heat olive oil in a large saucepan on high. Add garlic. Add Arborio rice and stir with a wooden spoon for 2 minutes.

Bring fumet to a boil. Using a ladle, slowly and carefully add fumet to rice, stirring constantly. Continue stirring for 8 minutes until all liquid is absorbed. Season with salt and pepper. Stir in butter and mascarpone cheese.

Add lobster meat to pan. Carefully add crabmeat and cook until just warmed through. Serve topped with Parmesan cheese.

Yields 4 servings

David Boyle, Executive Chef
Davio's Northern Italian Steakhouse, Philadelphia, PA

Pumpkin Risotto with Scallops

Recommended Wine

2001 Pepi Chardonnay, Napa Valley, CA
This rich risotto will be best suited by a dry, full-textured white wine. Pepi's unusual California Chardonnay does not have an overlay of oak barrel flavor, allowing the grape's soft, natural flavors of baked apple and almond shine through. Paired together, the subtle richness of both the wine and the dish will harmonize beautifully. Approximately $14

— Marnie Old
Old Wines LLC, Philadelphia

1 cup blended oil
2 or 3 shallots, finely chopped
1 pound unsalted butter
2 pounds Arborio rice
2½ cups white wine
3 quarts plus 4 ounces hot chicken stock
Salt to taste
1 small pumpkin
3 ounces roasted pinenuts
1 cup whipped cream
36 10-20 size dry scallops
Scallop Jus (Recipe appears on page 318.)

Heat a rondeau or wide shallow pot over medium flame for 2 or 3 minutes. Add oil, shallots, and ½ pound butter (in that order). Allow shallots to sweat and butter to melt away. (Control flame: Do not allow shallots and butter to change color.) Add rice and stir for 3 minutes until all fat is absorbed by the rice. Add white wine. Stir until liquid is evaporated. Add ⅓ of the warm chicken stock. Stir until almost dry and repeat process until rice is almost al dente. Add remaining butter and salt to taste. Transfer risotto to a buttered pan and cool in refrigerator.

Remove skin from pumpkin. Dice. Blend ⅓ of pumpkin in a blender until smooth. Sweat ⅓ of pumpkin in a sauté pan. Add any juice from remaining ⅓ diced pumpkin and enough chicken stock to cover. Discard pumpkin solids. Cook until soft and blended.

Place risotto in a sauté pan with pinenuts. Add remaining chicken stock and pumpkin puree. Cook until smooth. Add whipped cream and sautéed pumpkin. Season, if necessary.

Heat a nonstick sauté pan over medium-high heat with no oil or butter. Sear scallops on one side until almost cooked. Flip and cook briefly.

Place risotto on plates and top with scallops. Surround risotto with scallop jus.

Yields 12 servings

Dominique Filoni, Chef/Partner
Savona Restaurant, Gulph Mills, PA

Maine Lobster Risotto with Sweet Corn and Basil

Did you know?

Nutritional research and long-term heart disease studies show that seafood, including lobster, is good for you and can be included in a healthy diet.

Maine lobster contains less saturated fat, calories, and cholesterol than beef, pork, or even the light meat of chicken. In fact, lobster contains 15 percent less dietary cholesterol than chicken. In addition, the lobster calorie count is nearly half that of chicken, and contains only a fraction of the fat.

Maine Lobster Promotion Bureau

4 1-pound Maine lobsters

1 onion, chopped

1 carrot, chopped

5 ribs celery, chopped

2 tablespoons tomato paste

1 teaspoon thyme

2 bay leaves

Salt to taste

4 tablespoons butter

2 shallots, minced

4 cups Arborio rice

1 cup cognac

3 ears sweet corn, kernels only

4 tablespoons mascarpone cheese

1 tablespoon Parmesan cheese

4 large basil leaves, sliced

Roasted Red Pepper Coulis (Recipe appears on page 343.)

16 spears cooked asparagus

Bring 2 gallons water to a boil in a large lobster pot or stockpot. Cook lobsters for 4 minutes. Place lobsters in an ice water bath to stop the cooking process and cool. Clean lobsters and reserve meat.

Remove all but 1 gallon liquid from pot. Place shells and bodies in pot and crush. Add onion, carrot, celery, tomato paste, thyme, bay leaves, and salt. Bring to a boil. Reduce to a simmer and cook for 30 minutes. Strain out solids and return liquid to pot.

Melt butter in a sauté pan. Add shallots and sauté, being careful not to let them burn. Add rice and stir to coat with butter. Carefully add cognac. When the alcohol burns off, add 2 cups hot lobster broth to pan. Stirring frequently, add more stock in stages until rice is almost soft. Add lobster meat, corn, cheeses, basil, and season with salt and pepper. The risotto should not be thick and pasty. If too thick, add more broth.

Spoon coulis in the centers of 4 plates. Spoon risotto in the center of coulis. Garnish with cooked asparagus.

Yields 4 servings

Daniel Bethard, Executive Chef/Operating Partner
Iron Hill Brewery and Restaurant, West Chester, PA

Poultry

Herb Roasted Spring Chicken with Yellow Tomato Coulis

Culinary Quote

"There has always been a food processor in the kitchen. But once upon a time she was usually called the missus or Mom."

Sue Berkman
"Esquire" September 1984

½ cup butter, softened
1 tablespoon EACH chopped basil, parsley, chives, tarragon
2 cloves garlic
½ teaspoon freshly ground black pepper
Juice of 1 lemon
4 large boneless chicken breasts, skin on
Salt and pepper to taste
1 tablespoon blended oil
2 large yellow beefsteak tomatoes, peeled, seeded, and diced
2 tablespoons chopped shallots
1 teaspoon chopped garlic
¾ cup olive oil

Preheat oven to 400°. Combine butter, herbs, garlic, pepper, and lemon juice in a food processor and process until smooth. Remove from processor and place 2 tablespoons herb butter under skin of each breast. Season breasts with salt and pepper.

Heat blended oil and 2 tablespoons herb butter in a large sauté ovenproof pan over medium-high heat. Add chicken breasts, skin side down. Sauté until golden brown and crispy. Turn breasts and roast until fully cooked, about 10 to 15 minutes.

Place tomatoes, shallots, and garlic in a blender and blend smooth. With motor running, drizzle in oil until creamy and emulsified. Season with salt and pepper

Serve chicken topped with coulis.

Yields 6 servings

Eric Hall, Executive Chef
La Campagne, Cherry Hill, NJ

Chicken Paprikas

Whisk Wisdom

Cubanelle peppers are large and sweet with a light green skin that matures to red. They are also known as Italian frying peppers because the pepper's thin walls make it an excellent choice for frying. Cubanelle peppers are similar to banana peppers and can substitute for Anaheim peppers.

To prepare, slice with a paring knife around the edge of the stem. Remove the stem and you'll see that most of the seeds should be attached. Slice the pepper in half and remove any remaining seeds. Unwashed sweet peppers can be kept in a plastic bag in the refrigerator for up to a week.

5 chicken legs
5 chicken thighs
2 tablespoons butter
1 onion, minced
1 teaspoon minced garlic
2 tablespoons sweet Hungarian paprika
¼ teaspoon hot Hungarian paprika
2 teaspoons flour
1¼ cups white wine
4 canned peeled tomatoes, diced
1 Cubanelle pepper, diced
Salt to taste
Sour cream to taste

Brown chicken in a Dutch oven. Remove chicken from pot. Return pot to low heat and add butter. Add onion, garlic, and paprikas to pot and stir to release the flavor of paprikas. Stir flour into onions and cook for 30 seconds. Add wine, tomatoes, and Cubanelle pepper. Add chicken back to pot and season with salt.

Cover pot and put in a 300° oven for 1½ to 2 hours or until chicken is very tender and falls off the bone.

Remove chicken from sauce. Skim fat from sauce. Add sour cream to taste. Return chicken to pot and coat with sauce.

Yields 5 servings

Tracey Slack, Chef/Owner
The Red Hen Cafe, Medford, NJ

My Dad's Favorite Chicken

4 to 6 boneless, skinless chicken breasts
Seasoned breadcrumbs
Extra virgin olive oil
¾ cup fresh orange juice
¾ cup chicken broth, homemade or low sodium
¼ cup Creole mustard (such as Zatarain's)
1 tablespoon honey (or more to taste)
1 teaspoon hot sauce (like Tabasco or Crystal)
Salt and pepper to taste
Zest of 1 orange

Dredge chicken in breadcrumbs. Brown on both sides in olive oil in a heavy skillet over medium-high heat. Remove chicken from skillet and set aside.

Add orange juice and broth to pan and bring to a boil. Add mustard and honey to pan and whisk in. Cook until reduced, about 5 to 7 minutes, whisking occasionally. Stir in hot sauce and adjust seasonings. Return chicken and any accumulated juices to pan. Reduce heat and simmer for about 2 minutes per side or until done. Sprinkle zest over top and serve.

Chef's note ... This is a quick and easy pan sauce. Serve with whipped roasted sweet potatoes seasoned with a squeeze of fresh lime juice.

Yields 4 to 6 servings

Kathy S. Gold, Chef/Owner
Custom Cuisine Cooking Company, Cherry Hill, NJ

Greek Chicken Cutlets

½ cup olive oil
4 boneless chicken breasts, about 6 ounces each
2 tablespoons chopped garlic
4 red plum tomatoes
24 fresh leaves oregano, chopped
Salt and pepper to taste
½ cup black olives
½ pound feta cheese

Heat oil in a sauté pan. Add chicken breasts and brown on both sides. Add garlic, tomatoes, and oregano. Season with salt and pepper. Add olives and simmer. Top each chicken cutlet with feta cheese. Serve with couscous or rice.

Chef's note…Great with a cold beer or a glass of Merlot.

Yields 4 servings

**Joseph Shilling, Personal Chef/Dean of Education
Your Private Chef, Conshohocken, PA/
The Art Institute of New York City, NY**

Ginger-Soy Barbecued Chicken Breast

Recommended Wine

Wawerner Ritterpfad Riesling Kabinett feinherb Weingut Johann Peter Reinert 2001
The best vineyards along the Saar are the most difficult in Germany to cultivate. The vertiginous steepness of the slopes, the compactness of the rocky soil, and the extreme weather conditions result in wines that are "steelier" and lighter than those from the Mittel Mosel downriver. Reinert plants his vines wide apart so that sunlight reaches the clusters and ripens the grapes to perfection. The resulting wines balance delicate sweetness with high acidity and stony qualities. This 2001 Kabinett offers just a hint of how interestingly the wine will develop in time.

— Moore Brothers Wine Company
Pennsauken, NJ, and
Wilmington, DE

1 tablespoon paprika
2 teaspoons sugar
1 teaspoon salt
½ teaspoon cayenne pepper
⅓ cup red wine vinegar
1 egg
1 cup vegetable oil
¼ cup minced fresh onion
2 tablespoons dry mustard (Coleman's is best.)
2 teaspoons brown sugar
2 teaspoons bacon drippings
1 teaspoon soy sauce
1 teaspoon grated fresh ginger (do not use powder)
8 chicken breasts (butterflied, if making for a sandwich)

Combine paprika, sugar, salt, and pepper in a mixing bowl or food processor. Add vinegar and egg and mix well. Add oil in a slow stream. Mix in remaining ingredients except chicken.

Marinate chicken in mixture for at least 1 hour or more in the refrigerator, turning to cover with marinade every now and then.

Preheat grill. Grill chicken on medium high for a few minutes on each side or until no longer pink.

Yields 8 servings

Charlotte Ann Albertson, Owner/Director
Albertson's Cooking School, Wynnewood, PA

Chicken Sorrento

Chef's Notes

— This recipe is from our cookbook "Ralph's Italian Restaurant: 100 Years, 100 Recipes."

— Roux will keep for about 2 weeks in the refrigerator or can be frozen and defrosted when needed.

4 ounces water
6 rounded tablespoons flour
1 teaspoon Kitchen Bouquet (for color)
16 ounces chicken broth
8 boneless chicken breasts
3 cups flour
2 cups vegetable oil
½ pound butter
½ cup sherry
24 thin slices mozzarella

Place water in a mixing bowl. Whisk in flour and Kitchen Bouquet so that mixture is smooth with no lumps. Bring chicken broth to a boil. Whisk flour mixture into boiling broth, making sure there are no lumps. Cool, then refrigerate to form a roux.

Dredge chicken in flour. Heat oil in a large ovenproof fry pan. Sauté chicken breasts for 3 minutes on each side. Drain oil from pan when all chicken has been cooked.

Put butter, sherry, and 3 tablespoons cold roux (prepared flour mixture) in pan. Bring to a boil. Lower temperature and simmer for 4 minutes, stirring constantly. Lay 3 slices mozzarella on each breast. Set oven to broil. Place breasts in pan and broil until cheese has melted, about 1 minute.

Remove chicken from pan and reserve. Return pan to stovetop and bring sauce to a boil. Whip sauce, then spoon over chicken and serve.

Yields 4 to 8 servings

Jimmy Rubino, Jr., Owner/Chef
Jimmy Rubino's Ralph's of South Philadelphia, Ambler, PA

Chicken Monte Rosa

Recommended Wine

2001 Feudo di Santa Croce Bisanzio Primitivo di Manduria
This is a big, full and rich style of Primitivo that works with the creamy aspects of this dish and the bitterness of the spinach. $13

Tenuta di Travignano, "Misco," Verdicchio dei Castelle di Jesi, Classico Superiore
A ripe, nutty and silky smooth wine with flavors of lemon and pineapple. $13

— John McNulty
Corkscrewed, Cherry Hill, NJ

2 boneless chicken breasts
Flour
1 fresh plum tomato, cut up
1 sun-dried tomato, cut up
1 teaspoon chopped shallots
2 tablespoons sherry wine
1 cup heavy cream
4 tablespoons marinara sauce
2 tablespoons butter
1 cup roughly chopped spinach
2 slices mozzarella cheese

Dust chicken with flour. Heat a sauté pan over medium-high heat. Add fresh tomato, sun-dried tomato, shallots, and sherry wine. Cook until liquid is slightly reduced. Add chicken, heavy cream, marinara sauce, and butter. Add spinach and cook for 20 minutes over low heat.

Arrange chicken in an ovenproof pan. Add some spinach on top of each breast and cover each with mozzarella cheese. Place under broiler to melt cheese.

Transfer to serving plates and top with remaining vegetables and sauce.

Yields 2 servings

Gennaro Illiano, Chef
Lamberti's Cucina, Medford, NJ

Chicken Marsala

Recommended Wine

Valpolicella Classico Agricola Ca' La Bionda 2002
The Castellani family tends three adjacent vineyard plots on slopes of the prime Marano Valley planted to Corvina, Corvinone (a related clone), and Rondinella. The Fasanara vineyard provides most of the fruit for this delicious wine of plush fruit and vibrant, red berry aromatics.

— Moore Brothers Wine Company
Pennsauken, NJ, and
Wilmington, DE

1 pound boneless, skinless chicken breast cutlets
Flour (just enough to dust chicken)
3 tablespoons oil
1 pound mushrooms, sliced
1 to 2 cloves garlic, minced
3 tablespoons sun-dried tomatoes, soaked in warm water until soft, then drained
1 cup Marsala wine
2 tablespoons demi-glace
4 tablespoons butter
Salt and pepper to taste

Pound cutlets (not too thin) and dredge in flour. Heat oil in a sauté pan over medium-hot heat. Add chicken and sauté on both sides. Add mushrooms and garlic. Continue to sauté until mushrooms give off liquid. Add sun-dried tomatoes, Marsala wine, demi-glace, butter, and salt and pepper. (Be careful with the salt. You can always add more at the end.)

Cover and simmer for about 5 minutes. If sauce is too thin, reduce until correct consistency.

Yields 2 servings

Patrick Corvino, Chef
Lamberti's Cucina, Feasterville, PA

Drunken SoCo Chicken

Chef's Notes

Roux is a Southern Creole thickening paste that adds texture, flavor, and substance to most of Creole cooking as we know it. Basically, all roux are made up of equal parts of a fat and a starch. The fat used will dictate the flavor of the roux after it is cooked. You can use lard, oil, butter — it's your choice — but they will always have to be mixed with flour of some kind. Usually the roux has to be cooked; and the longer it is cooked, the deeper the flavor and the color. Roux is something that a bit of skill is needed to make an authentic Creole flavor. Roux are complex at times because they are painstaking to cook over a flame in a cast-iron skillet; and sometimes they burn, and you have to start all over again.

Quick little secret to make an easy roux … Melt some butter in a microwave. (You can also use oil or vegetable shortening.) Add an equal amount of flour and stir till batter-like in consistency. Pour into an oven pan and bake for 30 minutes at 350°. Stir occasionally. You will get a professional roux with the color and taste without burning it.

⅛ cup vegetable oil
8 chicken breast halves, lightly floured
¼ cup chopped green and red peppers
¼ cup chopped celery
¼ cup chopped onions
Creole seasoning to taste
Salt and pepper to taste
1 to 2 tablespoons roux (see sidebar)
2 teaspoons molasses
1 cup chicken stock
⅔ cup cooked black beans (Canned is fine.)
½ cup Southern Comfort 80 proof
4 cups steamed rice
¼ cup chopped green onion

Heat oil a large black iron skillet over high heat. Add chicken breasts. Let sear for about 1 minute, then turn over. Add peppers, celery, and onions and cook until vegetables wilt. Add Creole seasoning and salt and pepper to taste. Add roux and let roux melt. Stir in molasses and chicken stock. Add black beans.

Simmer for about 5 minutes and watch sauce start to get nice and thick. Now add the joy of Southern Comfort. Let dish cook for about 10 minutes until sauce is nice and thick and dark. Add more stock if sauce becomes too thick.

Place steamed rice in center of serving dish. Place breasts on rice and top with SoCo pan sauce. Finish with green onions and serve with a good glass of Chardonnay.

Yields 4 servings

Nick Ventura, Executive Chef/Partner
Nola on Head House Square, Philadelphia, PA

Jamaican Jerk Chicken Napoleon

Chef's Notes

— When cooking chicken, always be cautious with sanitation. Whatever the chicken touches should be washed immediately. I use a different cutting board for chicken to reduce the chance of contaminating other ingredients.

— Shocking means quickly transferring a cooked ingredient from boiling water to ice cold water. This stops the cooking process and keeps the vegetable's color and texture. This is also called blanching.

— When reducing the balsamic vinegar, I strongly recommend using an outside burner on the grill. Otherwise, the strong vinegar smell will linger in your house for days if you do it inside.

6 tablespoons Jamaican jerk seasoning

3 tablespoons honey

1 cup pineapple juice

4 6-ounce boneless, skinless chicken breasts, fat removed

1 cup balsamic vinegar

3 or 4 Idaho potatoes, thinly sliced lengthwise

½ cup extra virgin olive oil

Salt

1 firm ripe avocado

Justin's Salsa (Recipe appears on page 339.)

4 sprigs cilantro

In a large bowl, whisk together seasoning, 1½ tablespoons honey, and pineapple juice until blended and smooth. Add chicken and coat. Cover bowl with plastic wrap and refrigerate for 1 hour.

Meanwhile, cook balsamic vinegar over medium-high heat. Whisk often until liquid is reduced by half and is thick enough to coat the back of a spoon. Remove from heat. Add remaining 1½ tablespoons honey and whisk to combine. Return pan to heat and gently simmer until warm. Reserve.

Preheat oven to 450°. Boil potatoes until centers are clear, then transfer to a bowl of cold water to shock. Brush a baking sheet with oil. Arrange potato slices on sheet and brush with oil. Season with salt. Roast until golden brown but not burnt. Drain on paper towel.

When ready to serve, remove chicken from marinade. Discard liquid. Grill chicken on a preheated and oiled grill until cooked through. Let rest for about 4 minutes. Slice each piece on a bias into 6 equal pieces.

Slice avocado in half and remove stone and skin. Cut avocado into 4 equal pieces and then, without cutting all the way through, slice lengthwise. Fan out pieces.

Layer 1 tablespoon salsa in the middle of each plate. Cover with 2 slices chicken and 1 potato slice. Repeat 2 more times. Cover with a bit of salsa, fanned avocado, and a sprig of cilantro. Drizzle with balsamic honey sauce.

Yields 4 servings

Justin Sanders, Chef/Culinary Student

General Joe Chicken

Chef's Notes

— This is a very healthy recipe. Compare it to the General Tsao Chicken in most Chinese restaurants. They use heavy flour that absorbs a lot of the oil. I only dust with cornstarch. Lots of protein!

5 tablespoons chicken broth
4 tablespoons sugar
3 tablespoons Chardonnay
2 tablespoons soy sauce
1 tablespoon white vinegar
1 teaspoon garlic
1 teaspoon ginger
1 teaspoon hot sauce
2 tablespoons water
2 tablespoons flour
1 pound chicken breast
1 cup dry cornstarch
Oil for frying

Combine first eight ingredients in a saucepan. Cook until heated through. Mix together water and flour to form a slurry. Add to sauce and stir to combine well. Keep warm and reserve.

Cut chicken into 1-inch-wide slices. Dust very well with cornstarch until completely coated. Heat oil to 350°. Add chicken to oil and fry until cooked through and brown, about 5 to 10 minutes.

Place hot crispy chicken on a serving plate. Pour sauce over top. Serve!

Yields 2 servings

Joseph Poon, Chef/Nutritionist
Joseph Poon Asian Fusion Restaurant, Philadelphia

Chicken Cutlet with Assorted Vegetables

Chef's Note

This dish is also known as "Tauk Tauk Kyaw" in Burmese style of cooking.

1 cup fresh chopped chicken
1 egg, beaten
½ teaspoon salt
3 tablespoons wheat flour
½ cup vegetable oil
¼ cup grated carrot
¼ cup grated cabbage
¼ cup sliced string beans
¼ cup sliced cauliflower
½ cup chicken broth

Mix chicken, egg, salt, and wheat flour together. Form mixture into 4 round fritters, each about 5 inches in diameter and ½-inch thick.

Heat oil in a wok over medium-high heat. Slide one fritter into oil and fry on both sides for about 4 minutes or until golden. Drain on paper towels. Repeat with remaining fritters.

Stir-fry vegetables in wok for 1 minute. Stir in broth to make a gravy. Plate fritters and cover with gravy.

Yields 4 servings

Tun Myint, Chef
Rangoon Burmese Restaurant, Philadelphia, PA

Chicken Nilgiri Korma

Cafe Spice

Known for:
good food, good drinks, service, decor

Year opened:
2000

Most requested table:
our booths

Menu:
modern vibrant Indian bistro

Chef:
Bala Murugan

Chef's training:
degree in hotel management; worked ten years in hotels, restaurants, and cruise ships

Chef's hobbies/ accomplishments:
set up brand new kitchen at Cafe Spice and has been executive chef since day 1

Chef's favorite ingredient:
fennel seeds, fresh curry leaves

Chef's favorite food:
chicken chettinad

1 bunch fresh cilantro, roughly chopped
1 bunch fresh mint, roughly chopped
3 Thai peppers, chopped
5 green cardamom
4 cloves garlic, sliced
1 1-inch piece ginger root, chopped
1 tablespoon oil
2 onions, sliced
2 tomatoes, diced
3 pounds boneless chicken, cut into cubes
Salt to taste
1 14-ounce can coconut milk
Juice of 1 lemon

Put first six ingredients and a little water in a blender and puree. Reserve.

Heat oil in a sauté pan. Add onions and tomatoes. When onions are soft, add pureed mixture, chicken cubes, and salt to taste. When chicken is almost cooked through, add coconut milk. Add lemon juice. Serve with rice or bread.

Chef's note ... This is a very popular South Indian dish. The name came from the mass production of spices and herbs in Nilgiri. Chicken, lamb, or any seafood can be used for this recipe.

Yields 4 servings

Bala Murugan, Executive Chef
Cafe Spice, Philadelphia, PA

Chicken Casserole

Chef's Notes

— If you love garlic, substitute our Garlic Parmesan Sauce for Buffalo Sauce.

— To give this some Cajun flair, add 1 or 2 chopped chili peppers and 1 or 2 tablespoons of The Greatest Grub Ever Fire it up Sauce.

— For more tender vegetables, cook them first before combining with other ingredients.

½ pound elbow macaroni
1 pound boneless, skinless chicken, cooked and diced
1 12-ounce jar The Greatest Grub Ever Buffalo Mild or
    Buffalo Hot Sauce
10 slices crisp bacon, crumbled
1 large onion, diced
1 large red bell pepper, diced
1 large tomato, cored and diced
1 cup shredded mozzarella cheese
1 cup shredded sharp Cheddar cheese
1 cup light cream

Prepare macaroni according to package instructions.
Preheat oven to 375°. Mix pasta and all remaining ingredients, except cream, in a large bowl. Spoon into a large casserole dish. Pour in light cream. Cover and bake for 45 minutes to 1 hour. Mix well and serve.

Yields 6 to 8 servings

J. Scott Jemison, Chef/Owner
Buffalo Bill's BBQ Restaurant, Williamstown, NJ

Crispy Chicken Livers

Ravenna

Year opened:
2002

Most requested table:
32, the round by the fireplace

Menu:
Ravenna is the town in Ohio where I am from. It is named for the coastal city in the Emilia Romagna region of Italy.

Chef:
Shawn Sollberger

Chef's training:
International Culinary Academy
Pittsburgh, PA

Chef's favorite ingredient:
extra virgin olive oil

Chef's favorite food:
cheeseburgers

12 lobes cleaned chicken livers
Milk
2 cups balsamic vinegar
2 cups sugar
4 tablespoons oil
1 tablespoon Wondra flour
¼ cup reconstituted dried cherries
2 tablespoons toasted pinenuts
1 head frisee, leaves separated
8 grape tomatoes, halved

Soak livers in milk.

Heat balsamic vinegar and sugar to a simmer and cook until liquid is reduced by half and has reached a syrup consistency.

Heat oil in a skillet over moderate heat. Dust livers with Wondra flour. Fry in oil for 3 minutes on each side until crispy. Remove from skillet to paper towel.

Drain oil. Add balsamic reduction, cherries, and pinenuts and combine. Add livers to sauce and toss.

Plate livers on top of frisee. Garnish with tomatoes.

Chef's note ...This is our most requested recipe.

Yields 4 servings

Shawn Sollberger, Chef/Owner
Ravenna, Worcester, PA

Honey-Sake Roasted Duckling with Blood Orange Reduction

Chef's Notes

Why does the recipe call for cooking the marinade? Heating the marinade ingredients allows them to blend more thoroughly than if just combined at room temperature.

You'll notice the reduction calls for blood oranges. If they are not available, use 1 pint each of orange and grapefruit juices.

2 cups soy sauce
2 cups sake (any good brand)
2 cups honey
2 cups plus 1 quart water
1 whole duckling, approximately 3 pounds
2 stalks celery
2 medium onions
2 carrots
1 pint white mushrooms
1 piece fresh ginger, 6 inches long
1 leek
1 quart blood orange juice (fresh squeezed preferred)
1 cup Grand Marnier
Salt and pepper to taste
Oven-Dried Grape and Ginger Relish (Recipe appears on page 345.)

Place soy sauce, sake, honey, and 2 cups water in a medium saucepan and bring to a boil, then allow to cool. Pour marinade over duckling, rotating bird occasionally to ensure even marination. Marinate for 2 hours prior to roasting.

Preheat oven to 350°. Remove duckling from marinade (reserve marinade) and place in a shallow roasting pan. Coarsely chop all vegetables and add to pan. Add remaining 1 quart water. Pierce duckling skin on all sides to allow excess fat to drain during roasting. Roast for 2 hours, painting duckling with marinade every 15 minutes.

Remove from pan and allow to stand for 20 minutes before carving. Strain remaining liquid from roasting pan and reserve 1 quart for reduction sauce.

Meanwhile, heat fruit juice in a small saucepan over a low flame until reduced by one half. In a second saucepan, reduce roasting juices by one half. Combine the two liquids into one pot and continue to cook until reduced by one half. Add Grand Marnier and salt and pepper to taste. If sauce is too thin, mix a bit of cornstarch and water into a slurry, then gradually whisk into sauce over a low flame until it reaches desired consistency. Slice duckling and place on warm platter. Spoon reduction over duckling and garnish with relish.

Yields 2 servings

David Greer, Executive Chef
La Terrasse, Philadelphia, PA

Breast of Duck Au Poivre

2 duck breasts
2 tablespoons chopped shallots
½ cup brandy
1 tablespoon green peppercorns
1 cup chicken stock
2 cups heavy cream

Trim duck breasts of excess fat. Place skin side down in a large sauté pan. Cook over low heat until most of the fat is rendered and the skin is very crisp. Remove excess fat as it accumulates in pan. Turn breasts over and sear for 1 minute. Remove breasts from pan.

Add shallot and sauté for 1 minute. Add brandy and flambé until alcohol is cooked off. Add peppercorns, stock, and cream. Simmer until sauce is thick enough to coat the back of a spoon. Season to taste with salt and pepper.

Slice duck and serve with sauce.

Yields 4 servings

Eric Hall, Executive Chef
La Campagne, Cherry Hill, NJ

Roasted Pheasant Breast with Cranberry Compote

3 pheasants
Oil
Salt and pepper to taste
1 bag fresh cranberries
1 cup sugar
1 cup port wine
Zest and juice of 2 oranges
Wild Rice (Recipe appears on page 233.)

Preheat oven to 350°. Rub pheasants with oil and salt and pepper to taste. Roast for approximately 25 minutes; do not overcook.

Meanwhile, gently cook cranberries, sugar, wine, zest, and juice for approximately 10 minutes or until cranberries open.

Let roasted pheasants rest before carving. Serve breast meat with heated compote and wild rice on the side.

Yields 6 servings

Tom Hannum, Executive Chef
Hotel duPont, Wilmington, DE

Seafood

Salmon with Leeks and Morels 154

Herb Roasted Salmon 155 · Salmon for a Monday 156

Salmon with Black Bean Sauce 157

Ivory King Salmon with Black and White Truffle Butter 158

Pistachio and Basil Battered Salmon Fillet 159

Barbecued Salmon with Cucumber Salad 160

Sautéed Salmon "Saltimbocca" 161

Salmon Croquette with Creamy Cucumber Relish 162

Flounder Romana 163

Pan Seared Coconut Sea Bass 164

Sea Bass Baccala Style 165

Panko Crusted Sea Bass with Sun-dried Tomato Cream Sauce 166

Pan Seared Striped Bass with Lobster Saffron Sauce 167

Pan Seared Chilean Sea Bass with Leek and Cream Ragu 168

Skillet Wild Bass with Minted Zucchini Noodles 169

Napoleon of Seared Tuna and Hudson Valley Foie Gras 170

Grilled Tuna Steak with Mango Salsa 171

Polenta Crusted Halibut with Lobster Basil Sauce 172

Seared Alaskan Halibut with Grilled Pineapple-Mango Salsa 174

Catfish Nuggets with Leek and Ginger Sauce 175

Red Snapper Creole with Grilled Mangoes and Bananas 176

Sautéed Jumbo Lump Crab Cakes 178 · Mixmaster Crab Cake 179

What's For Dinner Crab Cakes 180 · Wasabi Crab Cake 181

Pan-Seared Crab Cakes with Yellow Pepper Cream Sauce 182

Soft-shell Crabs 183 · Garlic Shrimp 184

Shrimp Konbongyi 185 · Voodoo Shrimp 186

Yuzu Ginger Sea Scallops with Habañero Pineapple Salsa 187

Salmon with Leeks and Morels

Caribou Café

Known for:
classic French cuisine

Year opened:
1990

Most requested table:
patio

Menu:
classic bistro cuisine

Chef:
Olivier De Saint Martin

Chef's training:
Hotel School of Paris;
Apprentice with Guerard,
Lenôtre, Verger, and Le Coze

**Chef's hobbies/
accomplishments:**
family, sports

Chef's favorite ingredient:
root vegetables

Chef's favorite food:
anything simple with aroma

1½ pounds fresh salmon fillet
Salt and pepper to taste
6 tablespoons butter
1 ounce dry morels, soaked overnight
2 leeks, washed and cut into nickel-size diamond shapes
½ cup white wine
½ cup Noilly Prat vermouth
1 cup heavy cream

Cut salmon on a bias into 4 even pieces. Season with salt and pepper. Reserve.

Melt 2 tablespoons butter in a pan. Drain morels and add to pan. Cook for 2 minutes until flavors develop. Add leeks, wine, and vermouth. Season with salt and pepper. Cook for 5 minutes. Add cream and boil for 2 minutes.

In a separate pan, melt remaining 4 tablespoons butter over medium-high heat. Add salmon pieces. Pan sear until medium rare, about 2 minutes on each side.

Divide leeks and morels evenly between 4 plates. Spoon on sauce and top with salmon.

Chef's note ... You may want to substitute the morels with another mushroom of your liking. Simplicity is the key to good food. Less is more!

Yields 4 servings

**Olivier De Saint Martin, Chef/Owner
Caribou Café, Philadelphia, PA**

Herb Roasted Salmon

Whisk Wisdom

Star anise is native to China and Vietnam and was first introduced to Europe in the seventeenth century. It is a star-shaped fruit with eight points that comes from a small oriental tree. The fruit is picked before it can ripen and then dried. The dried fruit pods are usually added whole to cooking pots or ground and used as a powder. It has a powerful, somewhat bitter, licorice-like flavor that is stronger than anise. Traditionally associated with Asian cooking, especially Chinese, it gives depth and flavor to meat and poultry dishes, stews, and sauces. It is an ingredient of the mixture known as "Chinese Five-Spice." Vietnamese chefs add star anise to the beef soup, pho.

5 pounds salmon, cut into 12 fillets about 7 ounces each
Salt and pepper to taste
3 tablespoons chopped fresh parsley
2 tablespoons chopped fresh tarragon
½ cup olive oil
1 cup red wine
½ cup cranberry juice
1 star anise
2 pounds cold butter, cubed
Salt

Preheat oven to 400°.

Season fish with salt and pepper. Combine herbs and oil and spread on fish. Roast for 12 to 15 minutes.

Combine red wine, cranberry juice, and star anise. Cook until syrupy. Remove star anise. Slowly whisk in butter to form an emulsion. Season with salt.

Serve salmon with sauce. Shiitake Spinach Strudel (Recipe appears on page 302.) is a suggested accompaniment.

Yields 12 servings

Meg Votta, Executive Chef
Joseph Ambler Inn, North Wales, PA

Salmon for a Monday

Deux Cheminées

Year opened:
1979

Most requested table:
in the courtyard

Menu:
French

Chef de Cuisine/Propietor
Fritz Blank

Chef's training:
my grandmother's kitchen

**Chef's hobbies/
accomplishments:**
food history, food science,
bibliophile

Chef's favorite ingredient:
any and all

Chef's favorite food:
Chinese

1 cup lite soy sauce

2 cups orange juice

2 cloves garlic, finely chopped

1 teaspoon finely minced fresh jalapeño chiles

1 tablespoon finely chopped fresh ginger

1 tablespoon tomato paste

1 tablespoon toasted sesame oil

1 "side" fresh salmon, skin on, pin bones removed (allow 4
  to 6 ounces of salmon per person)

1 or 2 teaspoons light brown sugar

2 tablespoons cornstarch

2 tablespoons cold water

1 large ripe mango, peeled and cut into ½-inch cubes

Juice of 2 fresh limes

Chopped coriander

Combine first seven ingredients. Place salmon, skin side up, in a noncorrosive shallow ovenproof baking pan and pour marinade over fish, turning over once so that entire surface has been anointed with marinade. Refrigerate overnight.

Preheat oven to 425°. Drain and reserve any excess marinade from fish. Place fish back in pan and cook for 10 minutes for every inch of thickness.

Place 1 ounce or more of reserved marinade and brown sugar in a small saucepan and bring to a boil, stirring to dissolve sugar. Combine cornstarch and water to form a "slurry." Drizzle in just enough slurry (about 1 tablespoon) to produce a sauce that "coats a spoon." Strain into a small bowl. Add mango cubes and toss quickly. Taste carefully and season with lime juice. Arrange the sauce over fish and garnish with fresh coriander.

Yields 8 to 10 servings

Fritz Blank, Chef de Cuisine/ Proprietor
Deux Cheminées, Philadelphia, PA

Salmon with Black Bean Sauce

Alex Long New Asian Cuisine

Known for:
"Best of Philly" Dumplings

Year opened:
1998

Most requested table:
window

Menu:
new Asian

Chef:
Alex Long

Chef's training:
restaurant taught

Chef's hobbies/ accomplishments:
trying new restaurants with other chefs

Chef's favorite ingredient:
cilantro

Chef's favorite food:
anything made with fresh ingredients

½ cup water
1 tablespoon rice wine
1 tablespoon sugar
1 tablespoon sesame oil
1 tablespoon cornstarch
3 tablespoons chicken broth
3 cloves garlic, chopped
2 slices fresh ginger, cut into matchsticks
2 salmon fillets
2 tablespoons chopped black beans

Combine first six ingredients in a bowl and reserve.

Lightly sauté garlic and ginger in a little oil in a nonstick fry pan on medium heat. Remove garlic and ginger from pan and reserve. Return pan to medium heat and sauté salmon fillets, skin side down first, for about 5 minutes on each side, depending on the thickness of fish. (Be careful not to overcook.) Transfer fillets to two warm plates.

Return pan to heat. Add reserved liquid mixture, garlic, ginger, and beans. Simmer until thickened. Pour over salmon and serve with your favorite rice and vegetables.

Yields 2 servings

Alex Long, Chef/Owner
Alex Long New Asian Cuisine, Wynnewood, PA

Ivory King Salmon with Black and White Truffle Butter

Pinziminio Trattoria

Known for:
our unique style of service

Year opened:
2002

Most requested table:
the Chef's Room

Menu:
Italian cuisine

Chefs:
Manlon Randolph
(and Steve Petracelli)

Chef's training:
The Restaurant School in
Philadelphia

**Chef's hobbies/
accomplishments:**
reading and racquet ball

Chef's favorite ingredient:
spinach and tomatoes

Chef's favorite food:
hot pastrami and Swiss sandwich

1 cup plus 1 tablespoon whole butter, softened
2 ounces black truffles, shaved (Canned will do.)
1 ounce white truffle oil
Sea salt
6 white asparagus
6 green asparagus
3 tablespoons olive oil
2 Ivory King salmon fillets, 8 to 10 ounces each, skin
removed
Fresh cracked black pepper

Combine 1 cup softened butter, shaved truffles, white truffle oil, and sea salt to taste in a mixing bowl. Mix well. Place butter mixture in a pastry bag and pipe out rosettes on a sheet of waxed paper. Refrigerate.

Bring a pot of water to a boil. Blanch white asparagus, then green. Let dry on a paper towel. Combine 2 tablespoons olive oil and 1 tablespoon butter in a sauté pan. Add asparagus and sauté to desired doneness.

Preheat oven to 350°. Pat dry both sides of fillets and season with sea salt and fresh cracked black pepper. Heat an ovenproof sauté pan over medium-high heat and add remaining 1 tablespoon oil. Sear salmon, skin side down, until brown. Transfer to oven and cook to desired doneness.

Serve asparagus and fillet atop Seafood Saffron Risotto (Recipe appears on page 128.). Top fish with truffle butter.

Yields 2 servings

**Manlon Randolph, Chef
Pinziminio Trattoria, Cherry Hill, NJ**

Pistachio and Basil Battered Salmon Fillet

The Little Tuna

Known for:
cozy size, "little"

Year opened:
2003

Most requested table:
the back left corner

Menu:
classic and innovative seafood

Chef:
Marcus Severs

Chef's training:
self taught, worked at family's restaurant since the age of 9

Chef's hobbies/ accomplishments:
hunting, cooking/opening "The Little Tuna"

Chef's favorite ingredient:
honey

Chef's favorite food:
baby back ribs

4 salmon fillets, about 6 ounces each
Salt
1 cup water
½ cup pistachios
½ cup panko breadcrumbs
3 tablepoons fresh chopped basil
4 tablespoons melted unsalted butter
2 cloves garlic, minced
1 teaspoon lemon zest
Pinch of salt and pepper

Preheat oven to 375°.

Salt fish lightly. Place fillets in a nonstick baking pan or a baking sheet coated with nonstick spray. Place water in pan and bake until done, about 10 minutes.

Meanwhile, combine remaining ingredients. Remove fish from oven. Coat top of each fillet with pistachio mixture. Return to oven and bake until golden brown, about 4 minutes.

Excellent served with asparagus and roasted potatoes.

Chef's note ... I use panko because it helps to keep the nuts from being chewy and it adds a nice crisp to the dish.

Yields 4 servings

**Marcus Severs, Chef/Owner
The Little Tuna, Haddonfield, NJ**

Barbecued Salmon with Cucumber Salad

1 cup ketchup
½ cup chili sauce
½ cup orange juice
¼ cup molasses
½ cup brown sugar, packed
4 tablespoons chili powder
2 tablespoons chopped fresh garlic
Salt and pepper to taste
4 salmon fillets, about 7 ounces each
1 seedless cucumber, cut into half-moons
1 small red onion, sliced thin
2 tablespoons chopped fresh dill
¼ cup rice wine vinegar
1 tablespoon sugar

Combine first seven ingredients. Simmer on low heat for 1 hour. Season with salt and pepper.

Coat salmon with barbecue sauce. Marinate for 2 hours. Toss together cucumber, red onion, dill, vinegar, and sugar. Season with salt and pepper. Refrigerate.

On a medium hot grill, cook salmon on one side for 4 to 5 minutes. Turn and cook for approximately 2 to 3 more minutes. If desired, baste with additional sauce.

Chef's note…Great with a cold, crisp Chardonnay or a cold beer. Barbecue sauce can be cooled and refrigerated for future use.

Yields 4 servings

Joseph Shilling, Personal Chef/Dean of Education
Your Private Chef, Conshohocken, PA/
The Art Institute of New York City, NY

Sautéed Salmon "Saltimbocca"

Culinary Quote

*"Fish, to taste right, must swim three times —
in water,
in butter,
and in wine."*

Polish proverb

4 salmon fillets, about 4 to 5 ounces each
Salt and pepper to taste
4 thin slices prosciutto
8 fresh sage leaves
8 toothpicks
6 tablespoons butter
¼ cup dry white wine
2 tablespoons lemon juice
Flour

Season each fillet with salt and pepper. Place 1 slice prosciutto on top of each fillet. Place 2 sage leaves on each slice prosciutto. Skewer prosciutto and sage to fillets with toothpicks.

Heat 2 tablespoons butter in a sauté pan and sauté salmon, prosciutto side down, for 2 to 3 minutes. Flip and sauté for additional 2 to 3 minutes.

Transfer fish to heated serving plates and remove toothpicks. Add remaining butter, white wine, and lemon juice and cook for 1 to 2 minutes so that liquids reduces a little. Spoon sauce over salmon. Serve with your favorite vegetable and starch.

Chef's note ... Saltimbocca is a popular dish in Rome, classically prepared with veal. This makes for a light main course with salmon.

Yields 4 servings

Daniel Dogan, Executive Chef
Terrace at Greenhill, Wilmington, DE

Salmon Croquette with Creamy Cucumber Relish

Museum Restaurant

Known for:
Maryland crab cakes

Year opened:
1995

Most requested table:
table 10

Menu:
changes seasonally, theme revolves around exhibitions

Chef:
Tracey A. Hopkins, Sr.

Chef's training:
Baltimore Culinary College

Chef's hobbies/ accomplishments:
weightlifting, basketball

Chef's favorite ingredient:
crabmeat, Silver Queen corn

Chef's favorite food:
barbecued spare ribs

1 pound salmon fillet, blood line removed, cut into 3 pieces

1½ ounces blended oil

Lemon zest

½ teaspoon kosher salt

⅛ teaspoon white pepper

1 shallot, diced

½ medium onion, diced

2 tablespoons diced celery

1 Idaho potato, peeled and steamed

2 eggs

¼ teaspoon baking powder

1 tablespoon minced fresh dill

1 cup breadcrumbs

⅕ cup flour

1 teaspoon chives

Creamy Cucumber Relish (Recipe appears on page 344.)

Preheat oven to 400°.

Toss salmon with 1 ounce oil, zest, and salt and pepper. Roast until cooked through, about 5 to 6 minutes.

Sauté shallots, onion, and celery in remaining ½ ounce oil until softened. Do not brown. Cool and reserve.

Pass potato through a ricer and into a bowl. Reserve. Whip eggs and baking powder. Reserve.

Combine potatoes, eggs, shallot mixture, and dill. Stir to combine. Break salmon into ⅓-inch chunks and fold into mixture. Season with salt and pepper.

Combine breadcrumbs and flour. Mix well. Add chives.

Form mixture into 3-ounce cakes. Roll in breadcrumbs. Sauté in oil on both sides until golden brown. Transfer to a reheated 400° oven. Bake until heated through, about 3 to 4 minutes. Serve with relish.

Yields 4 to 6 servings

Tracey A. Hopkins, Sr., Executive Chef
Museum Restaurant at the Philadelphia Museum of Art, Philadelphia, PA

Flounder Romana

Recommended Wine

2002 Chateau Cambon
This juicy and earthy style of Beaujolais is the perfect red wine with fish. The Romano style of this flounder dish lends itself perfectly to a red wine. $11

2002 Staete Landt, Sauvignon Blanc
This wine is a classic, crisp, New Zealand Sauvignon from the Marlborough region. It has full body and an elegant style with a lengthy finish. $16

— John McNulty
Corkscrewed, Cherry Hill, NJ

2 tablespoons olive oil
2 cups chopped tomatoes
1 clove garlic, chopped
½ teaspoon salt
½ teaspoon black pepper
1 cup chicken broth
½ cup white wine
2 tablespoons chopped basil
2 flounder fillets, 4 to 6 ounces each, cleaned and deboned
2 cups cooked white rice

Preheat oven to 475°.

Heat olive oil in an ovenproof sauté pan over medium flame. Add tomatoes, garlic, salt, and black pepper. Cook for 5 to 7 minutes. Add chicken broth, white wine, and basil. Add flounder and cook for 5 more minutes. Transfer pan to oven and cook for 20 to 30 minutes.

Divide white rice between 2 plates. Top rice with flounder and pan juices. Buon Appetito!

Yields 2 servings

Massimo Criniti, Chef/Owner
Criniti Ristorante Italiano, South Philadelphia, PA

Pan Seared Coconut Sea Bass

Recommended Wine

Sanlúcar de Barrameda La Cosecha Oloroso Seco Sacristia de Bodega S. Francisco NV

"La Cosecha" Sherries are a collection of *Sacristia* wines from individual Bodegas (wineries). Sacristia are rarely bottled un-blended as they form the heart of "master blends" and represent a bodega's best effort. Wines destined to become rich, mahogany-colored Oloroso are fortified to a higher strength of nearly 18% alcohol to prevent the formation of flor. Many Olorosos are slightly sweetened before bottling with Pedro Ximénez, but pure Olorosos will typically be dry. This elegant Oloroso Seco has rich flavors and aromas of walnuts with a smooth and lingering finish. Serve it slightly chilled or at a cool room temperature with grilled meats, nuts.

— Moore Brothers Wine Company
Pennsauken, NJ, and
Wilmington, DE

2 tablespoons minced scallion

2 tablespoons minced fresh coriander

Salt and pepper to taste

1 pound boneless, skinless sea bass, cut into 4 pieces

8 ounces plus 2 tablespoons unsweetened shredded coconut

2 tablespoons canola or corn oil

2 teaspoons minced garlic

2 teaspoons minced shallot

2 tablespoons brandy wine

2 tablespoons peanut butter

1 cup chicken broth

4 tablespoons soy sauce

1 tablespoon sugar

½ cup sugar snap peas

½ cup chopped red bell pepper

½ cup sliced shiitake mushrooms

Combine scallion, coriander, and salt and pepper to taste. Pour over fish and toss lightly to coat. Cover with plastic wrap and let fish sit at room temperature for 1 hour. Pat 8 ounces coconut around fish pieces.

Heat a skillet over high heat and brush lightly with a little oil. Arrange fish in pan and sear for about 4 or 5 minutes per side or until fish is opaque. Reserve and keep warm.

Add 1 tablespoon oil to skillet. When oil is hot, add garlic and shallot and stir-fry for about 5 seconds. Add brandy wine, peanut butter, chicken broth, soy sauce, sugar, 2 tablespoons shredded coconut, and pepper to taste. Boil to thicken.

Meanwhile, add remaining oil to a separate pan. Sauté sugar snap peas, red bell pepper, and shiitake mushrooms. Season to taste with salt and pepper. Arrange fish on a platter and spoon sauce over fish. Place sautéed vegetables around fish and serve.

Yields 2 servings

James Huang, Chef
Cin Cin, Chestnut Hill, PA

Sea Bass Baccala Style

1 medium red onion, diced
2 ounces olive oil
1 tablespoon minced garlic
4 medium potatoes, diced
2 28-ounce cans plum tomatoes
8 anchovies
¼ cup capers
6 basil leaves
1¼ pounds sea bass, cut into 1-inch cubes
½ 8.5-ounce can black olives (add more or less to your liking)
½ 8.5-ounce can green olives (add more or less to your liking)

Sauté onion in oil until translucent. Add garlic and continue cooking for 3 or 4 minutes. Add potatoes, tomatoes, anchovies, capers, and basil. Cook over medium heat for 15 minutes or until potatoes are almost done. Add sea bass and olives and cook for 10 more minutes.

Yields 4 servings

Nick Tropiano, Pastry and Pasta Chef
Catelli Ristorante, Voorhees, NJ

Panko Crusted Sea Bass with Sun-dried Tomato Cream Sauce

Culinary Quote

"In the hands of an able cook, fish can become an inexhaustible source of perpetual delight."

Jean-Anthelme Brillat-Savarin
French lawyer, magistrate, and politician, who wrote one of the most celebrated works on food, "Physiologie du Gout" (The Physiology of Taste)

4 cups panko (Japanese) breadcrumbs
1 tablespoon chopped fresh parsley
1 tablespoon chopped fresh dill
1 teaspoon chopped fresh tarragon
1 teaspoon plus ½ teaspoon salt
¼ teaspoon plus ⅛ teaspoon fresh ground black pepper
1½ cups all-purpose flour
4 8-ounce Chilean sea bass fillets
3 eggs, beaten
2 tablespoons olive oil
1 cup Sun-dried Tomato Cream Sauce (Recipe appears on page 322.)

Preheat oven to 350°.

In a large bowl, combine breadcrumbs, parsley, dill, tarragon, 1 teaspoon salt, and ¼ teaspoon pepper. In a separate bowl, combine flour, ½ teaspoon salt, and ⅛ teaspoon fresh ground pepper. Season each fillet with additional salt and pepper. Dredge in flour mixture and shake off excess flour. Dip into beaten eggs. Coat with breadcrumb mixture, pressing to help to adhere.

Heat olive oil in a nonstick sauté pan over medium heat. Add fillets and sauté until each is golden brown. Transfer to a baking sheet and bake for 5 to 6 minutes until done. Serve with sun-dried tomato cream sauce.

Chef's note…Can be prepared up to 4 hours ahead. Keep refrigerated.

Yields 4 servings

Robert Mansfield, Executive Chef
Porterhouse Steaks and Seafood, Cherry Hill, NJ

Pan Seared Striped Bass with Lobster Saffron Sauce

Recommended Wine

2002 Santiago Ruiz, Albarino, Rias Baixas
A perfect wine for all types of fish and seafood, including this dish's fabulous lobster risotto. Brilliant freshness and a great lush texture and finish give this pairing a big thumbs up. $17

— John McNulty
Corkscrewed, Cherry Hill, NJ

2 lobsters, halved and cleaned
½ cup diced onions
½ cup diced celery
½ cup diced fennel
½ cup diced tomatoes
Pinch of saffron
3 cups fumet (fish stock)
2 tablespoons olive oil
4 striped bass fillets, 8 ounces each
Pinch of salt and pepper
Shellfish Risotto (Recipe appears on page 129.)

In a large saucepan, sear lobsters, onions, celery, fennel, and tomatoes over medium-high heat. When lobster is seared through (turns a bright red), remove tail meat and reserve for risotto. Continue cooking carcass and add saffron. Stir for 1 minute. Add fumet. Bring to a boil, then simmer for 30 minutes. Strain, season, and hold warm until ready to serve. (If not making risotto, lobster tail meat can be served as a garnish for the bass.)

Heat oil in a sauté pan on high. Season bass with salt and pepper. Carefully sear on both sides until done, approximately 2 to 4 minutes per side, depending upon the thickness of fish.

Arrange risotto on serving plates. Cover with fillets. Spoon sauce over fillets.

Yields 4 servings

David Boyle, Executive Chef
Davio's Northern Italian Steakhouse, Philadelphia, PA

Pan Seared Chilean Sea Bass with Leek and Cream Ragu

Chadds Ford Inn

Known for:
the haunted "Red Room"

Year opened:
1736

Most requested table:
the Wyeth table

Menu:
contemporary American with Asian and Latin influence

Chef:
Jason P. McHugh

Chef's training:
no formal training, self trained throughout kitchens in Europe

Chef's hobbies/ accomplishments:
nominated Best New Chef, Dublin, 1991

Chef's favorite ingredient:
ginger and bold spices

Chef's favorite food:
Japanese

5 to 8 red bliss potatoes
4 Chilean sea bass or black bass fillets
Salt and pepper
2 tablespoons grapeseed oil or olive oil
1 pound crimini or baby bella mushrooms, diced
1 bunch leeks, diced
1 bunch celery, diced
1 quart heavy cream
Black truffle oil to taste (Choose a high quality oil.)
Deep-fried leek greens or fresh shaved black truffle, optional

Boil potatoes in salted water for about 15 minutes or until fork tender. Immediately run potatoes under cold water to stop cooking process. Cool and cut into quarters. Reserve.

Preheat oven to 375°. Season fish with salt and pepper. Heat 1 tablespoon grapeseed in a medium sauté pan until oil starts to smoke. Place 2 fillets in pan. Cook on each side for 1½ minutes. Remove fish from pan and place on baking sheet. Repeat with remaining fillets. Transfer fish to oven and bake for 8 to 10 minutes.

Place mushrooms, leeks, celery, and cream in a pot and bring to a boil. Reduce heat to medium and continue to cook for 3 to 5 minutes until leeks are tender and cream is reduced by half. Drizzle in truffle oil and season to taste with salt and pepper.

Divide cream ragu between 4 shallow bowls and place 1 fillet in each bowl. Garnish with fried leeks or fresh shaved black truffle.

Yields 4 servings

Jason P. McHugh, Executive Chef
Chadds Ford Inn, Chadds Ford, PA

Skillet Wild Bass with Minted Zucchini Noodles

Recommended Wine

2001 Kabinett Reichsgraf von Kesselstatt Riesling, Mosel-Saar-Ruwer, Germany
A zesty, light-bodied white wine with a hint of sweetness is needed to handle the tomato jelly and rice vinegar tang of this dish. Germany's Mosel valley is among the world's coldest growing regions for wine, yielding delicate, racy wines from the classic Riesling grape. Snappy citrus and green apple flavors will help this lively white wine balance the minty zucchini and showcase the freshness of the wild striped bass.
Approximately $16

— Marnie Old
Old Wines LLC, Philadelphia

½ cup water
¼ cup plus 2 teaspoons sugar
2 cups chopped sun-dried tomatoes
3 tablespoons rice wine vinegar
2 teaspoons kosher salt
3 teaspoons cracked black pepper
1 teaspoon sirachi hot sauce
6 large firm zucchini, peeled
1 bunch mint, chopped
1 tablespoon olive oil
2 pounds wild bass fillet, cut into 4 portions (or other firm white flesh fish)

Boil water and ¼ cup sugar. Add sun-dried tomatoes, 2 tablespoons rice wine vinegar, 1 teaspoon salt, 1 teaspoon black pepper, and hot sauce. Bring to a boil and reserve.

Use a French mandoline to cut the flesh of each zucchini into "noodles." Toss with remaining 1 tablespoons rice wine vinegar, 1 teaspoon salt, 2 teaspoons pepper, 2 teaspoons sugar, and mint. Reserve.

Heat a pan over high heat. Add oil. Sear fish for 3 minutes per side until golden brown. Divide zucchini "noodles" between 4 plates. Place fish on top of noodles and top each with 1 heaping tablespoon tomato jelly.

Chef's note…Serve with a crisp, fruity Sauvignon Blanc.

Yields 4 servings

**Albert Paris, Executive Chef
Zanzibar Blue, Philadelphia, PA**

Napoleon of Seared Tuna and Hudson Valley Foie Gras

Eclipse

Known for:
fresh, eclectic fish preparations

Year opened:
1996

Most requested table:
table 4 — the corner table in the window

Menu:
creative/innovative American

Chef:
Patrick A. D'Amico

Chef's training:
Culinary Institute of America in Hyde Park, NY

Chef's hobbies/ accomplishments:
avid angler

Chef's favorite ingredient:
currently, a sweet Thai chile sauce

Chef's favorite food:
anything that is fresh!

4 bluefin tuna steaks, 6 ounces each
Salt and pepper to taste
½ cup blended oil
1 medium Vidalia onion, cut into ¼-inch slices
½ cup herb-infused olive oil
4 slices Hudson Valley Foie Gras, 2 ounces each, sliced ¼-inch thick
1 cup dry red wine
5 tablespoons unsalted butter

Season tuna with salt and pepper to taste. Heat sauté pan over medium-high heat and coat bottom with blended oil. Add tuna and sear until rare, about 2 minutes per side. Slice each piece in half, horizontally, to expose crimson color and set aside.

Preheat oven to 450°. Coat onion slices with herb-infused oil and place on a baking sheet. Cook for 10 minutes or until tender. Reserve.

Season foie gras with salt and pepper to taste. Heat sauté pan over medium-high heat and coat bottom with blended oil. Add foie gras and sear until done, about 1 to 1½ minutes per side. Reserve.

In a medium pot, cook red wine until reduced to ¼ cup. Add butter in small increments, whisking steadily until all butter has melted. Season to taste with salt and pepper.

To serve, stack one-quarter of onion slices in center of each serving plate. Cover with one piece tuna, one piece foie gras, and a second piece tuna. Spoon sauce around plates.

Yields 4 servings

Patrick D'Amico, Executive Chef
Eclipse Restaurant, Wilmington, DE

Grilled Tuna Steak with Mango Salsa

Chef's Note

— This dish is the essence of simplicity and beauty. It gives you time to mingle with your guests and talk with your family rather than slave over the grill for hours. The final dish will have your guests convinced that you did work on this for hours. Choose any firm-fleshed fish. We often use tuna, mahi mahi, and sometimes even salmon. You can use a whole fish, steak cuts, or fillets. Plan on 6 to 8 ounces per guest.

1 cup peeled, pitted, and diced into ¼-inch cubes ripe mango
¼ cup finely diced red onion
2 tablespoons coarsely chopped cilantro
1 tablespoon fresh lime juice
1 jalapeño pepper, minced (seeds and veins removed)
4 tuna steaks, 4 to 6 ounces each
Seasoned or herbed olive oil
Salt and pepper
Zucchini and/or yellow squash medallions
Strips of red pepper

Place first five ingredients in a bowl and combine thoroughly. Refrigerate. (Best when made 1 day in advance.)

Heat grill to medium-high. Brush steaks with oil. Sprinkle both sides with salt and pepper. Grill fish for a few minutes on each side. Do not overcook; fish can dry out very quickly on a char grill. Toss vegetable medallions and peppers with seasoned oil and grill.

Place fish on serving plates. Top fish with mango salsa and serve with grilled veggies.

Yields 4 servings

Andrew Maloney, Executive Chef
Nodding Head Brewery & Restaurant, Philadelphia, PA

Polenta Crusted Halibut with Lobster Basil Sauce

Recommended Wine

**Montlouis Clos Habert
François Chidaine 2001**
François Chidaine is establishing a reputation as one of the most important "jeune vignerons" in the middle Loire. A "biodynamie" farmer, Chidaine has transformed the often overlooked vineyards of Montlouis (always in the shadow of its famous neighbor to the north, Vouvray) and is producing wines of extraordinary richness and complexity. The touch of sweetness in this wine is balanced by powerful structure and makes this a delicious drink with aromatic cheeses, pâté, and roasted game birds.

— Moore Brothers Wine Company
Pennsauken, NJ, and
Wilmington, DE

12 Roma tomatoes, chopped

5 shallots, sliced

½ bulb garlic, peeled and chopped

2 tablespoons kosher salt

1 tablespoon tomato paste

1 teaspoon whole peppercorns

1 bay leaf

½ teaspoon crushed red pepper

2½ cups chicken stock

½ bunch basil

⅛ bunch cilantro

3 sprigs dill

2½ tablespoons butter, optional

½ pound pappardalle pasta (or fettuccine)

3 ounces lobster meat (Frozen or pasteurized is fine.
   Crabmeat or diced cooked shrimp is a good substitute.)

¼ cup vegetable oil

Salt and pepper

4 halibut fillets, 7 ounces each

1 cup cornmeal/polenta

Place tomatoes, shallots, garlic, kosher salt, tomato paste, peppercorns, bay leaf, crushed red pepper, and chicken stock in a medium saucepan. Bring to a boil, then simmer for 30 minutes. Pass sauce through a strainer. (The smaller the holes, the smoother the sauce will be. Sauce will be strained again after the addition of fresh herbs.)

Return sauce to stove. Tear herbs and add to sauce. Cook until reduced to desired consistency. Pass sauce through strainer again and return to stove. Whisk in butter and reserve.

While sauce is reducing, bring 2 quarts of salted water to a boil. Cook pasta until al dente and strain.

Add pasta and lobster meat to sauce. Season to taste and cover.

Heat vegetable oil in a Teflon-coated pan over medium heat for 3 minutes. Season fish on both sides with salt and pepper. Dredge fish in cornmeal on one side. Sauté fish,

cornmeal side down, for about 2 to 3 minutes or until golden brown, then flip. Cook for another 3 to 4 minutes to desired doneness.

Place pasta and sauce in bowls and top with fish. Enjoy!

Yields 4 servings

Alex Capasso, Executive Chef
Max's Fine Dining, Cinnaminson, NJ

Seared Alaskan Halibut with Grilled Pineapple-Mango Salsa

Recommended Wine

Alsace Gewürztraminer Herrenweg Domaine Barmès-Buecher 2001

Situated between the villages of Turckheim and Wintzenheim, the Herrenweg vineyard has a unique microclimate with sandy, well-draining soil and plenty of sun during the year. Elegant, sensuous wines are made from fruit grown here, particularly the beautiful Gewurztraminer, so palatable young as worth cellaring for a few years. The 2001 vintage, with its higher concentration and complexity, has emphasized these qualities and set a new standard for this varietal in the region.

— Moore Brothers Wine Company
Pennsauken, NJ, and
Wilmington, DE

6 Alaskan halibut fillets, 6 ounces each
Kosher salt and freshly ground black pepper to taste
Zest of 3 limes
2 tablespoons unsalted butter
1 tablespoon vegetable oil
Green Rice (Recipe appears on page 235.)
Black Beans (Recipe appears on page 230.)
Grilled Pineapple-Mango Salsa (Recipe appears on page 340.)
2 avocados, peeled and pitted

Arrange fillets in a baking dish. Season with salt and pepper and rub with zest. Preheat a cast-iron skillet over medium heat for 5 minutes. Raise the heat to high and add butter and oil. Working in batches, if necessary, sear fillets, turning once, until well browned and just cooked through, about 3 minutes per side.

Divide rice and beans among centers of 6 plates. Top with halibut fillets and spoon salsa over each. Cut avocados into thin slices and fan slices on each plate.

Yields 6 servings

Susanna Goihman, Chef/Owner
Azafran, Philadelphia, PA

Catfish Nuggets with Leek and Ginger Sauce

The Restaurant School at Walnut Hill College

Known for:
culinary school serving fresh seasonal foods

Most requested table:
in the courtyard

Menu:
three entirely different restaurants

Director of Culinary Arts:
Philip G. Pinkney

Chef's training:
European Masters in both Garde-Manger and Hot Kitchen

Chef's hobbies/ accomplishments:
skiing, biking, cooking, traveling

Chef's favorite ingredient:
whatever is at its peak of the season

Chef's favorite food:
simple roast chicken dinner or oven-fried chicken

1 cup rice vinegar
½ cup tamari soy sauce
⅓ cup lemon juice
3 tablespoons minced ginger
2 tablespoons minced garlic
3 tablespoons brown sugar, packed
3 pounds catfish fillets, cut into ½-inch strips
Flour, seasoned with coriander
8 tablespoons canola oil
2 leeks, blanched and julienned

In a nonreactive bowl or food processor, combine first six ingredients. Blend well and reserve.

Dust nuggets with seasoned flour. Preheat skillet or sauté pan over high heat. Add oil to pan. Pan-sear nuggets. Add leeks and toss to combine. Add ginger sauce and toss to combine. Cook until sauce reduces somewhat. Serve immediately.

Yields 8 servings

**Philip Pinkney CEC, CCE, Director of Culinary Arts
The Restaurant School at Walnut Hill College
Philadelphia, PA**

Red Snapper Creole with Grilled Mangoes and Bananas

Philadelphia Fish & Company

Known for:
upscale seafood, ahead of the curve with food, not trendy

Year opened:
1982

Most requested table:
#57

Menu:
innovative seafood

Owner:
Kevin Meeker

Chef's training:
self taught chef;
University of Maine

Chef's hobbies/ accomplishments:
snowboarding/opened seven restaurants since 1977

Chef's favorite ingredient:
cayenne pepper — it gives a little spice to everything

Chef's favorite food:
grilled island whole fish, red snapper, pompano

½ cup fresh orange juice
¼ cup fresh lemon juice
¼ cup fresh lime juice
3 tablespoons cider vinegar
¼ cup chopped fresh cilantro
¼ cup vegetable oil
2 medium cloves garlic, minced
1 medium onion, sliced
1 green bell pepper, julienne cut
1 red bell pepper, julienne cut
½ jalapeño pepper, julienne cut (use more if you prefer it hotter)
¼ cup dark rum, optional
2 tablespoons brown sugar
Salt and pepper to taste
1 large mango, peeled and pitted
2 ripe bananas, peeled
Juice of 1 lime
2 tablespoons unsalted butter, melted
2 red snapper fillets, 6 to 8 ounces each
Fresh cilantro sprigs

In a medium bowl, combine citrus juices, vinegar, and cilantro. Set aside.

In a large skillet, heat 2 tablespoons vegetable oil over medium-high heat. Add garlic, onions, and all peppers, including jalapeño, and sauté until soft. Add dark rum and allow alcohol to burn off; reduce to a simmer. Add citrus mixture and simmer until reduced by one half. Add brown sugar and simmer until dissolved and fully incorporated. Season to taste with salt and pepper. Reserve and keep warm.

Preheat grill to medium-hot temperature. Slice mango lengthwise into 1-inch-wide strips. Slice bananas lengthwise, then cut in half. Brush fruit pieces with lime juice, then with melted butter. Place on aluminum foil. Place foil

onto grill and cook until fruit is soft. Reserve and keep warm.

Brush snapper fillets on both sides with remaining oil. Season with salt and pepper. Grill for 4 to 5 minutes on one side, then turn and cook until done, approximately 3 minutes.

Place each fillet on a serving plate. Cover with warm Creole sauce and top with fruit slices. Garnish with a sprig of fresh cilantro and serve immediately.

Yields 2 servings

Kevin Meeker, Chef/Owner
Philadelphia Fish & Company, Philadelphia, PA

Sautéed Jumbo Lump Crab Cakes

Chef's Notes

— This is one of our signature dishes in our critically acclaimed Marker Restaurant.

— Cakes can be prepared in advance. Sauté and reserve, then heat in a 400° oven for 4 minutes until heated thoroughly.

¼ cup diced red pepper
¼ cup diced yellow pepper
1 tablespoon minced shallots
7 tablespoons olive oil
½ cup minced scallions
Salt and pepper to taste
3 pounds jumbo lump crabmeat
3 ounces ground panko breadcrumbs
3 tablespoons mayonnaise
2 tablespoons Dijon mustard
1 teaspoon Tabasco
1 tablespoon Old Bay Seasoning
Juice of 1 lemon

Sauté peppers and shallots in 1 tablespoon olive oil for 1 minute. Do not soften. Add scallions and cook for 30 seconds. Cool at once. Season with salt and pepper to taste.

In a mixing bowl, combine cooled vegetable mixture, crabmeat, and breadcrumbs. Mix very gently. In a separate bowl, combine mayonnaise, Dijon mustard, Tabasco, Old Bay, and lemon juice. Spread this mixture onto crabmeat mixture. Fold in gently — do not break up lumps of crabmeat. Adjust seasoning with salt and pepper. Form into 12 cakes, about 3 ounces each.

Heat a flat-bottomed sauté pan over medium heat for approximately 3 minutes until hot. Add remaining 6 tablespoons olive oil. Place crab cakes carefully in pan and gently shake pan to prevent sticking. Sauté for 2 minutes until bronze in color. Turn with a flat spatula and sauté for 2 more minutes. Remove cakes from pan and blot dry. Serve immediately alone or with Smoked Red Pepper Sauce (Recipe appears on page 321.).

Yields 12 cakes

Vince Alberici, Executive Chef
Marker Restaurant at Adam's Mark Hotel, Philadelphia, PA

Mixmaster Crab Cake

Recommended Wine

Coteaux d'Aix-en-Provence Cuvée Prestige Rosé Château Calissanne 2002
The largest single estate in the area with the best view of Mont-St.-Victoire, in the vicinity of Aix-en-Provence also makes some of the most refined and elegant wines. This is a blend of Cabernet Sauvignon and Syrah in equal proportions, vinified in the typical saignée method and uncompromised by barrel elevation. A true "rosé de repas," complex and full-bodied with a beautiful long and clean finish.

— Moore Brothers Wine Company
Pennsauken, NJ, and
Wilmington, DE

¼ cup Parmesan cheese
1 tablespoon Old Bay Seasoning
2 eggs
2 tablespoons mayonnaise
1 tablespoon grain mustard
1 teaspoon Worcestershire sauce
1 teaspoon fresh lemon juice
1 pound claw crabmeat
1 pound jumbo lump crabmeat
4 cloves garlic, minced
2 scallions, chopped
1 shallot, minced
½ bell pepper, chopped
½ bunch parsley, chopped
2 tablespoons breadcrumbs
2 tablespoons olive oil
½ cup flour
Saffron Aïoli (Recipe appears on page 333.)

Combine Parmesan cheese and Old Bay in a large bowl. In another bowl, whisk together eggs, mayonnaise, mustard, Worcestershire sauce, and lemon juice. Add to dry ingredients. Gently fold in crabmeats, garlic, scallions, shallot, bell pepper, and parsley. Slowly add breadcrumbs. (The consistency should be a little wet.) Form into 3- to 4-ounce cakes.

Preheat oven to 350°. Heat oil in a pan until just smoking. Dredge cakes in flour and shake off excess. Sauté cakes for 2 minutes. Flip over into an ovenproof pan and bake in oven for 8 to 10 minutes until golden brown. Serve with aïoli.

Yields 4 to 6 servings

Jon C. Hallowell, Chef/Owner
Mixmaster Café, Malvern, PA

What's For Dinner Crab Cakes

What's for Dinner ... It's a Mystery

Known for:
catering company featuring
in-home murder mysteries

Year opened:
2002

Menu:
ecelectic/murder
mystery parties

Chef:
John Caiola

Chef's training:
Johnson & Wales University

**Chef's hobbies/
accomplishments:**
writing, designing props, boating

Chef's favorite ingredient:
any seafood

Chef's favorite food:
pasta

2 large egg whites
6 tablespoons mayonnaise
2 teaspoons English dry mustard
2½ teaspoons Old Bay Seasoning
2 teaspoons Worcestershire sauce
Salt and black pepper to taste
2 pounds jumbo lump or colossal crabmeat
¼ to ½ cup unseasoned breadcrumbs

Preheat oven to 375°. Coat a sheet pan with breadcrumbs.

Mix together egg whites, mayonnaise, and seasonings. Gently fold in crabmeat, being careful not to break up the lump too much. Mix in breadcrumbs, starting with ¼ cup, adding more or less depending on how moist you want the cakes to be.

Form into 4-ounce cakes. Place on prepared pan. Bake for 15 to 20 minutes.

Yields approximately 8 cakes

John Caiola, Chef/Owner
What's for Dinner ... It's a Mystery, Mount Laurel, NJ

Wasabi Crab Cake

Brasserie Perrier

Known for:
Art Deco design

Year opened:
1997

Most requested table:
#32

Menu:
French with Asian
and Italian influence

Chef:
Chris Scarduzio

Chef's training:
Culinary Institute of America

**Chef's hobbies/
accomplishments:**
golf/popularity and success of
Brasserie Perrier

Chef's favorite ingredient:
basil

Chef's favorite food:
pasta

6 ounces crabmeat, picked over
2 teaspoons minced fennel
2 teaspoons minced celery
2 teaspoons minced shallot
4 tablespoons wasabi mayonnaise (add more, if you like)
1 teaspoon chopped chives
1 teaspoon chopped cilantro
Salt and pepper
Drizzle of sesame oil
Japanese panko breadcrumbs
1 tablespoon blended oil
1 cup juliennned daikon radish
1 cup picked pea leaves
Olive oil

Place crabmeat in a chilled bowl. Place fennel, celery, and shallot in a food processor and pulse to combine well. Squeeze to remove excess moisture and add to crabmeat.

Stir in wasabi mayonnaise, chives, and cilantro. Season to taste with salt and pepper and sesame oil. Mix in enough breadcrumbs to tighten mixture. Form mixture into 2 crab cakes and coat with additional breadcrumbs.

Heat blended oil in a sauté pan over medium-high heat. Sauté crab cakes until hot and crispy on both sides.

Combine daikon radish, pea leaves, salt and pepper, and olive oil to taste. Place crab cakes on plates and garnish with vegetables.

Yields 2 servings

**Chris Scarduzio, Executive Chef
Brasserie Perrier, Philadelphia, PA**

Pan-Seared Crab Cakes with Yellow Pepper Cream Sauce

Chef's Notes:

— 1998 Pinot Grigio is an excellent complementary wine for this dish.

— Chef Andrea suggests fresh peaches to garnish the plate.

1 pound crabmeat
1 egg white
2 tablespoons Dijon mustard
2 tablespoons mayonnaise
Chopped parsley
1 teaspoon lemon juice
Salt and pepper
1 cup breadcrumbs
½ quart heavy cream
3 tablespoons butter
Pinch of saffron
Fresh chives

In a large bowl, combine crabmeat, egg white, Dijon mustard, mayonnaise, and chopped parsley. Stir in lemon juice. Season with pinch of salt and pepper. Refrigerate for 15 minutes.

Preheat oven to 400°. Shape mixture into cakes. Cover with breadcrumbs and place on an oiled sheet pan. Bake for approximately 15 minutes.

While cakes are baking, prepare sauce. Bring heavy cream to boil in a skillet over medium heat, stirring occasionally so hot cream does not overflow. Stir in butter. Season with saffron and salt and pepper to taste. Heat on low for 10 minutes or until desired thickness.

Increase temperature to 450° and set oven to broil. Carefully watch crab cakes and remove from oven when a brown crust forms.

Serve on a plate and pour sauce on top. Garnish with fresh chives.

Yields 4 servings

Andrea Pugliese, Chef
Lamberti's Cucina, Mt. Holly, NJ

Soft-shell Crabs

Whisk Wisdom

Soft-shell crabs are blue crabs that have shed their hard outer shell. The shell is completely soft and edible so the entire crab can be eaten once it has been properly cleaned (or dressed). You can buy them fresh and fully dressed or frozen during the off-season.

To dress crabs, cut across the face at an upward angle and remove the eye sockets and scaly section of the lower mouth. Lift each side of the shell and remove gills. Turn crab over and cut off the bottom apron.

1 cup flour
2 tablespoons cornstarch
1 tablespoon granulated garlic
1 tablespoon ground pepper
2 tablespoons Old Bay Seasoning
1 tablespoon paprika
8 soft-shell crabs
1 cup clarified butter
1 cup canola or blended oil
¼ cup white wine
¼ pound butter
1 head garlic, minced
Juice of 1 lemon

Mix flour with cornstarch and seasonings. Dredge crabs in seasoned flour.

Heat a large sauté pan over medium heat. Add clarified butter and oil and combine. Place crabs, tops down, in pan for about 3 to 4 minutes until bright red in color and puffy. Turn <u>carefully</u>: moisture from crabs may cause oil to splatter. (You may want to cover with a lid.)

Add wine, butter, garlic, and lemon juice. Raise heat to high and cook for about 2 minutes to reduce liquid. Serve immediately alone or with Creole Tartar Sauce (Recipe appears on page 334.).

Yields 8 servings

Laura Kaplan, Chef/Owner
Emerald Fish, Cherry Hill, NJ

Garlic Shrimp

Mixmaster Café

Known for:
crab cakes, risotto, filet mignon

Year opened:
1999

Most requested table:
table #8

Menu:
Mediterranean-American

Chef:
Jon C. Hallowell

Chef's training:
Restaurant School, Philadelphia

Chef's hobbies/ accomplishments:
skiing, Grateful Dead music/our bruschetta was named "Best of Mainline"

Chef's favorite ingredient:
garlic and saffron

Chef's favorite food:
foie gras, bacon and eggs, ramen noodles

¼ cup olive oil
1 pound large shrimp, peeled and deveined
4 cloves garlic, minced
1 shallot, chopped
½ bunch parsley, chopped
Salt and pepper

Heat oil in a 12-inch sauté pan over medium-high heat. Add shrimp and cook for 2 minutes. Flip over and add remaining ingredients. Cook for 3 more minutes. Season with salt and pepper to taste.

Yields 2 servings

Jon C. Hallowell, Chef/Owner
Mixmaster Café, Malvern, PA

Shrimp Konbongyi

Rangoon Burmese Restaurant

Known for:
spicy food

Year opened:
1993

Chef:
Tun Myint

Chef's training:
20 years experience in Burmese and Chinese cooking

Chef's hobbies/ accomplishments:
appetizers and garnishes

Chef's favorite ingredient:
curry and spicy ingredients

Chef's favorite food:
Burmese-Chinese food

½ pound medium shrimp, shelled and deveined
½ teaspoon salt
¼ cup vegetable oil
4 small whole dried hot red chiles
4 tablespoons sliced onion
2 cloves garlic, sliced
½-inch fresh ginger, sliced
2 tablespoons mushroom soy sauce
1 scallion, cut into 1-inch pieces
½ teaspoon monosodium glutamate

Marinate shrimp in salt for 5 minutes.

Heat oil in a wok or skillet over moderate heat. Fry dried red chiles until brown. Add onion, garlic, and ginger and cook for 30 seconds. Add shrimp and stir-fry for 2 minutes. Add soy sauce, scallion, and MSG. Mix together for a few seconds. Serve warm with rice.

Yields 4 servings

Tun Myint, Chef
Rangoon Burmese Restaurant, Philadelphia, PA

Voodoo Shrimp

Chef's Note

This item is our #1 seller and just about everyone tries it and loves it. Marie Claire will bless all after eating this dish.

1 pound large shrimp, peeled and deveined
Flour
2 tablespoons Creole seasoning
Olive oil as needed
¼ cup chopped celery
1 ounce Voodoo sauce (hot pepper sauce)
2 cups steamed rice
2 teaspoons chopped parsley

Dredge shrimp in flour, then toss with Creole seasoning. Heat olive oil in a sauté pan. Add shrimp and celery and sear shrimp for approximately 30 seconds on each side. Splash shrimp with Voodoo sauce. Turn off heat and cover for 2 minutes to let Voodoo sauce steam until all is tender.

Serve shrimp over warm rice and finish with parsley.

Yields 2 to 4 servings

Nick Ventura, Executive Chef/Partner
Nola on Head House Square, Philadelphia, PA

Yuzu Ginger Sea Scallops with Habañero Pineapple Salsa

Denim Lounge

Known for:
Latin-Asian inspired dishes done with finesse

Year opened:
2003

Most requested table:
crystal lounge

Menu:
American with heavy Latin/ Asian influences

Chef:
Scott D. McLeod

Chef's training:
L'Academie de Cuisine; ¡Pasión! alumni

Chef's hobbies/ accomplishments:
tattoos, working out, dining out

Chef's favorite ingredient:
yuzu

Chef's favorite food:
foie gras

5 giant sea scallops, about 1½ ounces each
1 cup chopped fine, thin strips fresh cilantro
1½ cups orange juice
½ cup yuzu juice (sold at Asian markets)
1 tablespoon minced ginger
1 tablespoon red chili pepper flakes
2 cups diced golden pineapple
2 tablespoons diced red onion
2 tablespoons diced red bell pepper
1½ habañero chili peppers, very finely diced
1 jalapeño chili pepper, finely diced
½ cup thinly chopped fresh culantro leaves (sold at Latin
   markets or substitute with cilantro)
1 tablespoon sliced scallion, green part only
3 tablespoons lime juice
3 tablespoons rice wine vinegar
3 tablespoons extra virgin olive oil
Kosher salt to taste
Sea salt to taste

Slice sea scallops in half lengthwise. Reserve.
   In a shallow dish, combine half the cilantro, orange juice, yuzu juice, ginger, and red chili pepper flakes. Marinate sea scallops in mixture in the refrigerator for at least 3 hours.
   Combine pineapple, red onion, red bell pepper, habañero, jalapeño, culantro, scallion and remaining cilantro in a bowl. Add lime juice, rice wine vinegar, olive oil, and a pinch of kosher salt to taste.
   Sprinkle scallops with sea salt and arrange on top of salsa.
   Chef's note … Before serving, adjust acidity to taste, using yuzu juice for the scallops and lime juice for the salsa.

Yields 2 servings

Scott McLeod, Executive Chef
Denim Lounge, Philadelphia, PA

Meats

Grilled Rib-eye with Gorgonzola Butter

Sotto Varalli

Known for:
giant squid at bar and jazz band on weekend

Most requested table:
bar area

Menu:
seafood with contemporary American and French influences

Chef:
William Carroll

Chef's training:
Culinary Institute of America

Chef's hobbies/ accomplishments:
fishing, family, wine

Chef's favorite ingredient:
fresh herbs, wild mushrooms, sea salt

Chef's favorite food:
French with Asian influence

12 ounces Hen of Wood mushrooms (Portobello can be substituted.)
½ cup walnut oil
6 tablespoons sherry vinegar
3 tablespoons chopped garlic
2 tablespoons chopped shallot
2 teaspoons chopped thyme
4 tablespoons Gorgonzola cheese
4 tablespoons soft sweet butter
2 roasted red peppers, peeled and seeded
1 tablespoon diced carrots
1 tablespoon diced fennel
½ cup dry vermouth
1 sprig thyme
4 rib-eye steaks, 12 ounces each
Salt and pepper to taste

Combine mushrooms, walnut oil, 4 tablespoons vinegar, 2 tablespoons garlic, shallots, and thyme. Marinate for 4 hours.

Mix cheese and butter with a fork. Reserve. Combine remaining 2 tablespoons sherry vinegar and roasted peppers in a food processor or blender and puree. Reserve.

Preheat oven to 375°. Roast mushrooms for 15 minutes.

Meanwhile, sauté remaining garlic, carrots, and fennel until soft. Add vermouth and thyme sprig. Cook until liquid is reduced by half. Add puree to carrot mixture and cook until slightly thickened (a fondue consistency).

Season steaks with salt and pepper. Grill to medium-rare.

Place steaks on serving plates. Top with Gorgonzola butter, then roasted pepper fondue. Cover with roasted mushrooms.

Yields 4 servings

William Carroll, Executive Chef
Sotto Varalli, Philadelphia, PA

Grilled Chimichurri Steak

Fork

Known for:
creative bistro cooking with seasonal ingredients; hand painted lamp shades that illuminate the room

Year opened:
1997

Most requested table:
B1

Menu:
new American bistro

Chef:
Thien Ngo
sous chef, Christina McKeogh

Chef's favorite ingredient:
scallions

Chef's favorite food:
wine

½ pound ginger, peeled and roughly chopped
1 bunch cilantro, washed and chopped
2 bunches parsley, washed and chopped
¼ cup fresh squeezed lime juice
2 cloves garlic, chopped
1 tablespoon cumin
2 bunches scallions, chopped and ends removed
2 cups olive oil
6 center cut strip steaks, about 10 ounces each (or chicken breasts or fish fillets)

Mix all ingredients, except steaks, in a blender or food processor. Marinate steaks in mixture for at least 24 hours. (Marinate chicken for at least 24 hours; fish for 1 hour.)

When ready to cook, season with salt and pepper to taste. Cook on a hot grill to your liking.

Yields 6 servings

Thien Ngo, Executive Chef
Fork, Philadelphia, PA

Filete Toluca

Recommended Wine

Marcillac Lo Sang del Païs Domaine du Cros 2002
Marcillac (the town) lies 1,500 feet above sea level in a sheltered, enclosed amphiteatre called Le Vallon. The wine made here is mostly red, from a local grape variety called Fer Servadou that gives rustic, tannic wines. A partial exception to the rule, Domaine du Cros produces a more fragrant and better-balanced wine with red berry and licorice aromatics, a dry, velvety palate, and spicy, peppery finish.

— Moore Brothers Wine Company
Pennsauken, NJ, and
Wilmington, DE

¾ cup vegetable oil
3 to 6 dried or 2 canned chipotle chiles
1 ancho chile
½ pound chorizo sausage
1½ white onions, quartered plus 2 thick slices white onion
4 medium cloves garlic, whole
Salt to taste
25 canned or fresh tomatillos, husked
½ cup chopped cilantro plus extra for garnishing
⅓ cup plus ½ cup olive oil
2 tablespoons butter
8 beef fillets (filet mignon), 5 to 6 ounces each
¾ tablespoon freshly ground pepper
1½ cups beef broth
8 tortillas
8 slices Chihuahua cheese, about 3 ounces each

Heat vegetable oil in a frying pan. Fry chiles and chorizo. Remove, drain, and reserve.

Add quartered onions and garlic to same pan and brown. Season with salt. Add tomatillos and 3 cups water. Increase heat and boil for 15 minutes if tomatillos are fresh; just a few minutes if canned. Transfer contents of pan plus reserved chile mixture to a blender. Add ½ cup chopped cilantro. Blend until smooth.

Heat ⅓ cup olive oil in same pan. Add onion slices and brown on both sides. Remove and discard onion. Add blended sauce back to pan and cook on low heat for 40 minutes or until fat rises to the surface.

In a heavy skillet, heat ¼ cup olive oil and 1 tablespoon butter. Add 4 fillets and fry for 3 to 4 minutes per side. When juices begin to rise to the surface, sprinkle with salt and pepper. Remove fillets from pan and keep warm. Repeat with remaining oil, butter, and fillets. Stir beef broth into pan juices. Boil until liquid is reduced by half. Add chipotle-chorizo sauce and simmer for 25 minutes. Add meat to skillet. Heat for 5 to 8 minutes.

Place 1 tortilla on each plate. Place a fillet on each tortilla and cover with a slice of cheese. Place under broiler to melt cheese. Remove from broiler. Cover with chipotle-chorizo sauce. Sprinkle with cilantro. Serve with rice and refried beans.

Yields 8 servings

Rogelio Flores, Chef
El Sarape Mexican Restaurant & Tequila Bar, Blue Bell, PA

El Sarape Cortadillo

El Sarape Mexican Restaurant

Known for:
authentic Mexican food

Year opened:
2000

Menu:
Mexican food

Chef:
Rogelio Flores

Chef's training:
in Mexico

Chef's favorite ingredient:
chipotle, fresh cilantro

Sauce

½ cup butter
½ cup olive oil
4 medium white onions, sliced diagonally
15 serrano chiles, sliced into thin strips
6 tomatoes (about 2 pounds), finely chopped
Salt and pepper to taste

Beef

16 slices bacon, finely chopped
½ cup olive oil
1 medium white onion, finely chopped
4 pounds beef tenderloins, cut in strips
4 jalapeño chiles, sliced into thin strips
¾ cup finely chopped cilantro

Heat a frying pan over medium heat for 5 minutes. Add butter and oil. Stir in onion and chiles and cook until onion is golden brown. Add tomatoes. Season with salt and pepper. Stir and bring to a boil. Reduce heat and simmer for 30 minutes or until the sauce thickens and the fat rises to the surface.

Heat a separate frying over medium heat for 15 minutes. Fry bacon until crisp. Remove, drain on paper towels, and reserve. Add oil to pan. Add onions and beef and stir. Sauté until onion is golden brown, about 7 minutes. Season with salt and pepper. Remove beef from frying pan and keep warm. Add sauce to onion frying pan. Stir in bacon and cook until sauce thickens.

Divide beef between 8 plates. Cover with sauce. Garnish each plate with chile strips and sprinkle with cilantro.

Yields 8 servings

Rogelio Flores, Chef
El Sarape Mexican Restaurant & Tequila Bar, Blue Bell, PA

Spicy Beef with Basil

Recommended Wine

2000 Santa Barbara Winery Pinot Noir
Bright fruit and a racy finish will help this wine to combine with this spicy dish. Deep berry flavors help with the savory aspects of this complex dish. $17

2001 Olivier Dumaine Crozes-Hermitage Blanc
A fabulous alternative to Chardonnay and a great white wine for this spicy beef dish. Red wine with fish was only the beginning! $20

— John McNulty
Corkscrewed, Cherry Hill, NJ

¼ cup oil

1 teaspoon chopped garlic

½ teaspoon minced ginger

2 ounces fresh chile peppers, sliced

16 ounces flank steak, thinly sliced

2 tablespoons oyster sauce

¼ cup brown sugar, packed

3 ounces basil leaves, chopped

1 sprig mint, chopped

Heat oil in a medium sauté pan over medium heat. Add garlic and ginger and sauté until garlic begins to sizzle. Add chili peppers and cook until seeds begin to bubble. Add beef and sauté until meat changes color and is cooked almost to desired doneness. Combine oyster sauce and brown sugar and stir into pan. Add basil and mint and serve.

Chef's Note ... This is a Thai-influenced dish which may be served with steamed rice or noodles.

Yields 4 servings

Jerome C. Seeney, Chef
Jack Kramer's Catering, Philadelphia, PA

BBQ
Beef Tips

Chef's Notes

— You can cook this in a crockpot.

— To give this some Cajun flair, add 1 or 2 chopped chili peppers and 1 or 2 tablespoons of The Greatest Grub Ever Fire it up Sauce.

— For more tender vegetables, cook them first before combining with other ingredients.

2 pounds London broil or beef tips, cooked and diced
1 12-ounce jar The Greatest Grub Ever Honey BBQ or Honey Hot BBQ Sauce
1 large onion, cut into strips
1 large red bell pepper, cut into strips
1 large yellow or orange bell pepper, cut into strips
1 green bell pepper, cut into strips
1 large tomato, cored and diced
3 stalks celery, minced very small
2 heaping tablespoons The Greatest Grub Ever Garlic Parmesan Sauce
2 teaspoons lemon or lime juice

Preheat oven to 375°.

Combine all ingredients and pour into a large casserole dish. Cover and bake for 45 minutes. Mix well before serving. Serve over rice or noodles or in a hoagie roll.

Yields 6 to 8 servings

J. Scott Jemison, Chef/Owner
Buffalo Bill's BBQ Restaurant, Williamstown, NJ

Southwestern Brisket

Recommended Wine

Vin de Pays des Collines Rhodaniennes Syrah Domaine Louis Cheze 2001
A member of the Rhône Vignobles, Louis Cheze farms 18 hectare of vines in St. Joseph, Condrieu, the Vin de Pays des Collines Rhodaniennes, and the appellation of Côtes du Rhône. This Vin de Pays Syrah comes from vineyards in the high hills west of St. Joseph. The vines produce wines of rich, mouthfilling character, with a hint of smoke on the nose. A wonderful accompaniment to grilled meats.

— Moore Brothers Wine Company
Pennsauken, NJ, and
Wilmington, DE

1 first-cut brisket, about 4½ to 5 pounds
Salt and pepper
1 cup apple cider vinegar
1 cup ketchup
⅔ cup brown sugar, packed
½ cup water
4 cloves garlic, minced
2 chipotle peppers in adobo, chopped (or more to taste)
2 tablespoons Worcestershire

Preheat oven to 325°. Season brisket with salt and pepper. Dry sear on both sides in a heavy-bottomed skillet and then place in a roasting pan.

In a separate saucepan, combine remaining ingredients and bring to a simmer. Pour sauce over brisket, cover with foil, and roast for about 3½ hours. (Make sure brisket is covered by liquid; if not, baste occasionally.)

Remove brisket from pan. Slice into thin pieces across the grain and return to liquid to serve.

Yields 6 to 8 servings

Kathy S. Gold, Chef/Owner
Custom Cuisine Cooking Company, Cherry Hill, NJ

Blanquette de Veau

La Campagne

Known for:
known for fine French cuisine and country charm

Year opened:
1990

Most requested table:
fireplace table

Menu:
Provençale French

Chef:
Eric Hall

Chef's training:
Widener University; 20 years of experience in kitchens

Chef's hobbies/ accomplishments:
fishing, home remodeling

Chef's favorite food:
anything that's home cooked!

3 pounds veal cubes
1 large onion, diced
2 stalks celery, diced
1 large carrot, diced
1 leek, white part only, diced
8 ounces mushrooms
2 cloves garlic
1 cup white wine
1 tablespoon lemon juice
1 bay leaf
1 sprig thyme
2 egg yolks
1 cup heavy cream
Pinch of nutmeg
Salt and pepper to taste

Place veal in a Dutch oven with onion, celery, carrot, leek, mushrooms, garlic, wine, lemon juice, and spices. Cover with cold water and bring to a simmer. Simmer gently for 1 hour, skimming surface of any scum that rises to the top.

When meat is tender, strain off cooking liquid and transfer liquid to a saucepan. Reserve veal and vegetables and keep warm. Cook liquid until reduced to 1 cup.

Combine egg yolks, cream, and nutmeg in a mixing bowl. Temper mixture into reduced cooking liquid. Heat mixture over a low flame and cook, stirring constantly, until thickened. Do not allow it to boil.

Season with salt and pepper and pour over veal and vegetables.

Yields 6 servings

Eric Hall, Executive Chef
La Campagne, Cherry Hill, NJ

Veal Oscar

The Prime Rib

Known for:
exquisite flowers, furnishings,
and carpets; lithographs

Year opened:
1997

Most requested table:
table 42

Menu:
top-level American steaks,
chops, and seafood

Chef:
Victor Ossorio

Chef's training:
self-training plus long experience
in restaurants in New Jersey and
Pennsylvania

**Chef's hobbies/
accomplishments:**
basketball

Chef's favorite ingredient:
cilantro

Chef's favorite food:
Cuban cuisine

2 large artichokes, leaves and stems removed
1 teaspoon unsalted butter
¼ cup mascarpone cheese
¼ cup goat cheese
1 cup milk
1 cup heavy cream
Pinch of salt and black pepper
6 medallions veal
2 lobster tails, 8 ounces each
10 asparagus spears
6 ounces Choron Sauce (Recipe appears on page 320.)
2 sprigs tarragon

Clean artichokes down to the hearts. Place in a small saucepan with ¼-inch water. Bring to a boil, cover tightly, and steam over low heat until tender. Drain and place into a food processor or blender. Add butter and blend until incorporated. Add cheeses, milk, cream, and salt and pepper. Puree until smooth. Set aside and keep warm.

Season veal and lobster with salt and pepper. Sauté in a pan over medium heat until cooked medium. Remove and set aside. Add asparagus to pan and sauté for 3 to 5 minutes until cooked *al dente* (firm, but tender).

Place a 2-ounce scoop of artichoke puree in center of each plate. Arrange veal and lobster so that they cover puree. Place asparagus on top and drizzle 2 ounces Choron sauce on asparagus and veal and around plate. Garnish with tarragon sprig and serve immediately.

Yields 2 servings

**Victor Ossorio, Chef
The Prime Rib, Philadelphia, PA**

Pan-Seared Veal Saltimbocca with Parma Prosciutto

McCrossen's Tavern

Known for:
friendly tavern atmosphere/ best wings to great rack of lamb

Year opened:
1993

Most requested table:
table 8

Menu:
Mediterranean/American

Chef:
Bill Strobel

Chef's hobbies/ accomplishments:
Irish erotica/honorarium - top 3 artist in city of Camden

Chef's favorite ingredient:
fresh cracked black pepper

Chef's favorite food:
anything spicy or really hot

3 tablespoons olive oil
4 ½-inch-thick veal chops
Salt and pepper
2 tablespoons minced shallot
2 tablespoons minced fresh sage
1 cup white wine
2 tablespoons butter
½ pound Parma prosciutto, very thinly sliced
¼ pound Parmesan Reggiano, freshly shaved
1 lemon, quartered
Fresh sage leaves

Preheat oven to 400°.

Heat olive oil in an ovenproof pan over high heat. Season dry veal chops with salt and pepper and place in pan. Sear for 2 minutes, then turn and place pan in oven for 8 to 10 minutes (for medium) or to desired doneness. Remove chops from pan and reserve.

Add shallots and sage to pan. Add wine and deglaze. Add butter and cook over medium heat, stirring until sauce is silky.

Place chops on 4 plates and top each with pan sauce. Decoratively place prosciutto on top of chops, then garnish with Parmesan shavings. Garnish with lemon wedge and fresh sage leaves.

Chef's note … Sautéed Italian greens, such as broccoli rabe or escarole, are a great side for this classic dish.

Yields 4 servings

Bill Strobel, Chef
McCrossen's Tavern, Philadelphia, PA

Veal Saltimbocca

Thommy G's

Known for:
restaurant is housed in a bank
built in 1929

Year opened:
1999

Most requested table:
private table in vault

Menu:
fine Italian cuisine with a New
Orleans flair

Chef:
Thommy Geneviva

Chef's training:
Culinary Institute of America

**Chef's hobbies/
accomplishments:**
reading/Star Chefs of New
Jersey 1999, 2000, 2001, 2002

Chef's favorite ingredient:
basil

Chef's favorite food:
veal

½ pound veal medallions, approximately 6 slices, pounded
Flour
2 ounces clarified butter
4 ounces Chablis
4 ounces Parma prosciutto
6 ounces imported sharp provolone, sliced
4 ounces chicken stock
4 ounces marinara sauce
Juice of 1 lemon
½ cup whole unsalted butter
Salt and pepper to taste
1 tablespoon chopped parsley
1 tablespoon grated Pecorino Romano cheese

Dredge veal in flour and shake off excess. Sauté in clarified butter over medium-high heat. Add Chablis and stir. Top each medallion with prosciutto and sharp provolone. Add chicken stock, marinara sauce, and lemon juice to pan. Simmer until cheese is melted. Add whole butter and stir until incorporated. Season with salt and pepper.

Place 3 veal medallions on each plate. Top with sauce. Garnish with chopped parsley and grated cheese.

Yields 2 servings

**Thommy Geneviva, Executive Chef
Thommy G's, Burlington, NJ**

Veal Capricciosa

Ralph's Italian Restaurant

Known for:
being the oldest family-owned Italian restaurant in the United States

Year opened:
1900

Menu:
Italian

Chef:
Jimmy Rubino, Jr.

Chef's training:
grew up in the business; was cooking by the age of 12

Chef's favorite ingredient:
basil

Chef's favorite food:
veal capricciosa

1 large Spanish onion, chopped

6 cups vegetable oil

1 28-ounce can tomatoes, crushed by hand

1 tablespoon salt

1 tablespoon black pepper

2 large eggplants, peeled and cut into ¼-inch-thick slices

4 cups flour

8 eggs, beaten

12 medallions milk fed veal, about 2 ounces each

¼ cup grated Pecorino Romano cheese

12 thin slices prosciutto, 3 inches x 2 inches

24 slices mozzarella cheese, sliced ⅛-inch thick

½ cup sauterne wine

¼ cup chopped fresh parsley

In a 4-quart pot, sauté onion in 1 cup vegetable oil until golden in color. Add tomatoes, salt, and black pepper. Bring to a boil. Lower flame and simmer for 45 minutes.

While sauce is cooking, dip eggplant slices in flour, then into beaten egg. Heat 3 cups oil in a large ovenproof frying pan. Working in batches, add eggplant slices and sauté for 2 minutes on each side. Drain on paper towels. Drain oil from pan when all eggplant has been cooked.

Add remaining 2 cups oil to frying pan and heat over medium-high heat. Dip veal in flour and sauté for 2 minutes on each side. Drain on paper towels. Drain oil from pan.

Preheat oven to 375°. Coat bottom of frying pan with 1 cup tomato sauce. Add veal and sprinkle with grated cheese. Layer each medallion with 1 slice eggplant, 1 slice prosciutto, and 2 slices mozzarella. Top with remaining sauce and sauterne wine. Bake for 45 minutes. Top with fresh parsley. Serve 2 or 3 veal medallions per person.

Yields 4 to 6 servings

Jimmy Rubino, Jr., Owner/Chef
Ralph's Italian Restaurant, Philadelphia, PA

Pork Normandy

Chef:
Justin Sanders

Chef's training:
Axelsson's Blue Claw; freshman at Culinary Institute of America

Chef's hobbies/ accomplishments:
fishing, weightlifting/cooking with Tony Clark; appearance on the Food Network

Chef's favorite ingredient:
salt

Chef's favorite food:
steak

½ cup brandy

1 tablespoon vanilla liqueur

3 tablespoons peach preserves

1½ cups apple cider

2 teaspoons anise seeds

2 cinnamon sticks

½ shallot, finely minced

2 tablespoons unsalted butter

8 ounces heavy cream

1 tablespoon all-purpose flour

½ large Granny Smith apple, peeled, cored, and finely chopped

4 12-ounce French-cut pork chops

Extra virgin olive oil

Kosher salt

Whisk together brandy, vanilla liqueur, and 2 tablespoons peach preserves. Refrigerate for at least 1 hour.

Combine apple cider, anise seeds, cinnamon sticks, and shallot in a saucepan. Cook over medium-high heat until liquid is reduced to about ½ cup. Strain through a sieve. Discard solids and return liquid to pan. Add 1 tablespoon butter and whisk until completely melted. Return pan to stove and slowly bring to a simmer over low heat. Stir in brandy mixture and cream. Raise temperature to medium-low and cook for 10 to 15 minutes until smooth and light caramel in color, being careful not to burn the cream. Remove pan from heat.

If sauce is too liquidy, melt remaining 1 tablespoon butter in a separate pan. Add flour and stir until well incorporated. When mixture reaches a light brown color, remove from heat and add a small amount to apple cream sauce. Stir until sauce is smooth and coats the back of a spoon. (Add more flour mixture if the sauce still isn't thick enough.) Stir in chopped apple and a splash of brandy and stir well. Reserve.

Wrap tin foil around bone of each pork chop. Brush meat with oil and season with salt. Place chops on a medium-low preheated grill. Cook slowly, so chops do not burn, until desired doneness. (I recommend medium-well or well done.) Remove from heat and let rest for 5 to 7 minutes.

Carefully remove foil from bones and slice pork chops on an angle all the way to the

bone. Slowly, maintaining chops' shape, carefully transfer to plates and fan out slices. Spoon warm sauce over chops and serve hot.

Chef's note ... This is a nice fall dish when the apples are ripe for the picking. I would encourage you to use Granny Smith green apples because of their tartness, which works well with the brandy cream sauce.

Yields 4 servings

Justin Sanders, Chef/Culinary Student

Java Pork Tenderloin

333 Belrose Bar & Grill

Known for:
great food, wine, outdoor dining

Year opened:
1999

Most requested table:
52

Menu:
American cuisine; menu changes 6 times a year

Executive chef:
Carlo deMarco; chef du cuisine, Anna Marie Karlsen

Chef's training:
University of Massachusetts

Chef's favorite ingredient:
cilantro

1 cup mocha java coffee

1 cup blended oil

½ cup molasses

½ cup ground macadamia nuts

½ cup pure maple syrup

2 jalapeño peppers

1 tablespoon fresh minced ginger

1 tablespoon fresh minced garlic

1 tablespoon kosher salt

1 tablespoon ground black pepper

2 tablespoons mirin

Juice of 2 limes

1 whole pork tenderloin, about 2 pounds

Combine all ingredients, except tenderloin, in a robot coupe or food processor and process until smooth.

Marinate trimmed whole tenderloin for 36 to 48 hours. Grill over medium flame, covered, turning often until cooked to an internal temperature of 165 degrees, about 15 to 25 minutes. Let rest for 10 minutes prior to service. Serve with Mango Habañero Salsa (Recipe appears on page 342.).

Yields 4 servings

Carlo deMarco, Chef/Owner
333 Belrose Bar & Grill, Radnor, PA

Pan Seared Pork Loin

Recommended Wine

1997 Torre del Bardo
This "Super Tuscan" blend of Sangiovese and Cabernet Sauvignon will pick up the richness of the sauce and not overpower the pork flavors. $12

— John McNulty
Corkscrewed, Cherry Hill, NJ

1 Vidalia onion
½ cup butter
2 tablespoons sugar
6 tablespoons olive oil
1½ pounds pork tenderloin, cut into 1½-inch medallions
1 cup flour
16 ounces red wine (Chianti)
4 ounces veal stock

Peel and cut onion in half, then slice into thin sections in the opposite direction. Melt 2 tablespoons butter in a sauté pan over medium heat. Add onion and cook until lightly brown, approximately 20 minutes. Add sugar and stir, cooking for another 5 minutes, until onions turn golden brown in color. Reserve and keep warm.

Heat oil in a large sauté pan until just smoking. Dredge medallions in flour and place in pan. Sauté for approximately 5 to 8 minutes until golden brown on both sides.

When pork is almost fully cooked, drain off excess oil. Add remaining butter, wine, and stock. Simmer for 5 minutes, stirring occasionally. (The sauce should thicken as the mixture cooks down.) Add caramelized onions.

Divide pork medallions between 4 serving plates and cover with sauce and onions. (The pork can be served over mashed potatoes. Port wine can be used in place of red wine to attain a sweeter taste.)

Yields 4 servings

John Pilarz, Chef/Owner
Anthony's Creative Italian Cuisine, Haddon Heights, NJ

Port Roasted Pork Chops

The Chef Did It

Known for:
Setting the mood and cooking anything you desire for 2 to 100 people.

Year opened:
2002

Most requested table:
Most people go for the one in their dining room, but we'll do it anywhere you want.

Menu:
It's always up to you, but we can be of service if a little imagination is required.

Chef:
Trish Morrissey

Chef's Training:
Drexel University and The Restaurant School at Walnut Hill College

Chef's hobbies/ accomplishments:
shoe shopping and owning far too many pairs

Chef's favorite ingredient:
anything edible from the sea

Chef's favorite food:
anything from Bruce Kim's Sishikazu in Blue Bell, PA

6 pork chops, 6 to 8 ounces each
1 clove garlic, minced
1 teaspoon crushed caraway seeds
½ teaspoon salt
½ teaspoon fresh cracked pepper, optional
½ cup port
½ cup beef broth
½ cup sour cream

Place pork chops in an ovenproof casserole. Mix remaining ingredients, except sour cream, and pour over chops. Marinate for 2 to 3 hours in refrigerator.

Preheat oven to 325°. Bake chops for 1 hour or until tender. Add more port or stock, if needed.

Remove chops from baking dish and set aside on a serving platter.

Whisk sour cream into pan juices. Heat gently and do not boil.

Pour sauce over chops and serve with Twice Baked Vidalia Onions (Recipe appears on page 223.) or egg noodles.

Yields 6 servings

**Trish Morrissey, Chef/Partner
The Chef Did It, Personal Chef and Catering Service,
Philadelphia, PA**

Peppers Pork Chop with Shallot Au Jus

Recommended Wine

Moulin-à-Vent "La Reserve d'Amélie" Gérard Charvet 2001
Gérard Charvet farms nearly 35 acres of vineyards in the appellation of Moulin-A-Vent, one of the most famous of the "Cru" Beaujolais. Severe pruning and "vendages verte" ensures low yields and concentrated flavors from his old-vine Gamay. This intensely flavored, richly textured cuvée will provide delicious drinking over the next five years.

— Moore Brothers Wine Company
Pennsauken, NJ, and
Wilmington, DE

2 chipotle peppers
1 roasted red pepper
½ bunch cilantro
Juice of 1 lime
1 clove garlic, minced
2 pork chops
5 shallots, julienned
1 teaspoon chopped garlic
½ teaspoon salt
½ teaspoon pepper
½ cup white wine
2 cups veal stock or demi-glace

Put first five ingredients in a blender and puree until a smooth consistency is achieved. Cover pork chops with mixture and marinate for 24 hours in the refrigerator.

When ready to prepare, combine shallots, garlic, salt, and pepper in a sauté pan over medium heat. Cook until caramelized. Add wine and deglaze pan. Add demi-glace. Cook until reduced to a thick consistency.

Preheat grill. Preheat oven to 400°. Grill pork chops for 10 minutes and finish in oven for about 5 minutes or until desired doneness. Serve chops topped with au jus. Great when paired with Shrimp and Garlic Mashed Potatoes (Recipe appears on page 224.).

Yields 2 servings

Brian Watson, Sous Chef
Bourbon Blue, Philadelphia, PA

Guava Barbeque Ribs

Cuba Libre

Known for:
colorful, lively, open-air tropical atmosphere set in 1940's Havana street scene

Year opened:
2000

Menu:
Cuban cuisine

Chef:
Guillermo Veloso

Chef's training:
originally an archaeologist; later attended Johnson & Wales University

Chef's hobbies/ accomplishments:
appearance on national TV, regularly hosts cooking classes

Chef's favorite ingredient:
garlic

Chef's favorite food:
seafood

10 pounds St. Louis cut pork ribs
2 cups prepared barbecue sauce
1 cup hot sauce
1 cup Worcestershire sauce
Water to cover
1 cup chopped garlic
4 to 5 bay leaves
Guava Barbecue Sauce (Recipe appears on page 326.)

Place pork ribs in a large roasting pan or a large stockpot. Mix together barbecue sauce, hot sauce, and Worcestershire and add to pan with enough water to cover ribs. Add garlic and bay leaves. Place pan in refrigerator and marinate for 2 or more hours.

Preheat oven to 325°. Cover ribs and place in oven for 2 hours or until meat is very tender and almost falls off bones. (If cooking ribs on grill, leave racks whole and baste continuously until fully glazed and caramelized.) Remove from liquid and allow to cool.

Serve with guava barbecue sauce.

Yields 8 servings

Guillermo Veloso, Executive Chef
Cuba Libre Restaurant & Rum Bar, Philadelphia, PA

Pennsylvania Dutch Ham and Cabbage

¼ cup oil
1 small onion, diced
2 pounds ham, diced
1 head cabbage, diced
Salt and pepper to taste
¼ pound butter

Heat oil in a large skillet. Add onion and ham. Cook until onion begins to caramelize and ham browns. Add cabbage and season with salt and pepper. Cook until cabbage is soft. Add butter and simmer on low for 5 minutes. Stir often.

Chef's note…A great meal or side dish. Great with scrambled eggs, hot biscuits, and a cup of hot Java!

Yields 6 servings

Joseph Shilling, Personal Chef/Dean of Education Your Private Chef, Conshohocken, PA/ The Art Institute of New York City, NY

Lamb Roasted Over Potatoes "Crying Leg of Lamb"

Recommended Wine

2000 Chateau de Grand Moueys Premieres Cotes de Bordeaux, Bordeaux, France
This simply prepared dish requires a medium weight dry red wine, intense enough to handle the lamb and subtle enough not to overwhelm it. This Merlot based blend from France's famed Bordeaux region will fit the bill nicely. Its woodland berry and cedar flavors are a perfect accent for this herb-roasted preparation. Approximately $12

— Marnie Old
Old Wines LLC, Philadelphia

1 8- or 9-pound leg of lamb, either whole, partially, or fully deboned (may substitute boned and rolled shoulder)

4 or 5 pounds potatoes, unpeeled

2 cups best quality extra virgin olive oil, divided

15 to 20 or more cloves fresh garlic, peeled and either cracked or rough chopped, divided

2 tablespoons coarse kosher salt, divided

2 tablespoons freshly cracked black peppercorns, divided

6 large bunches rosemary (may substitute fresh thyme or sweet marjoram)

6 bay leaves, preferably fresh

2 tablespoons Kitchen Bouquet, optional

Lamb Stock (Recipe appears on page 315.)

Preheat oven to 425°. Boil or steam potatoes until half cooked (very al dente). Drain and quickly lay potatoes out to cool. Peel as soon as they are cool enough to handle. Cut peeled potatoes into 2-inch cubes or slice into ¼-inch-thick rounds. Place in a bowl and toss with some of the olive oil, garlic, salt, and pepper. Set aside.

Oil the inside bottom of a roasting pan which is large enough to accommodate lamb and potatoes. Place half the fresh rosemary and bay leaves in pan. Arrange seasoned potatoes in layers, approximating the area of the lamb, directly on top of the herbs. Place remaining whole herbs on top of potatoes.

Deeply pierce lamb with a sharp paring knife and insert as many whole cloves of garlic as personal preferences dictate. Rub leg with remaining olive oil and a mixture of salt and pepper.

Arrange four custard cups (or four pieces of wood cut from a clean two-by-four), placing one in each of the four corners of roasting pan. Set a roasting or cooling rack on cups or woodblocks, then place lamb on center of rack. Put this entire setup into the oven on the middle or lower shelf. Do not place pan directly on the very bottom of oven else potatoes will burn.

Roast for 20 minutes, basting every 7 minutes with lamb stock. Keep an eye on potatoes and anoint as necessary to keep from drying out as they cook. Lower oven temperature to 350° and continue to baste for another 10 to 15 to 20 minutes, depend-

ing on degree of doneness desired.

Remove from oven and rest for 10 or 12 minutes before carving and serving. Avoid bay leaves and stems of rosemary on which potatoes were cooked.

Chef's note … The heart of this recipe is the cooking method which stems from open hearth cookery. A well-seasoned leg of lamb (or any joint of any species of meat) is positioned and roasted over a bed of potatoes so that the cooking juices drip onto the potatoes, and they cook. The endpoint of this one-pot effort is truly epicurean.

Yields 6 to 8 servings

Fritz Blank, Chef de Cuisine/ Proprietor
Deux Cheminées, Philadelphia, PA

Pan Roasted Rack of Lamb

Chef's Note

— Frenched lamb will give you a clean bone. Lamb has been "frenched" when the meat is cut away from the end so that part of the bone is exposed.

— Steele Pinot Noir is an excellent complementary wine for this dish.

4 frenched and chimed lamb racks, 14 ounces each
Salt and pepper to taste
1 cup olive oil
1 shallot, peeled and diced
1 cup Merlot
1 cup fresh raspberries
1 tablespoon peeled and grated horseradish root
2 tablespoons honey
1 pound French green beans, tips trimmed
Sweet Potato Almond Dumplings (Recipe appears on page 225.)

Preheat oven to 450°.

Season lamb with salt and pepper. Heat oil in an ovenproof skillet over medium-high heat. Sear lamb on both sides, then place in oven for 15 minutes. Remove and let stand for 10 minutes.

In a separate pan, sauté shallot. Add Merlot, raspberries, and horseradish. Simmer until liquid is reduced by half. Add honey and strain. Reserve.

Steam green beans until tender.

Cut each lamb chop off of rack. Place sauce on each serving plate. Place lamb in center of sauce. Surround with dumplings and green beans.

Yields 4 servings

Sean Sellaro, Chef
Lamberti's Cucina, Manalapan, NJ

Lamb with Okra

1½ pounds small okra

Salt

½ cup lemon juice

3 tablespoons unsalted butter

3 tablespoons virgin olive oil

2½ pounds boneless lamb shoulder or shank, trimmed of excess fat and cut into 1-inch chunks

1 small Spanish onion, finely diced (about ½ cup)

4 cloves garlic, minced

1 tablespoon tomato paste

4 medium tomatoes, peeled, seeded, and finely chopped (about 2½ cups)

2 cups lamb stock or water

Freshly ground pepper

¼ teaspoon Turkish red pepper or ground red pepper

1 teaspoon dried mint

Gently pare around cone-shaped tops of okra. Place in a bowl and sprinkle with salt and just over half the lemon juice. Toss well and set aside for at least 20 minutes.

Heat butter and oil in a heavy medium saucepan over high heat. Add lamb and brown, stirring with a wooden spoon, for about 6 minutes. Add onion and garlic and cook gently, stirring for 1 minute. Add tomato paste, tomatoes, and stock. Season with salt and pepper. Bring mixture to a boil. Lower heat, cover saucepan, and simmer for about 45 minutes. Skim surface occasionally to remove any scum that rises to the top.

Drain okra and rinse well under cold running water. Add okra, Turkish red pepper, and mint to lamb. Cover saucepan and simmer for another 25 minutes or until tender. Stir in the remaining lemon juice. Serve hot or warm.

Yields 4 to 6 servings

Melek Basaran, Chef
Authentic Turkish Cuisine, Voorhees, NJ

Pan-Seared Venison Medallions with Bourbon-Mushroom Sauce

Recommended Wine

Barbaresco Canova Cascina Vano 1999
Terreno bianco, a unique, friable but compact limestone soil of volcanic origin, is the theatre of choice of the Nebbiolo grape to perform at its best. Varietal Nebbiolo, this young Barbaresco is vinified for 26 months in 1- and 2-year-old tonneaux of 500 litres and large Slavonic oak botti. The wine is very ample and concentrated, with ripe fruit and chocolate flavors interacting with high acidity, elements of spice, and powerful tannins. Best after 2003.

— Moore Brothers Wine Company
Pennsauken, NJ, and
Wilmington, DE

1½ pounds venison tenderloin, fat trimmed, silver skin removed
2 cups red burgundy wine
3 medium shallots, chopped
2 garlic cloves, finely chopped
1 sprig fresh rosemary, leaves pulled
1 teaspoon dry rubbed sage
2 teaspoons unsalted butter
1 medium leek, white part only, well rinsed and cut into
  2-inch lengths and finely julienned
1½ cups sliced button mushrooms
½ cup bourbon
2 cups City Tavern Demi-glace (Recipe appears on page 317.)
Salt and freshly ground black pepper

Slice the venison into ¼-inch-thick medallions (about 3 ounces each). Place the venison in a medium shallow dish. Add the red wine, shallots, garlic, rosemary, and sage. Cover with plastic wrap and marinate in the refrigerator for 8 hours or overnight.

Remove the venison from the marinade; discard the marinade. Pat the venison dry with paper towels. In a large skillet, cook the venison in the butter over high heat for 3 minutes on each side (for medium-rare), until brown. Remove the venison from the pan. Reserve and keep warm.

Add the leek to the pan and sauté for about 2 minutes, until soft. Add the mushrooms and sauté for 3 minutes, until soft. Add the bourbon to deglaze the pan, loosening any browned bits on the bottom of the pan with a wooden spoon. Stir in the Demi-glace. Reduce the heat and simmer for about 3 minutes, until Demi-glace comes to boil. Season with salt and pepper to taste.

Fan out the venison on the serving plate and top with the mushroom mixture. Any kind of mashed root vegetable makes a good accompaniment.

Yields 4 to 6 servings

Walter Staib, Executive Chef/Proprietor
City Tavern, Philadelphia, PA

Rabbit Bolognese with Cavatelli Pasta

2 tablespoons extra virgin olive oil
2 pounds ground rabbit meat
1 carrot, finely diced
3 shallots, finely diced
2 ribs celery, finely diced
3 cloves garlic, finely chopped
1 tablespoon tomato paste
2 cups red wine
3 pints chicken stock
3 pints veal stock
6 sprigs fresh thyme, chopped
3 sprigs fresh rosemary, chopped
Pinch of hot red pepper flakes
Salt and pepper to taste
Cavatelli Pasta (Recipe appears on page 112.)

Heat a large pot until very hot. Add oil and coat bottom of pan. Add rabbit meat and cook, stirring until dark brown. Add vegetables and tomato paste and cook until browned. Pour in wine and scrape bottom of pot until smooth. Continue to cook until almost dry.

Add chicken and veal stocks and fresh herbs. Bring to a boil. Reduce heat and simmer for 45 minutes or to desired thickness. Season with hot pepper flakes and salt and pepper.

Spoon cavatelli and rabbit Bolognese into serving bowls.

Yields 6 servings

Alex Capasso, Executive Chef
Max's Fine Dining, Cinnaminson, NJ

Sides

Stuffed Artichokes

6 artichokes
2 cups seasoned breadcrumbs
½ cup grated Romano cheese
1 tablespoon granulated garlic
Salt and pepper to taste
¼ cup olive oil
1 quart chicken broth

Using scissors, cut off sharp points of artichokes. Remove outer leaves. Spread open artichokes with thumbs and remove the tender leaves and hairy parts in the middle of artichokes.

Combine breadcrumbs, grated cheese, garlic, and salt and pepper. Fill center of each artichoke with some crumb mixture. Sprinkle mixture between outer leaves.

Heat oil in a sauté pan over medium heat. Add artichokes and cook over medium heat for 3 or 4 minutes. Add chicken broth. Cover and continue to cook for 20 minutes.

Yields 6 servings

Nick Tropiano, Pastry and Pasta Chef
Catelli Ristorante, Voorhees, NJ

Asparagi Parmigiano e Tartufi Nero

Chef's Notes

— This is a fantastic spring dish. The asparagus is fresh, thin, and tender in the first months of spring.

— Parmigiano cheese is recommended for this dish, but any other grated cheese can be substituted.

— Black truffle paste is available at specialty/gourmet food stores.

1 pound thin asparagus
Pinch of salt
1 cup freshly grated Parmigiano Reggiano cheese
3 tablespoons melted butter
2 teaspoons extra virgin olive oil
2 tablespoons black truffle paste
Freshly ground black pepper to taste

Cut off the woody ends of asparagus and discard. Fill a large pot with water and bring to a boil. Add salt and asparagus and cook for 2 to 3 minutes. Drain well and immerse in cold water. (Or put washed asparagus in a dish and microwave for approximately 1 to 2 minutes. Remove, turn asparagus, and repeat.)

Preheat oven to 350°. Place asparagus in an 8 x 8-inch glass baking dish and sprinkle with ½ cup cheese. Mix melted butter, extra virgin olive oil, and truffle paste together and drizzle over asparagus. Sprinkle with remaining cheese. Bake for 5 to 7 minutes.

Serve warm with crusty Italian bread.

Yields 4 servings

Lisa Bogan, Manager
DiBruno Brothers House of Cheese, Philadelphia, PA

Sauté Broccoli Rabe

Chef's Notes

— The longer you cook the broccoli rabe, the softer it will become.

— Cooked fresh ground sausage can be added to the dish.

2 bunches broccoli rabe, stems removed, bunches halved
6 ounces olive oil
¼ cup chopped roasted garlic
Salt and pepper to taste
15 sun-dried tomatoes, halved

Bring a large pot of water to boil. Parboil broccoli rabe by placing in water for approximately 20 seconds. Remove rabe from water and reserve water.

Combine olive oil, garlic, and pinch of salt and pepper in a large sauté pan over medium heat. When garlic begins to brown, add broccoli rabe, sun-dried tomatoes, and 2 ounces of reserved cooking water. Cook for 3 or 4 minutes, stirring often so that ingredients are well combined.

Yields 4 servings

John Pilarz, Chef/Owner
Anthony's Creative Italian Cuisine, Haddon Heights, NJ

Broccoli Rabe with White Beans and Tomato

4 cloves garlic, peeled
½ cup extra virgin olive oil
2 or 3 bunches fresh broccoli rabe, chopped, heads removed
1 8-ounce can cannelloni beans
¼ cup chicken stock
Salt and pepper to taste
3 to 4 Roma tomatoes, cut into sticks

Preheat oven to 400°.

Toss garlic in some olive oil. Place in a pan and roast for 8 to 10 minutes. Chop coarsely.

Heat remaining oil in a sauté pan. Add garlic and broccoli rabe to pan and lightly sauté. Add white beans and chicken stock. Bring to a boil for 1 minute. Remove from stove. Season to taste with salt and pepper. Add tomatoes and serve.

Yields 4 servings

Jason McMullen, Chef/Owner
Valentes, Mt. Laurel, NJ

Sautéed Wild Mushrooms

Morton's the Steakhouse

Known for:
steak, wine, atmosphere

Year opened:
1985

Most requested table:
12 or any booth

Menu:
steakhouse

Chef:
Dan Barbuto

Chef's training:
Morton's University

Chef's hobbies/ accomplishments:
snowboarding, rock climbing

Chef's favorite ingredient:
garlic

Chef's favorite food:
steak

2 ounces portobella mushrooms
2 ounces crimini mushrooms
2 ounces shiitake mushrooms
2 ounces chanterelle or oyster mushrooms
2 tablespoons butter
1 tablespoon chopped parsley
1 teaspoon chopped garlic
1 teaspoon chopped shallots
¼ teaspoon minced anchovies
2 slices bread
Pinch of salt
Pinch of white pepper
1 teaspoon Pernod

Remove stems from portobella mushrooms. Using a spoon, gently scrape dark fronds from bottom of mushrooms. Slice portobellas and remaining mushrooms approximately ⅛-inch thick.

Melt butter in a medium-size sauté pan warmed over medium heat. Add parsley, garlic, shallots, and anchovies. Sauté for approximately 1 minute. Add mushrooms and sauté for 3 minutes more.

Cut each bread slice into a round shape and toast. Reserve.

Add salt and white pepper. Sauté for 30 seconds. Pour in Pernod and sauté for 30 seconds more. Serve mushrooms atop toasted bread.

Yields 2 servings

Dan Barbuto, Executive Chef
Morton's the Steakhouse, Philadelphia, PA

Twice Baked Vidalia Onions

Culinary Quote

"The kitchen, reasonabley enough, was the scene of my first gastronomic adventure. I was on all fours. I crawled into the vegetable bin, settled on a giant onion and ate it, skin and all. It must have marked me for life, for I have never ceased to love the hearty flavor of raw onions."

James Beard

6 large sweet onions (Vidalia or Maui)
Salt and pepper
¾ cup beef or chicken stock
½ cup red wine
3 medium potatoes (Yukon gold preferred), peeled and
   quartered
⅓ cup heavy cream or milk
2 tablespoons butter

Preheat oven to 375°.

Cut tops and bottoms off onions and remove outside layer of each. Cut each onion in half and single layer in a shallow ovenproof dish. Sprinkle with salt and pepper, then pour in stock and wine. Cover with foil and bake for 45 minutes or until tender. Remove foil and bake until slightly browned. Set onions aside to cool. Reduce oven to 350°.

While onions are in oven, bring a medium pot of salted water to boil and add potatoes. Cook over medium-high heat until fork tender, about 25 minutes. Drain well.

Heat cream and butter in a saucepan over medium heat. Add potatoes. Using a potato masher or fork, coarsely mash ingredients together. (The potatoes will be a little lumpy and thicker than mashed potatoes.) Set aside.

When onions are cool enough to handle, scoop out the center of each half onion to make a cup. Leave the three outer layers intact and patch the bottom with loose pieces removed from the center. Mince remaining onion centers and fold into potato mixture. Divide onion potato mixture into 6 equal parts and fill each onion cup. Place in a greased baking dish.

About 30 minutes before serving, bake for 20 to 30 minutes or heated through. For nice color you can quickly brown under a broiler with a dab of butter on each cup. Serve immediately as a side for meat or poultry.

Yields 6 servings

Trish Morrissey, Chef/Partner
The Chef Did It, Personal Chef and Catering Service, Philadelphia, PA

Shrimp and Garlic Mashed Potatoes

Bourbon Blue

Chef:
Brian Watson

Chef's training:
studied under a wide variety of chefs on the East Coast; previous endeavor was in a southwestern style restaurant; spent time in Acapulco learning that style of cuisine.

Chef's hobbies/ accomplishments:
traveling, playing and watching sports, watching the Iron Chef. Brian is the father of a baby boy named Zachary.

Chef's favorite ingredient:
all kinds of fresh peppers

Chef's favorite food:
chicken

1½ pounds baking potatoes, peeled and quartered
Milk
¼ cup chopped shrimp
1 teaspoon chopped garlic
1 teaspoon butter
1 teaspoon chopped parsley

Bring a pot of salted water to a boil. Add potatoes and cook until tender but still firm, about 15 minutes. Drain. Using a potato masher or electric beater, slowly mash or beat potatoes, adding milk as needed until desired consistency.

Sauté shrimp and garlic in butter until shrimp is cooked. Add to mashed potatoes. Add parsley and mix thoroughly.

Yields 2 servings

Brian Watson, Sous Chef
Bourbon Blue, Philadelphia, PA

Sweet Potato Almond Dumplings

2 large sweet potatoes, peeled and diced
2 tablespoons butter
½ cup brown sugar, packed
1 tablespoon peeled and grated ginger root
1 vanilla bean, split
1 teaspoon flour
1 egg
¼ cup toasted sliced almonds
½ cup oil

Boil sweet potatoes until tender. Strain and put through a food mill.

Melt butter in a pan. Add brown sugar, ginger root, and vanilla bean. Strain into potatoes. Mix in flour and egg. Stir almonds into batter.

Heat oil in a skillet. Form dumplings by rolling batter between two spoons. Place in hot oil and cook until brown.

Yields 4 servings

Sean Sellaro, Chef
Lamberti's Cucina, Manalapan, NJ

Smashed Yams

Whisk Wisdom

Even though they look alike, yams and sweet potatoes are not related. The sweet potato (which is not related to the potato) is a large edible root that belongs to the morning-glory family and is a native to tropical areas of the Americas. The yam is a member of the Dioscoreaceae family of tropical and subtropical climbing herbs and shrubs which grow in the Americas and parts of Asia and Africa. Yams are sweeter than sweet potatoes. Yams are higher in moisture, while sweet potatoes are higher in vitamins A and C. Sweet potatoes are smaller than yams which can grow to be 7 feet in length and weigh up to 150 pounds. Yams, when eaten raw, can be toxic.

2 pounds Idaho potatoes, peeled
1 pound yams, peeled
Milk
Butter
½ cup maple syrup
1 teaspoon cinnamon
1 teaspoon allspice
Pinch of nutmeg
Salt and pepper to taste

Boil potatoes and yams until fork tender. Mash, adding as much milk and butter as you like. Add syrup and spices. Season to taste with salt and pepper.

Yields 4 servings

Carlo deMarco, Chef/Owner
333 Belrose Bar & Grill, Radnor, PA

African Peanut Yams

Your Private Chef

Known for:
personalized in your home chef

Year opened:
1996

Most requested table:
in your home

Menu:
cooking to the desire and wants of clients/innovative fresh cooking

Chef:
Joseph E. Shilling

Chef's training:
Penn State University; Culinary Institute of America; Le Cordon Bleu; La Carenne

Chef's hobbies/ accomplishments:
education: currently Dean of Education at the Art Institute of New York City

Chef's favorite ingredient:
garlic! garlic! garlic!

Chef's favorite food:
fish — pan seared/sautéed

2 large yams, diced small
2 tablespoons peanut oil
½ small onion, diced
1 green pepper, diced
1 red pepper, diced
½ cup peanut butter
½ cup orange juice
Salt and pepper to taste
½ pound roasted peanuts, chopped

Boil yams until tender. Reserve.

Heat oil in a sauté pan. Add onions and peppers and sauté until tender. Add peanut butter and orange juice and stir to form a sauce. Season with salt and pepper. Toss yams with sauce. Top with peanuts.

Yields 4 servings

**Joseph Shilling, Personal Chef/Dean of Education
Your Private Chef, Conshohocken, PA/
The Art Institute of New York City, NY**

Kabak Mucveri (Zucchini Fritters)

Authentic Turkish Cuisine

Known for:
fresh to order

Year opened:
2000

Menu:
lamb, chicken, vegetables, seafood, vegetarian dishes

Chef:
Melek Basaran

Chef's training:
from family

Chef's hobbies/ accomplishments:
reading, traveling, tasting different foods

Chef's favorite ingredient:
all vegetables, flour

Chef's favorite food:
imam bayildi — a roasted eggplant dish

1½ pounds small, firm zucchini, grated (about 4 cups)
1 bunch scallions, trimmed and finely chopped, white parts only (about ½ cup)
2 tablespoons finely chopped fresh dill
2 tablespoons finely chopped fresh Italian parsley
3 eggs
1 tablespoon paprika
Salt and fresh ground black pepper
1 cup crumbled feta cheese
1 cup all-purpose flour
1½ cups light olive oil or vegetable oil

Place grated zucchini in a colander. Sprinkle with salt and let drain for about 15 minutes. Squeeze out excess juice. Place zucchini in a large bowl. Add scallions, dill, parsley, eggs, and paprika and mix well. Season with salt and pepper. Stir in feta cheese and flour, a little at a time, until well incorporated.

Heat oil in a large skillet on high, and then lower heat to medium. Scoop out tablespoons of zucchini mixture and gently drop into the hot oil. (Make sure you do not crowd the fritters in the skillet.) Fry until golden brown all over, about 5 minutes. Drain fritters on paper towels.

Serve immediately. Alternatively, serve at room temperature with yogurt and garlic sauce.

Yields 4 to 6 servings

Melek Basaran, Chef
Authentic Turkish Cuisine, Voorhees, NJ

Green Mango Escabeche

2 green hard mangoes
1 small habañero chile, seeded and finely minced
6 tablespoons mild olive oil
¼ cup fresh lime juice
4 teaspoons finely chopped garlic
2 teaspoons sugar
2 teaspoons kosher salt
¼ cup chopped cilantro

Pare away the mango skins. Find the large, flat, tongue-shaped pit in the center of each fruit. Slice each side of the mango into paper-thin shavings paralleling the pit until your slices get too close to it. Discard the pit section.

Whisk together the remaining ingredients and toss with the mango. Cover and refrigerate for at least 30 minutes, up to 2 days. Just before serving, drain the excess liquid from the mango and toss with the cilantro.

Yields 1½ cups

Guillermo Pernot, Executive Chef/Owner
¡Pasión!, Philadelphia, PA

Black Beans

Azafran

Known for:
Cuban, Venezuelan, Columbian
influences

Year opened:
1997

Menu:
eclectic South American/
Nuevo Latino

Chef:
Susanna Goihman

Chef's training:
grandmother's kitchen; self taught

**Chef's hobbies/
accomplishments:**
artist, design/
"Best Nuevo Latino" from
Philadelphia magazine

Chef's favorite ingredient:
plantains and ginger

Chef's favorite food:
French fries,
cheese with lots of pepper

3 tablespoons olive oil
1 teaspoon cumin seeds
2 red bell peppers, cored, seeded, and chopped
1 large Spanish onion, chopped
3 12-ounce cans black beans
½ teaspoon sugar
Red wine vinegar to taste
Kosher salt and freshly ground pepper to taste

Heat oil in a saucepan over medium-high heat. Add cumin seeds. Cook and stir until fragrant, about 30 seconds. Add bell peppers and onion and cook, stirring, until soft, about 8 minutes. Stir in black beans and sugar. Bring to a boil. Lower heat and simmer for 5 minutes. Add vinegar and season with salt and pepper.

Yields 6 servings

**Susanna Goihman, Chef/Owner
Azafran, Philadelphia, PA**

Savory Black Beans

Custom Cuisine Cooking Company

Known for:
foods full of flavor and gorgeous presentations

Year opened:
1997

Most requested table:
your dining room or kitchen table!

Menu:
spice it up!

Chef:
Kathy S. Gold

Chef's training:
Le Cordon Bleu

Chef's hobbies/ accomplishments:
acting in community theater/ founder and president of United States Personal Chef Association South Jersey; National Advisory Council

Chef's favorite ingredient:
chipotle peppers in adobo

Chef's favorite food:
anything hot — bring on the heat!

2 cans black beans, drained
1 medium onion, diced
1 tablespoon minced garlic
3 tablespoons mild molasses
3 tablespoons freshly squeezed orange juice
2 teaspoons cumin
1½ teaspoons ancho chili powder
1 to 2 teaspoons hot sauce (such as Crystal or Tabasco)
Salt and freshly ground black pepper to taste
2 tablespoons chopped cilantro

Combine all ingredients, except cilantro, in a large skillet and simmer on stovetop for 20 minutes to blend flavors. Taste and adjust seasoning as desired. Garnish with cilantro.

Yields 6 servings

**Kathy S. Gold, Chef/Owner
Custom Cuisine Cooking Company, Cherry Hill, NJ**

Nicola Shirley's Rice and Beans

Jamaican Jerk Hut

Known for:
best Jamaican food in the hemisphere

Year opened:
1994

Menu:
traditional Jamaican with melting pot influences

Chef:
Nicola Shirley

Chef's training:
Johnson & Wales University

Chef's hobbies/ accomplishments:
studying herbs and homeopathic medicine, badminton

Chef's favorite food:
anything sweet and sour

3 cups dried kidney beans

12 cups water

1 medium yellow onion, coarsely chopped

1 cup coarsely chopped scallions

1 Scotch Bonnet pepper, chopped

4 teaspoons fresh thyme or 2 teaspoons dried thyme

¼ cup butter

½ block (or 3.5 ounces) coconut cream (I use Grace brand.)

2 teaspoons minced garlic

10 pimento seeds

6 cups rice

Soak beans for several hours or overnight in enough water to cover. Drain and rinse. Place beans and 12 cups water in a large pot. Cook at a medium boil for at least 1 hour or until beans are tender but still firm.

Add remaining ingredients except rice. Return to boil. When coconut cream is dissolved, add rice and stir. Cook until water line is level or just below rice line. Cover and reduce heat. Cook for about 25 minutes or until rice is still firm but cooked through.

Yields 6 servings

Nicola Shirley, Chef/Owner
Jamaican Jerk Hut, Philadelphia, PA

Wild Rice

Culinary Quote

"Rice is a beautiful food. It is beautiful when it grows, precision rows of sparkling green stalks shooting up to reach the hot summer sun. It is beautiful when harvested, autumn gold sheaves piled on diked, patchwork paddies. It is beautiful when, once threshed, it enters granary bins like a (flood) of tiny seed-pearls. It is beautiful when cooked by a practiced hand, pure white and sweetly fragrant."

Shizuo Tsuji
culinary educator, author
"Japanese Cooking: A Simple Art"

2 cups steamed wild rice
3 tablespoons honey
¼ cup diced dried fruits
¼ cup diced walnuts
Cracked black pepper

Preheat oven to 350°. Combine cooked rice, honey, dried fruits, and walnuts. Season with cracked pepper. Place in timbale molds and bake for approximately 30 minutes in a water bath. Carefully unmold onto plates when ready to serve.

Yields 6 servings

Tom Hannum, Executive Chef
Hotel duPont, Wilmington, DE

Thai Sweet Black Rice

Marker Restaurant

Known for:
seasonally changing menu/
ambiance of dining room

Most requested table:
table # 40

Menu:
contemporary American

Chef:
Vince Alberici

Chef's training:
Culinary Institute of America

**Chef's hobbies/
accomplishments:**
American Academy of Chefs,
Order of the Golden Toque

Chef's favorite ingredient:
any Mediterranean food product

Chef's favorite food:
extra virgin olive oil

½ gallon water
2 tablespoons kosher salt
1 cup Thai black rice
1 tablespoon extra virgin olive oil
2 tablespoons finely diced shallots
2 tablespoons finely diced carrots
1 tablespoon finely diced zucchini
1 tablespoon finely diced yellow squash
2 tablespoons tomato concassé (peeled, seeded, and coarsely chopped)
1 ounce Chardonnay
1 tablespoon butter
Salt and cracked black pepper to taste

Bring water to a boil in a stainless steel pot. Add kosher salt. Add rice and partially cover. Cook at a rolling boil for 40 minutes, stirring once or twice while cooking. Drain in a china cap and rinse under cold water until rice is cool and water runs clear. Let rice drip dry, then spread out in an even layer on a sheet pan. Refrigerate.

Heat oil in a 12-inch sauté pan. Add shallots and cook for 15 seconds. Add carrots, zucchini, and yellow squash. Sauté for 30 seconds. Add tomatoes and cook for 1 minute. Add Chardonnay and cook for 2 minutes. Add cooked rice. Stir in butter until incorporated. Season with salt and pepper to taste.

Yields 4 servings

**Vince Alberici, Executive Chef
Marker Restaurant at Adam's Mark Hotel, Philadelphia, PA**

Green Rice

Whisk Wisdom

According to the *Food Lovers' Companion,* chimichurri is a thick herb sauce as common in Argentina as ketchup is in the United States. This fresh and tangy sauce is commonly used on many types of Cuban and Argentine style steaks. It is a flavorful companion to any grilled food from chicken to vegetables. It's also good for bread dipping.

1 Spanish onion
⅓ cup olive oil
1 bunch fresh flat-leaf parsley
1 bunch fresh cilantro
Leaves of 3 sprigs fresh oregano
2 large cloves garlic
Juice of 2 limes
Kosher salt and freshly ground pepper to taste
2 cups long-grain rice
3½ cups water
Kosher salt to taste

Place onion in a food processor and pulse until finely chopped but not pureed. Transfer onion to a bowl. Add olive oil, parsley, cilantro, oregano, garlic, and lime juice to food processor and pulse until finely chopped. Add herb mixture to bowl with onion and stir to combine. Season with salt and pepper to taste. Reserve. (This mixture is called chimichurri.)

Combine rice and water in a saucepan with a tight-fitting lid. Season water with salt. Bring to a boil, lower heat, and simmer, covered, until tender, about 20 minutes. Set rice aside, covered, for 10 minutes. Fluff rice with a fork and stir in 2¼ cups chimichurri.

Yields 6 servings

**Susanna Goihman, Chef/Owner
Azafran, Philadelphia, PA**

Spicy Polenta

2 cups corn meal

6 cups cold water

½ cup red bell pepper, seeded and diced

½ cup green bell pepper, seeded and diced

1 tablespoon finely chopped garlic

1 tablespoon finely chopped shallots

1 tablespoon chopped fresh rosemary

1 tablespoon chopped fresh thyme

1 tablespoon chopped fresh cilantro

6 tablespoons whole butter

3 ounces grated Parmesan cheese

2 jalapeño peppers, seeded and chopped

2 tablespoons olive oil or butter

Soak corn meal in 2 cups cold water.

Bring 4 cups water and peppers to a boil. Add soaked corn meal and stir constantly for 20 minutes. Add garlic, shallots, and fresh herbs. Add butter and Parmesan cheese and stir until butter is melted. Pour into a round mold or pie plate and top with jalapeño peppers. Refrigerate until set, about 30 minutes. Cut into wedges. Sauté wedges in olive oil or butter until golden in color.

Yields 4 servings

Joseph Stewart, Executive Chef
GG's Restaurant at the Doubletree Hotel, Mt. Laurel, NJ

Risotto Cakes Milanese

Zanzibar Blue

Known for:
live jazz

Year opened:
1990

Most requested table:
#11

Menu:
international

Chef:
Albert Paris

Chef's training:
35 years hands on

Chef's hobbies/ accomplishments:
martial arts, my family

Chef's favorite ingredient:
love

Chef's favorite food:
life

4 tablespoons butter
½ pound Arborio rice
2 tablespoons olive oil
1 ounce shallots, diced
1 carrot, diced
1 rib celery, diced
½ tablespoon saffron threads
½ tablespoon chopped parsley
½ cup white wine
1 quart chicken stock
¼ pint cream
2 ounces grated Pecorino Romano
1 ounce seasoned breadcrumbs
3 ounces shredded fontina cheese

Melt butter in a thick bottom pot. Add rice, olive oil, shallots, carrot, celery, saffron, and parsley. Stir continually with a wooden spoon until rice begins to take color slightly.

Add wine and begin to ladle in stock slowly, a little at a time, while continually stirring. (Do not add additional stock until the first ladle is totally absorbed.) Continue until all stock is used. (This will take approximately 15 minutes.) Stir in cream. Transfer to a shallow pan and cool for 15 minutes.

Preheat oven to 500°. Combine pecorino cheese and breadcrumbs. Add fontina cheese and half the pecorino-breadcrumb mixture to risotto and toss lightly. Create risotto balls using a 4-ounce scoop. Flatten lightly with hands and place cakes on a baking sheet. Top cakes with remaining pecorino-breadcrumb mixture. Cook for 15 minutes.

Yields 8 servings

Albert Paris, Executive Chef
Zanzibar Blue, Wilmington, DE

Sandwiches and Pizzas

Original Pat's King of Steaks® Philadelphia Cheese Steak 240

White Dog Cafe's Philly Cheese Steak 241

Lobster Hoagie 242

Muffuletta Hoagie 243

Georges Perrier's Hoagie Francais 244

Tony Luke's Belly Buster 245

Open-faced Salmon BLT 246

Caviar and Smoked Salmon Club Sandwich 247

Grilled Gruyere Cheese and Apple Currant Chutney 248

Grilled Chicken and Sweet Potato Burrito 249

Portabella Special Pizza 250

Mexican Pizza 251

Original Pat's King of Steaks® Philadelphia Cheese Steak

Pat's King of Steaks

Known for:
inventing the "Philly Steak and Cheese Steak"

Year opened:
1930

Most requested table:
any and all

Menu:
comfort food

6 tablespoons soya bean oil
1 large Spanish onion, sliced thin
24 ounces thinly sliced rib-eye or eye-roll steak
Cheese (We recommend Cheez Whiz®, but American or provolone works fine.)
4 crusty Italian rolls
Sweet green and red peppers sautéed in oil, optional
Mushrooms sautéed in oil, optional

Heat an iron skillet or a nonstick pan over medium heat. Add 3 tablespoons oil to pan and sauté onions to desired doneness. Remove onions and reserve.

Melt Cheez Whiz® in a double boiler or in the microwave. Reserve.

Add remaining oil to pan and sauté meat slices quickly on both sides. Place 6 ounces meat into each roll. Add onions and pour Cheez Whiz® over top. Garnish with hot or fried sweet peppers, mushrooms, ketchup.

Chef's note ... For all the people who cannot get to South Philadelphia to get the Orginial, here is the recipe for you home cooks. Put on the theme song to the first *Rocky* movie and enjoy!

Yields 4 steaks

Frank E. Olivieri, Owner
Pat's King of Steaks, Philadelphia, PA

White Dog Cafe's Philly Cheese Steak

Chef's Notes

A Philadelphia tradition, the cheese steak is now known the world over. According to local legend, the cheese steak was invented by Pat and Harry Olivieri, two brothers who had a hot dog stand during the Depression. They grew tired of eating hot dogs day in and day out; so, one afternoon they went to the butcher to see if he had any scraps. He gave them some beef, which they cooked up on their hot-dog griddle along with the onions from the condiment tray. A cab driver happened to pull up just as they were about to eat their new sandwich and asked if he could buy it from them. He loved it, and the rest is history. Provolone cheese was added in 1950, and today has been replaced by Cheez Whiz. Our cheese steak doesn't follow traditional guidelines, but we'd match it against a South Philly steak any day.

2 tablespoons olive oil

2 large yellow onions, thinly sliced (about 4 cups)

2 large portobello mushroom caps, thinly sliced (about 3 cups)

1½ teaspoons salt

1 pound trimmed flank steak, sliced as thinly as possible (preferably on a slicer)

½ teaspoon freshly ground black pepper

1½ cups grated Pepper-Jack cheese

2 soft-crusted long baguettes, or 4 Italian-style hoagie rolls

Preheat the oven to 400°.

Heat the oil in a large nonreactive sauté pan set over medium-high heat until it ripples. Add the onions and cook until soft, about 5 minutes. Add the mushrooms and 1 teaspoon of the salt and sauté until tender, about 5 minutes. Add the flank steak, the remaining ½ teaspoon salt, and the pepper and sauté until the meat is cooked through, about 5 minutes more.

Remove the pan from the heat. Sprinkle the cheese over the top, cover the pan, and set aside until the cheese melts, about 5 minutes.

Meanwhile, slice the baguettes lengthwise. Place, cut sides up, on a baking sheet, and toast in the oven until crisp, 4 to 5 minutes.

Fill the baguettes with the meat and cheese. Cut each into 2 portions. Serve immediately—with or without ketchup.

Yields 4 servings

Judy Wicks and Kevin von Klause, Owner/Executive Chef
White Dog Cafe, Philadelphia, PA

Lobster Hoagie

Chef's Notes

— To prepare the lobster meat, steam a live 2-pound lobster or two 1-pound lobsters or four 4-ounce lobster tails. (As a less expensive alternative, substitute a lobster-flavored processed seafood product or cooked monkfish.)

— For oven-dried tomatoes, place the peeled, seeded halves of 5 ripe plum tomatoes on a lightly oiled baking sheet. Brush with extra virgin olive oil and sprinkle with fresh or dried thyme and salt and pepper to taste. Roast at 175° until dry but still soft, about 3 hours.

1 pound steamed lobster meat, cut into bite-size pieces
6 tablespoons Roasted Garlic Aïoli (Recipe appears on page 330.)
Pinch of fresh herbs (parsley, thyme, tarragon)
Salt and pepper to taste
1 24-inch French baguette, split
¼ cup Boursin cheese
4 ounces thinly sliced pancetta (Italian cured bacon)
4 shallots, sliced
1 teaspoon grapeseed oil
10 slices oven-dried plum tomatoes
4 ounces mâche

Mix lobster meat, aïoli, herbs, and salt and pepper in a bowl. Refrigerate.

Warm baguette in a hot oven. Spread Boursin cheese on inside of baguette. Grill or fry pancetta for 2 minutes per side and layer it over the cheese. Spread lobster mixture over pancetta.

In a hot skillet, sauté shallots in oil, stirring constantly, until lightly browned, about 5 minutes.

Top sandwich with shallots, dried tomatoes, and mâche. Close sandwich and slice into desired number of servings. Wrap in plastic and chill until read to serve.

Yields 2 to 4 servings

**Gene Betz, Executive Chef
The Saloon, Philadelphia, PA**

Muffuletta Hoagie

Did you know?

The muffuletta is to New Orleans as the hoagie is to Philadelphia. And they both owe their origins to Italian immigrants.

New Orleans is a true cultural and culinary melting pot. Influences from France, Spain, Africa, and especially Italy can be tasted in every Big Easy bite. The muffuletta, some say the quintessential sandwich of New Orleans, is pure Italian. Italians, especially those from Sicily, have been coming to New Orleans since the 1880s. And although they were not always welcomed with open arms in those days, their contribution to local culture and cuisine is unmistakable. So much so that you'll often see "Creole-Italian" referred to as one of the local cuisines.

According to legend, the muffuletta sandwich was invented in 1906 by Signor Lupo Salvadore, the owner of the Central Grocery on Decatur Street in the French Quarter. It was named for a favorite customer. Central Grocery is still there, and you can find a fine "muff" there and at many restaurants and groceries around New Orleans.

1 cup pitted Spanish green olives
1 cup pitted kalamata olives
¼ cup chopped red onion
2 tablespoons chopped fresh basil
2 tablespoons lemon juice
1 tablespoon grated horseradish
1 tablespoon chopped garlic
1 tablespoon Dijon mustard
1 teaspoon Worcestershire sauce
Dash of hot sauce
Salt and pepper
¼ cup plus 4 teaspoons olive oil
2 French baguettes, cut in half
12 slices provolone
12 slices spicy Italian ham
12 slices hard salami
Shredded lettuce
12 slices tomato

Combine first ten ingredients in a food processor and blend, just a few times, until coarse. With processor running, gradually add ¼ cup olive oil. Transfer to a mixing bowl. Season to taste with salt and pepper. Cover and refrigerate for at least 1 hour. (Mixture may be kept refrigerated for up to 24 hours.)

Split open baguettes. Coat inside of each with 1 teaspoon olive oil. Spread a thick layer of muffuletta salad over rolls. Evenly layer on cheese and meats. Cover with lettuce, tomato slices, and more muffuletta salad.

Yields 4 servings

**Joe Brown, Executive Chef/Owner
Melange Cafe, Cherry Hill, NJ**

Georges Perrier's Hoagie Francais

Chef's Notes

— French duck foie gras (flash frozen, $30 a pound) is sold at Caviar Assouline shops at Liberty Place (215-972-1616) and at Reading Terminal Market (215-629-9200), both in Philadelphia.

— Fresh North American duck foie gras (1.5 pounds, $76 plus shipping) may be ordered from D'Artagnan, 280 Wilson Avenue, Newark, NJ (800-327-8246).

— Jambon de francais ($10.99 a pound) and saucisson (10-ounce roll, $10.99) are sold at DiBruno Bros. in Philadelphia (215-665-9220) or online at www.dibruno.com.

1 cup sherry vinegar

½ cup sugar

1 teaspoon salt

1 small Spanish onion, sliced into thin rings

½ cup kosher salt

1 teaspoon cayenne pepper

½ pound fresh raw foie gras, optional

2 tablespoons freshly cracked black peppercorns

1 20- to 24-inch French baguette

6 tablespoons Pommery or other whole-grain mustard

½ pound thinly sliced jambon de francais (French ham)

½ pound thinly sliced Gruyere cheese

¼ pound saucisson (French salami)

½ head frisee (curly endive), rinsed and dried, about 6 ounces

1 tablespoon extra virgin olive oil

1 heirloom tomato, thinly sliced

2 hard-cooked eggs, thinly sliced

The day before serving, mix vinegar, sugar, and 1 teaspoon salt in a small saucepan. Bring to a boil. Put onions in a bowl and cover with hot liquid. Refrigerate for 12 to 24 hours.

Mix kosher salt with cayenne. Coat foie gras with salt mixture and wrap in plastic wrap. Refrigerate for 2 hours. Rinse off salt and pat dry. Coat foie gras with black pepper and refrigerate.

Split baguette and spread with mustard. Layer ham, Gruyere, and salami on the bottom half.

In a bowl, toss frisee with oil and a pinch of salt. Add frisee and tomatoes. Add pickled onions, reserving juice. Top with thin slices cured foie gras and eggs.

Drizzle with a little pickling juice. Close sandwich, press lightly, and cut into portions, as desired.

Yields 2 or 3 servings

Georges Perrier, Chef/Owner
Le Bec-Fin, Philadelphia, PA

Tony Luke's Belly Buster

Chef's Notes

— I invented this about one year ago. It started as sort of a joke, but we sell a ton of these at night. The Belly Buster is not for the weak of heart and seems to appeal to people who have had more than one beer. It's THE sandwich to eat at 1 a.m. on a Saturday night.

½ cup mayonnaise
¼ cup ketchup
2 tablespoons horseradish
1 tablespoon pickle juice
2 7-inch Italian rolls
14 ounces thinly sliced cold roast beef
8 slices tomato
12 slices dill pickle
1 handful thinly sliced raw onion
8 strips bacon, cooked
1 order curly fries or regular French fries

Mix together mayonnaise, ketchup, horseradish, and pickle juice and stir until well combined. Reserve.

Slice rolls. Spread a thick layer of horseradish sauce on bottom of each roll. Cover sauce with a layer of roast beef. Top with (in this order) tomatoes, pickles, onion, and bacon. Mound a large handful hot curly fries on top of bacon. Drizzle fries with more horseradish sauce.

Yields 2 sandwiches

Tony Luke, Jr., Co-Owner
Tony Luke's Old Philly Style Sandwiches
Philadelphia, PA

Open-faced Salmon BLT

4 small fresh plum tomatoes

1 teaspoon salt

1 teaspoon freshly ground black pepper

2 teaspoons balsamic vinegar

Fresh basil and oregano, chopped, optional

2 tablespoons capers, drained

1½ cups mayonnaise

Juice of 2 lemons

8 slices good quality smoked bacon

4 boneless salmon fillets, 5 ounces each, skinned

Butter, oil, or nonstick spray for grilling

4 slices sunflower honey wheat bread or Branola

4 pieces green leaf lettuce, washed and dried

Flat-leaf Italian parsley, washed and dried

Slice tomatoes into 4 slices per tomato. Sprinkle each slice with salt, pepper, and vinegar. Toss gently in a bowl with herbs. Allow to stand at room temperature.

Crush capers slightly and combine with mayonnaise. Stir in lemon juice to taste; set aside. Cook bacon in a single layer in a 350° oven. (Do not allow bacon to get too crisp.) Drain on paper towels and set aside. Leave oven on.

Heat a charcoal grill or a raised-grill skillet on high heat. Coat fillets with butter, oil or nonstick spray. Grill, skin side up, until deep brown grill marks appear. Turn fish over and briefly grill other side. (Fish should not be cooked through or this will hinder the slicing.) Remove fish from heat or remove from pan. Cut fillets one time diagonally and put into hot oven to finish cooking. (The fish is best left slightly rare.)

Toast bread in oven but not too much: inside of each slice should be "spongy." Spread an even layer of lemon-caper mayonnaise on toast. Cover with 1 piece lettuce and 1 piece salmon. Top with 2 slices bacon and another piece salmon. Layer 4 slices tomatoes in center of sandwich and spread a generous amount lemon-caper mayonnaise on tomatoes. Garnish with parsley and serve.

Yields 4 servings

David Leo Bank, Executive Chef
Harry's Savoy Grill, Wilmington, DE

Caviar and Smoked Salmon Club Sandwich

Chef's Notes

Caviar Assouline's caviar and smoked salmon club sandwich is a long-standing favorite of the store's lunch crowd. Lately, rave reviews have been coming from a new crowd: savvy travelers out of Philadelphia International Airport have been tucking them into their carry-on bags as an affordable luxury for flights. Many out-of-towners have discovered us through our Web site www.caviarassouline.com.

1½ cups crème fraîche
24 slices bread, lightly toasted
8 ounces salmon roe
16 slices smoked salmon
Mixed greens, roughly chopped
2 ounces Ossetra caviar

Spread 1 tablespoon crème fraîche on each slice of bread. Gently spread 1 tablespoon salmon roe on 8 slices and top each with a slice of smoked salmon. Cover with a second slice of bread, crème fraîche side up. Cover with a second layer of salmon roe and smoked salmon. Layer on mixed greens. Top with a third slice of bread, crème fraîche side down.

Garnish with a dollop of Ossetra caviar.

Yields 8 sandwiches

Joel Assouline, President
Caviar Assouline, Philadelphia, PA

Grilled Gruyere Cheese and Apple Currant Chutney

Metropolitan Bakery

Known for:
naturally leavened breads

Year opened:
1993

Menu:
breads and pastries

Owners:
James Barrett and
Wendy Smith Born

16 slices gruyere cheese, ⅛-inch thick
8 slices country white bread (traditional peasant-style bread)
8 heaping tablespoons apple currant chutney

Lay 2 slices gruyere on each slice of bread. Spread 2 heaping tablespoons apple chutney on 4 slices of bread. Close to make 4 sandwiches. Place in a heated sandwich press for 4 to 5 minutes until bread is toasted and cheese is melted. Serve warm.

Alternatively, melt 1 tablespoon butter in a large skillet over medium heat. Place sandwich in melted butter and cover, cooking lightly, for 2 to 3 minutes. Remove lid, flip sandwich, and cook for another 2 to 3 minutes until bread is toasted and cheese is melted.

Chef's note ... This sandwich was inspired by a delicious lunch we had in a pub in London: a terrific combination of country bread, sharp cheese, and pungent chutney.

Yields 4 sandwiches

James Barrett and Wendy Smith Born, Owners
Metropolitan Bakery, Philadelphia, PA

Grilled Chicken and Sweet Potato Burrito

The Tortilla Press

Known for:
guacamole made to order

Year opened:
July 2002

Most requested table:
all of them!

Menu:
Mexican influenced gourmet cuisine

Chef:
Mark E. Smith.

Chef's training:
spent 22 years as a chef in resorts

Chef's hobbies/ accomplishments:
traveling, exploring new restaurants

Chef's favorite ingredient:
chipolte peppers

Chef's favorite food:
ceviche

2 medium sweet potatoes
1 pound boneless, skinless chicken breasts
4 flour tortillas, 12 inches each
3 ounces EACH Chihuahua cheese (Queso), Monterey
   Jack, and Cheddar, grated
½ to ¾ cup Pasilla Chile Salsa (Recipe appears on page 336.)
2 cups shredded lettuce
8 slices ripe tomato
1 ripe Haas avocado

Roast sweet potatoes in their skins. Remove skins and cut potatoes in half.

While potatoes are roasting, grill chicken breasts and cut into strips.

Wrap tortillas in foil and warm in oven. Place one-quarter of cheese, chicken, and salsa and a one-half piece sweet potato in the middle of the bottom half of tortilla. Top filling with ½ cup lettuce, 2 slices of tomato and one-quarter avocado. Fold up both sides over filling, then roll. Repeat with other 3 tortillas. Serve with red rice or refried beans.

Yields 4 burritos

Mark E. Smith, Chef/Owner
The Tortilla Press, Collingswood, NJ

Portabella Special Pizza

Mom's Bake at Home Pizza

Known for:
We make it, you bake it.

Year opened:
1987: This is the original franchise.

Menu:
gourmet, international pizza developed by Mom

Chef's favorite food:
cheese pizza

1 16-ounce unbaked pizza crust
1 teaspoon olive oil
4 ounces Cheddar cheese or the cheese of your choice, grated
2 to 3 portabella mushrooms, sliced
1 cup thinly sliced fresh spinach
Red onions, sliced
¾ cup feta cheese
8 ounces mozzarella cheese, grated
Black pepper, dried basil, dried parsley and grated Romano cheese to taste

Preheat oven to 450º.

Glaze pie crust with oil. Spread Cheddar on crust. Cover with a single layer of portabellas. Sprinkle with spinach. Add red onion and feta cheese. Cover with mozzarella cheese. Season to taste with pepper, basil, parsley, and Romano cheese. Bake until golden, about 20 minutes.

Yields 8 slices

Mom Zee, Owner
Mom's Bake at Home Pizza, Manayunk, PA

Mexican Pizza

Did you know?

— Basic pizza most likely began in prehistoric times with bread cooked on flat, hot stones.

— Italians started making round herb and spice covered baked dough about 1,000 years ago in Naples. They were called focaccia and served as an appetizer or snack.

— Legend has it that Gennaro Lombardi's, an Italian restaurant in New York City, served America's first pizza in 1905.

— The first Pizza Hut restaurant was in Wichita, Kansas.

— October is National Pizza Month. It was first so designated in 1987.

1 16-ounce unbaked pizza crust
1 teaspoon olive oil
6 ounces refried beans
6 ounces salsa
10 ounces Cheddar cheese or the cheese of your choice, grated
15 strips roasted red peppers
1 tomato, thinly sliced
1 onion, thinly sliced
½ cup diced green peppers
4 ounces black olives, chopped
Taco seasoning, dried garlic, and grated Romano cheese to taste
Light sour cream

Preheat oven to 450º.

Glaze pie crust with oil. Spread crust with refried beans and then salsa. Cover with cheese. Layer with red peppers, tomato, and onion. Sprinkle with green peppers and black olives. Season to taste with taco seasoning, garlic, and Romano cheese. Bake until golden, about 20 minutes.

Cut into 8 slices. Serve sour cream as a dipping sauce.

Yields 8 slices

Mom Zee, Owner
Mom's Bake at Home Pizza, Manayunk, PA

Desserts

Carrot Cake with Cream Cheese Icing

Homemade Goodies by Roz

Known for:
coziest kitchen in Philly

Year opened:
1997

Most requested table:
front table by the window

Menu:
homemade baked goodies

Chef:
Roz Bratt

Chef's training:
self taught

Chef's hobbies/ accomplishments:
volunteering, teaching, baking, being a wife and mother, loving animals

Chef's favorite food:
chocolate cake, pretzels, chocolate ice cream, M&M's

2 cups sifted flour
2 teaspoons baking soda
2 teaspoons cinnamon
1 teaspoon baking powder
1 teaspoon salt
1¾ cups sugar
1 cup oil
3 eggs
2 teaspoons vanilla
2 cups shredded carrots
1 cup chopped nuts
1 8¼-ounce can crushed pineapple
3 ounces cream cheese
½ cup margarine
3 cups confectioners' sugar
Crushed nuts, optional

Preheat oven to 350°.

Sift first five ingredients together. Add sugar, oil, eggs, and 1 teaspoon vanilla. Mix well. Stir in carrots, nuts, and pineapple. Pour into pan(s). Use your choice of a 10-inch tube pan, a 13 x 9-inch pan, or two 9-inch round layer cake pans. Bake 13 x 9-inch pan for 30 minutes or until an inserted toothpick comes out clean. (For 10-inch tube pan, bake for 40 to 45 minutes. For 9-inch pans, bake for 20 to 25 minutes.)

Combine remaining vanilla, cream cheese, margarine, and confectioners' sugar and beat until smooth. Add more confectioners' sugar, if needed. Ice cooled cake. Top with nuts, if desired.

Yields 1 cake

Roz Bratt, Owner/Baker
Homemade Goodies by Roz, Philadelphia, PA

Gingerbread Upside-Down Cake

The Red Hen Cafe

Known for:
Eastern/Central European cuisine

Year opened:
1998

Chef:
Tracey Slack

Chef's training:
B.S. Marketing from Rutgers University; chef's training from The Restaurant School

Chef's favorite food:
homemade Hungarian sausages — kelbasz

¾ cup unsalted butter

1¼ cups light brown sugar, packed

3 Bosc pears, peeled, cored, and cut into 6 pieces

½ cup dark molasses

1 egg

1½ cups all-purpose flour

1 teaspoon baking soda

1 teaspoon ground ginger

¾ teaspoon ground cinnamon

½ teaspoon ground cloves

½ teaspoon salt

½ cup hot water

Melt ¼ cup butter over low heat in a 10-inch oven-ready sauté pan. Crumble ¾ cup brown sugar into pan and cook for 1 to 2 minutes or until melted. Arrange pear slices over entire bottom of pan and heat for 1 minute. Remove pan from heat and cool slightly.

Preheat oven to 350°. Melt remaining ½ cup butter in a separate pan. Transfer butter to a mixer fitted with a whisk attachment. Add remaining ½ cup brown sugar and molasses. Mix. Add egg and mix.

Sift together flour, baking soda, spices, and salt. Add to wet ingredients and mix on low speed until just combined. Mix in hot water.

Pour batter over pears in pan. Bake for 35 minutes or until a tester inserted in the middle comes out clean. Invert cake immediately onto serving plate. Serve warm or cool.

Chef's note … You may need to put a baking sheet on the oven rack below the cake because sugar and butter may bubble over.

Yields 8 servings

Tracey Slack, Chef/Owner
The Red Hen Cafe, Medford, NJ

Chef Blank's Favorite Olive Oil Cake

Chef's Note

Many recipes for olive oil cakes exist. They are generally considered Italian. By and large these cakes are orange flavored, but many also contain finely ground toasted almonds. The following recipe does not contain almonds and is very simple, easy, and delicious.

Breadcrumbs

Butter

3 whole eggs

2½ cups sugar

1½ cups extra virgin olive oil

1½ cups milk

Zest of 3 large oranges (preferably Navel)

2 cups all-purpose flour

½ teaspoon baking powder

½ teaspoon baking soda

¼ teaspoon salt

Freshly peeled orange segments or thick-sliced orange
   rounds

Confectioners' sugar

Preheat oven to 350°. (Avoid using a convection oven.) Butter and breadcrumb a round 12-inch diameter cake pan.

Whisk together eggs and sugar until blended well. Continue to whisk and add olive oil, milk and orange zest until well mixed.

In a separate bowl sift and mix together flour, baking powder, baking soda, and salt, making sure baking powder and baking soda are evenly distributed throughout the mixture. Quickly mix the combined dry ingredients into the egg and sugar mixture just until a smooth batter results. (Do not "over mix.") Immediately pour batter into prepared baking pan.

Place on center middle rack and bake for 50 to 55 minutes. (Start checking for doneness after 45 minutes.) When the cake and pan are thoroughly cooled, loosen rim edges with a knife, if necessary, and invert onto a serving plate. Serve garnished with orange segments or rounds and confectioners' sugar.

Chef's note…The size of the baking pan is very important.

Yields 1 12-inch cake

Roger Johnson, Pastry Chef
Deux Cheminées, Philadelphia, PA

Chocolate Whiskey Cake with Chocolate Glace

Culinary Quote

"Always carry a large flagon of whisky in case of snakebite and furthermore always carry a small snake."

W.C. Fields

8 ounces white seedless raisins

1 cup plus 2 teaspoons whiskey

2 eggs, separated plus 2 additional yolks

1 cup sugar

1 pound butter, softened

8 ounces semi-sweet chocolate, melted

¼ cup strong coffee

1 teaspoon vanilla

½ cup flour, sifted

1½ cups heavy cream

Pinch of salt

12 ounces semi-sweet chocolate, coarsely chopped

Preheat oven to 350°. Butter and flour two 10-inch-round cake pans.

Poach raisins in 1 cup whiskey for 3 minutes. Drain and cool.

Beat 2 yolks and sugar till light and fluffy. Whisk in soft butter. Beat in melted chocolate and slowly beat in coffee. Add vanilla and 2 teaspoons whiskey.

Whip egg whites to firm peaks. Fold whites into chocolate in thirds. Fold in sifted flour. Fold in raisins.

Pour batter into prepared pans. Bake for 18 to 22 minutes. Cool for 10 minutes before turning out. Brush cooled cakes with additional whiskey.

Boil heavy cream. Whisk in remaining 2 yolks and salt. Pour boiling cream into chopped chocolate while whisking. Pour glace over cakes.

Yields 2 10-inch cakes

Garry Waldie, Senior Pastry Chef Instructor
The Restaurant School at Walnut Hill College, Philadelphia, PA

Chocolate Pecan Torte

Braddock's Tavern

Known for:
colonial, historic inn

Year opened:
1980

Most requested table:
porch

Menu:
America

Chef:
Glenn Reinhardt

Chef's hobbies/ accomplishments:
fly fishing, skiing, mountain biking

Chef's favorite ingredient:
chocolate

Chef's favorite food:
beef

1 cup pecan pieces
⅓ cup light brown sugar, packed
2 tablespoons all-purpose flour
¼ teaspoon nutmeg
2 tablespoons chilled butter
12 ounces semi-sweet chocolate
4 ounces bittersweet chocolate
1¾ cups heavy cream
2 egg yolks

Blend pecans, brown sugar, flour, nutmeg, and butter in a food processor until fully mixed. Press crust into a 10-inch fluted tart pan. Reserve.

Melt chocolates over a double boiler. In a separate pan, heat heavy cream to a gentle boil. Whisk egg yolks into chocolate. Whisk in hot cream. Pour mixture into prepared tart pan. Refrigerate for 2 hours.

Remove from pan. Slice, using a dry, warm knife. Serve with your choice of seasonal fruit sauce.

Yields 12 servings

Glenn Reinhardt, Executive Banquet Chef
Braddock's Tavern, Medford, NJ

Chocolate Framboise Torte

The Night Kitchen Bakery

Known for:
cakes, wedding and special occasion cakes, breakfast pastries

Year opened:
1983

Pastry chef:
Alex Kujawa

Chef's training:
Johnson & Wales Pastry Arts program

Chef's hobbies/ accomplishments:
gardening

Chef's favorite ingredient:
chocolate

Chef's favorite food:
anything I don't have to cook

½ cup water

1 cup plus ½ cup sugar

6 ounces semi-sweet chocolate (Valhrona is an excellent, quality chocolate.)

7 ounces unsweetened chocolate

3 tablespoons framboise liqueur

½ pound plus 1 ounce unsalted butter, cubed

6 eggs

1 cup heavy cream

1 tablespoon confectioners' sugar

Fresh raspberries

Preheat oven 350º. Butter a 9- or 10-inch-round cake pan and place a parchment paper circle inside.

Bring water and 1 cup sugar to a boil. Remove from heat and add chocolates and framboise. Stir until chocolate is melted. Add butter and stir until melted.

Combine remaining ½ cup sugar and eggs in a mixer. Whip until light and fluffy. Gently fold chocolate mixture into egg mixture. Place batter in cake pan and bake in a water bath for about 40 minutes.

Cool cake to room temperature and unmold. Whip together heavy cream and confectioners' sugar. Garnish cake with whipped cream and fresh raspberries.

Yields 10 servings

Alex Kujawa, Pastry Chef
The Night Kitchen Bakery, Philadelphia, PA

Chocolate Gateau

8 ounces bittersweet chocolate, chopped
7 ounces unsalted, lightly sweetened butter, cut into pieces
8 eggs yolks
1 cup sugar
5 egg whites

Preheat oven to 350°. Grease or butter a springform pan fitted with a removable bottom.

Place chocolate and butter in a glass or metal bowl. Place bowl over a water bath (pot of simmering water). Melt chocolate and butter together, stirring occasionally. Remove from heat.

Place egg yolks and sugar in a mixer. Whip with paddle until pale and ribboned. In a separate bowl, whip egg whites until soft peaks form. Stir chocolate mixture into egg yolks until completely incorporated. Fold in egg whites.

Pour into prepared pan. Place pan in center of oven and bake for 35 minutes. Cool slightly. Remove from collar and serve with fresh berries and ice cream.

Yields 8 to 10 servings

Daniel Grimes, Co-Chef/Co-Owner
Chlöe, Philadelphia, PA

Chocolate Soufflé

Davio's

Known for:
best veal chop!

Year opened:
1999

Most requested table:
by fishtank (#10) and by flowers (#13)

Menu:
northern Italian steakhouse

Chef:
David Boyle

Chef's training:
The Restaurant School and then at the Four Seasons

Chef's hobbies/ accomplishments:
remodeling of home, especially kitchen

Chef's favorite ingredient:
truffles and caviar

Chef's favorite food:
pho (Vietnamese soup)

18 ounces bittersweet chocolate
4½ ounces butter
5 egg yolks
6 egg whites
1 cup granulated sugar
1 tablespoon vanilla extract

Preheat oven to 350°.

In a small saucepan, melt chocolate and butter together, stirring until blended.

In a mixing bowl, whisk together eggs (yolks and whites), sugar, and vanilla. Gently fold chocolate mixture into egg mixture until all ingredients are fully incorporated.

Pour into a 3-inch-round soufflé mold. Bake for 15 minutes; serve immediately.

Yields 2 servings

David Boyle, Executive Chef
Davio's Northern Italian Steakhouse, Philadelphia, PA

Pumpkin Roulade

Miel Patisserie

Known for:
creator/owner of Miel

Year opened:
2002

Menu:
traditional and classical French pastries, chocolates, breads, ice creams, sorbets

Chef:
Robert W. Bennett

Chef's training:
New England Culinary Institute; France: Paris and Lyon

Chef's hobbies/ accomplishments:
President Reagan's guest pastry chef; U.S. Rep in World Cup, Lyon

Chef's favorite ingredient:
chocolate

Chef's favorite food:
French

3 eggs
1 cup plus ⅓ cup plus 2 tablespoons sugar
⅔ cup pumpkin puree
1 cup cake flour
1 teaspoon baking soda
½ teaspoon cinnamon
½ teaspoon ground ginger
¼ teaspoon cloves
¼ teaspoon ground nutmeg
¼ teaspoon salt
⅓ cup water
¼ cup brandy
2 cups crème fraîche or heavy cream

Preheat oven to 425°. Brush a 9 x 13-inch jelly-roll pan with butter, shortening, or nonstick baking spray. Line with parchment paper.

Beat eggs and 1 cup sugar at high speed until soft and ribbon-like. Beat at medium speed for a couple minutes more. Add in pumpkin puree.

Sift together dry ingredients. With mixer still running, slowly incorporate dry ingredients into pumpkin mixture.

Spread in prepared pan, making sure batter is smooth and even. Bake for 9 to 10 minutes. Let cool. Transfer to freezer paper and reserve.

Bring ⅓ cup sugar and water to a boil. Let cool, then add brandy. Brush half of the syrup over roulade.

Whip together cream and remaining 2 tablespoons sugar and spoon over roulade. Roll halfway, then repeat, brushing with remaining syrup and continue to roll. Close ends and chill. Garnish with powdered sugar and slice. Serve cold.

Chef's note … Optionally, brush roulade with an apricot glaze and roll in toasted walnuts, or sprinkle walnuts on top of cream and proceed to roll.

Yields 6 servings

Robert Bennett, Owner
Miel Patisserie, Cherry Hill, NJ

Passion Fruit Cheesecake

Philadelphia Fish & Company

Known for:
innovative seafood and large metal fish sculpture

Year opened:
1982

Most requested table:
#57

Menu:
upscale seafood, eclectic/fusion California

Chef:
Amy Coben

Chef's training:
California Culinary Academy; 16 years experience in restaurants

Chef's hobbies/ accomplishments:
mom to two beautiful pit bulls, Lani and Kai

Chef's favorite ingredient:
hoisin, thyme, chipotle

Chef's favorite food:
Thai food

1 pound ricotta cheese
1 pound cream cheese, softened
4 large eggs
½ cup sugar
4 tablespoons fresh lime juice
1½ cups passion fruit puree
36 pieces ladyfinger cookies (any high-quality commercial brand)
½ cup unsalted butter, softened
1 tablespoon sugar

Combine cheeses, eggs, sugar, and lime juice in a mixer and mix until smooth. Add passion fruit puree and continue to mix until thoroughly incorporated. Chill for 10 minutes.

Place ladyfingers in a food processor and grind until the consistency of coarse crumbs. Pour into a mixer. Add butter and sugar. Mix until mixture becomes a soft dough that can be formed by hand.

Preheat oven to 325°. Using either a nonstick muffin pan (for individual cakes) or a springform pan (for one large cake), press dough into bottom and up sides of cups or pan. Pour cheese mixture into cups until three-quarters full or entire mixture into pan. Bake for 15 to 20 minutes or until tops are firm to the touch and centers do not move when pan is shaken.

Allow to cool completely before removing from cups or pan.

Yields 12 servings

Amy Coben, Executive Chef
Philadelphia Fish & Company, Philadelphia, PA

Oreo Cheesecake

Catelli Ristorante

Known for:
receiving Five Diamond award

Year opened:
1995

Menu:
northern Italian cuisine

Chef:
Nick Tropiano

Chef's training:
The Restaurant School of Philadelphia

Chef's hobbies/ accomplishments:
winemaking

Chef's favorite ingredient:
fresh fruits and vegetables

Chef's favorite food:
pasta

5 cups crushed Oreo cookies
5 ounces melted butter
2 pounds cream cheese, softened
1 cup sugar
3 ounces heavy cream
5 ounces sour cream
5 large eggs
1 teaspoon vanilla

Preheat oven to 350°. Wrap bottom and sides of a 10-inch springform pan with aluminum foil.

Combine 4 cups Oreo crumbs and butter and press into bottom and up sides of prepared pan. Bake for 10 minutes. Lower oven temperature to 300°.

Beat cream cheese and sugar on low speed for 10 minutes until smooth. Add heavy cream, then sour cream. Add eggs, one at a time, until well incorporated. Mix in vanilla. Fold in remaining 1 cup Oreo crumbs. Pour into pan. Bake in a waterbath for 1 hour.

Yields 8 servings

**Nick Tropiano, Pastry and Pasta Chef
Catelli Ristorante, Voorhees, NJ**

Key Lime Cheesecake with Macadamia Crust

Joseph Ambler Inn

Known for:
elegant country inn, inventive American cuisine

Year opened:
1983

Most requested table:
Tack Room

Menu:
New American

Executive Chef:
Meg Votta

Chef's training:
BA from Hamilton College; AAS from Parsons; ANS from Culinary Institute of America

Chef's hobbies/ accomplishments:
skiing, golf, art, travel/ Les Dames Escoffier scholarship; 2003 Philly Cooks Dessert of the Year

Chef's favorite ingredient:
salt

Chef's favorite food:
any pork product!

Crust
1 cup graham cracker crumbs
½ cup chopped toasted macadamia nuts
3 tablespoons sugar
⅓ cup butter, melted

Cheesecake
32 ounces cream cheese, softened
4 eggs
1½ cups sugar
3 tablespoons key lime juice
Zest of 1 lime

Glaze
¼ cup sugar
¾ cup blood orange juice
1 tablespoon cornstarch

Mix graham cracker crumbs, macadamia nuts, sugar, and butter in a bowl. Press into a 10-inch springform pan. Chill until firm.

Preheat oven to 350°. Beat cream cheese at a low speed in a mixing bowl until smooth. Add eggs, sugar, key lime juice, and zest and continue to beat until well incorporated and smooth. Pour mixture into prepared pan. Bake cheesecake for 40 to 50 minutes or until set. Remove from oven and cool completely.

Heat sugar, blood orange juice, and cornstarch in a saucepan. Bring to a simmer and cook, stirring constantly, until mixture thickens. Pour evenly over cheesecake. Chill until ready to serve.

Yields 12 servings

Meg Votta, Executive Chef
Joseph Ambler Inn, North Wales, PA

Lime Mousse Pie

Marigold Dining Room

Known for:
homemade meatloaf; dining in
an old Victorian home

Year opened:
1934

Most requested table:
#2

Menu:
comfort food served with style

1½ cups graham cracker crumbs
¼ cup sifted confectioners' sugar
½ cup dry coconut flakes
½ teaspoon cinnamon
6 tablespoons butter, melted
½ tablespoon unflavored gelatin
¼ cup dark rum
4 eggs
1 cup sugar
⅔ cup fresh lime juice
2 tablespoons grated lime zest
1 cup chilled whipping cream
Whipped cream
Mint

Preheat oven to 350°.

Combine graham cracker crumbs, confectioners' sugar, coconut, and cinnamon in a large bowl. Stir in melted butter to moisten. Press moistened crumbs into bottom and partially up the sides of a 9-inch springform pan. Bake for approximately 10 minutes or until golden brown. Cool on a rack.

Dissolve gelatin in rum. Reserve.

Whisk eggs, sugar, and lime juice over medium-high heat until mixture thickens, about 6 to 8 minutes. Do not boil. Remove from heat and stir in gelatin mixture and lime zest. Refrigerate mixture until cold but not completely set, stirring occasionally, about 30 minutes.

Whip cream to soft peaks. Fold into chilled lime mixture until thoroughly mixed. Pour into cooled crust and refrigerate until set, about 4 hours.

Remove from pan by releasing sides. Cut into wedges and garnish with whipped cream and mint.

Yields 8 servings

Richard DeMatt, Owner
Marigold Dining Room, Philadelphia, PA

Apple Pear Ginger Pie

Diane's La Patisserie

Known for:
French and Italian pastries and wedding cakes

Year opened:
1986

Menu:
beautifully decorated cakes and pastries

Pastry chef:
Diane Nussbaum

Chef's training:
self taught

Chef's hobbies/ accomplishments:
dance, art history

Chef's favorite ingredient:
chocolate

Chef's favorite food:
any dessert made with chocolate

2 pounds Bartlett pears, sliced
½ pound Granny Smith apples, sliced
2 tablespoons fresh lemon juice and rind
2 tablespoons cornstarch
2 to 4 tablespoons sugar (to taste)
2 tablespoons chopped candied ginger (or ground ginger)
2 tablespoons butter
Your favorite pastry for a two-crust 10-inch pie
Cream or milk
Granulated sugar

Preheat oven to 350°.

Combine pears and apples and toss with lemon juice and rind. Combine cornstarch, sugar, and ginger in a separate bowl. Line pie plate with unbaked pie crust. Fill crust half-full with fruit. Sprinkle half dry ingredient mixture over fruit. Dot with 1 tablespoon butter. Repeat with remaining fruit, dry ingredients, and butter.

Cover with top crust. Brush with cream or milk and sprinkle with granulated sugar. Bake for 45 minutes to 1 hour until juices bubble.

Chef's note ... This can be made a day ahead. Just reheat and serve.

Yields 1 10-inch pie

Diane Nussbaum, Head Pastry Chef/Owner
Diane's La Patisserie, Bellmawr, NJ

Almond Financier with Diced Apples

Fountain Restaurant

Year opened:
1983

Most requested table:
windows

Executive chef:
Martin Hamann

Chef's training:
The Restaurant School,
Philadelphia, PA

**Chef's hobbies/
accomplishments:**
tennis

Chef's favorite ingredient:
thyme

Chef's favorite food:
Provençal

½ cup plus 3 tablespoons butter
1 apple, peeled and diced
6½ ounces confectioners' sugar
3 ounces all-purpose flour
3 ounces almond flour
6 ounces egg whites

Preheat oven to 375°. Grease four 3-inch-round pans.

Melt butter in a sauté pan until nut brown. Remove and reserve all but 1 tablespoon butter. Sauté apple pieces in remaining 1 tablespoon butter. Reserve apples.

Combine all dry ingredients. Add egg whites and whisk to combine. Add reserved melted butter and continue whisking. Spoon into prepared pans. Top with apples. Bake for 10 minutes.

Yields 4 servings

**Martin Hamann, Executive Chef
Fountain Restaurant, Philadelphia, PA**

Spiced Pear Cobbler

The Restaurant School at Walnut Hill College

Known for:
pastry arts, chocolate and sugar show pieces

Chef:
Garry Waldie CEC, CCE, CEPA, AAC

Chef's training:
apprenticeship at Canadian Federation of Cooks; certifications from America Culinary Federation

Chef's hobbies/ accomplishments:
travel

Chef's favorite ingredient:
any citrus fruit or zest

Chef's favorite food:
bread

2 pears
1 tablespoon grated lemon rind
3 tablespoons lemon juice
3 tablespoons butter
1 cup flour
1 teaspoon baking powder
½ teaspoon baking soda
¼ teaspoon salt
½ teaspoon ginger
¼ teaspoon cinnamon
¼ teaspoon allspice
¼ teaspoon nutmeg
¼ cup molasses
8 ounces plain yogurt
½ cup heavy cream
1 tablespoon milk

Preheat oven to 400°. Grease a 9-inch baking dish.

Place pears in a pot with enough water to cover and simmer until tender. Remove pears, cut into slices, and reserve.

Remove all but ½ cup water from pot. Add lemon rind, lemon juice, and 1 tablespoon butter. Simmer until a syrupy consistency.

Combine flour and other dry ingredients. Cut remaining 2 tablespoons butter into flour.

Combine molasses and yogurt. Add to dry ingredients along with heavy cream and milk. Mix until a soft dough is formed.

Turn out onto a floured table and shape into a 7-inch circle. Cut into 6 wedges. Place pears and syrup in prepared dish. Place dough wedges over pears and bake for 20 minutes.

Yields 6 to 8 servings

Garry Waldie, Senior Pastry Chef Instructor
The Restaurant School at Walnut Hill College, Philadelphia, PA

Shortbread Triangles with Apple Chutney Filling

City Tavern

Known for:
unique historic ambiance and fresh from the farm to the table cuisine

Year opened:
1774

Most requested table:
any table in the Cincinnati Room where George Washington spent most of his time

Menu:
Colonial American

Chef:
Walter Staib

Chef's training:
over four decades of culinary experience having received formal training in fine European hotels and restaurants

Chef's favorite ingredient:
leeks

Chef's favorite food:
medallions of venison

Vanilla Shortbread

¾ pound (3 sticks) unsalted butter, softened

1 cup confectioners' sugar, sifted

½ teaspoon vanilla extract

3 cups all-purpose flour, sifted

½ teaspoon salt

1½ teaspoons granulated sugar, for garnish

Apple Chutney Filling

¼ pound (1 stick) unsalted butter, softened

½ cup packed dark brown sugar

¼ cup molasses

¼ teaspoon salt

2 sticks cinnamon

2 teaspoons grated fresh ginger

4 Granny Smith apples, peeled, cored, and cubed

1 tablespoon grated lime rind, about 1 medium lime

2 tablespoons lime juice, about 1 medium lime, strained

½ cup raisins

½ cup walnuts, lightly toasted and chopped (see Chef's note)

In the bowl of an electric mixer, cream the ¾ pound butter, confectioners' sugar, and vanilla on medium to high until light and fluffy.

In a separate bowl, combine the flour and salt. With the mixer on low, slowly add the dry ingredients to the butter/sugar mixture, and beat just until the dough begins to hold together. Form the dough into a disc shape, wrap in plastic wrap, and chill in the refrigerator for at least 1 hour before using.

In a large sauté pan, melt the ¼ pound butter over medium heat. Stirring constantly, add the brown sugar, molasses, and salt. Add the cinnamon sticks and ginger and bring the mixture to a boil. Reduce the heat to low, and add the apples, lime rind, and lime juice. Cook just until the apples start to soften. Add the raisins and walnuts, and remove from heat. Set aside.

Preheat the oven to 325°. Line the baking sheet with parchment paper.

On a lightly floured surface, roll out the shortbread to ¼-inch thick. Cut the dough into eighteen 3-inch triangle shapes and place them 1 inch apart on prepared baking sheets. Sprinkle the granulated sugar over the top of each triangle.

Bake for 15 to 20 minutes, until golden brown around the edges. Cool on a wire rack.

When the triangles are cool, spoon ¼ cup of the warm apple chutney onto each of six triangles. Top each with another triangle and more chutney. Top with a third triangle. You should have a total of six, three-layer apple chutney triangles. Dust the plate with confectioners' sugar and, if desired, serve with purchased caramel praline ice cream.

Chef's note … Preheat oven to 350°. Spread out the nuts in a single layer on a sheet pan. Bake for about 20 minutes, until golden brown. Let cool.

Yields 6 servings

Walter Staib, Executive Chef/Proprietor
City Tavern, Philadelphia, PA

From the *City Tavern Cookbook*, ©1999 by Walter Staib
Running Press Book Publishers, Philadelphia and London, http://www.runningpress.com

Pineapple Crisp Napoleon

Jeffrey Miller Catering

Known for:
our food quality and taste

Menu:
international (Really! We do a broad range of cuisines.)

Pastry chef:
Michael Dengler
Executive chef: Anthony G. Lucas

Chef's training:
Baltimore International College, Baltimore, MD

Chef's hobbies/ accomplishments:
golf, photography/mutiple newspaper interviews

Chef's favorite ingredient:
fruit purees, especially tropical or exotic ones

Chef's favorite food:
prime rib, foie gras, anything with nuts

1 cup water
2 cups sugar
1 pineapple, peeled and sliced into 1/16-inch rounds (You'll need 24 rounds.)
2½ ounces cornstarch
½ teaspoon salt
3 large eggs
1 quart whole milk
½ vanilla bean, split and scraped
1 mango, peeled, seeded, and diced

Preheat oven to 200°. Bring water to a boil. Remove from heat and add 1 cup sugar, stirring until sugar is dissolved. Cool slightly. Dip pineapple slices into sugar syrup, shake off excess liquid, and lay on a silicone baking sheet. Place in oven and bake for 1 to 2 hours until thoroughly dry and crisp.

Combine remaining 1 cup sugar, cornstarch, and salt in a bowl. Whisk in eggs until smooth and light yellow in color.

Place milk and vanilla bean in a 3-quart saucepan. Heat until just boiled. Whisking constantly, slowly add hot milk to egg mixture. Return mixture to pan and bring to a boil over medium-high heat, stirring constantly and vigorously. Boil for 2 to 3 minutes, being careful not to burn, until custard becomes very thick. Remove from heat and strain through a fine mesh strainer into a medium bowl. Cool immediately over an ice bath, stirring occasionally to prevent a skin from forming. Stir mango into cooled custard.

Place a small dollop of custard in the center of 8 plates. Cover with a slice of pineapple. Top with 2 tablespoons custard. Stack another layer of pineapple and custard on top. Finish with a final slice of pineapple. Serve immediately with your choice of sauce: raspberry puree or a pomegranate syrup are recommended.

Yields 8 servings

Michael Dengler, Pastry Chef
Jeffrey Miller Catering, Lansdowne, PA

Creamy Caramel Banana Napoleon

Chez Colette

Menu:
contemporary French cuisine

Year opened:
2000

Pastry chef:
Amy Clemento

Chef's training:
The Restaurant School

Chef's hobbies/ accomplishments:
spending time with family and friends/Fruit Sushi (a hot menu item!); National Dessert Competition, Los Angeles (August 2001)

Chef's favorite ingredient:
vanilla bean

Chef's favorite food:
fresh bread

¼ cup sugar
2 tablespoons cinnamon
12 sheets phyllo
¼ cup melted butter
½ cup butter
1 cup brown sugar, packed
¼ cup corn syrup
¼ cup heavy cream
6 ripe bananas, sliced
½ gallon vanilla ice cream
¼ cup chocolate chips, optional

Preheat oven to 350°.

Combine sugar and cinnamon in a small bowl. Place 1 phyllo sheet on a cutting board. Lightly brush top with melted butter. Sprinkle with sugar and cinnamon. Cover with another sheet phyllo. Repeat this step until you have a stack of 4 sheets. Brush top sheet with butter and sprinkle on sugar and cinnamon. Assemble two more stacks of 4 sheets each.

Cut each stack into 8 squares (about 4 x 2 inches each) for a total of 24 squares. Place squares on a cookie sheet and bake for 5 to 10 minutes or until golden brown.

Melt ½ cup butter in a sauté pan. Add brown sugar and cook until combined. Add corn syrup and bring to a boil. Slowly add heavy cream: be careful because it will begin to bubble. Return mixture back to a boil. Remove pan from heat and stir in sliced bananas.

To assemble, place one phyllo square on a plate. Top square with a small scoop vanilla ice cream and spoon some warm banana sauce on top. Place another phyllo square on top and repeat with another scoop of ice cream and more sauce. Add one more phyllo square and top with sauce. Repeat procedure seven times. For more added fun, sprinkle plates with chocolate chips. Serve immediately.

Yields 8 servings

Amy Clemento, Pastry Chef
Chez Colette, Hotel Sofitel, Philadelphia

Lamberti's Tiramisu

Whisk Wisdom

What are ladyfingers? Known in Italy as *"savoiardi,"* ladyfingers are sweet, somewhat dry, sponge cakes shaped like a large finger. They date from the House of Savoy in 11th- century France, and the recipe has changed little in 900 years. Folklore has it that Czar Peter the Great of Russia and his wife, the peasant empress Catherine, enjoyed ladyfingers so much when they visited Louis XV of France, that they purchased the baker and sent him immediately to Saint Petersburg. You can make ladyfingers yourself or purchase them at most supermarkets. If you do decide to bake them at home, Le Cordon Bleu advises cooks to be careful, because ladyfinger batter is very fragile.

5 egg yolks
½ cup plus 2 tablespoons sugar
1 pint heavy cream
8 ounces mascarpone cheese
3 packages lady fingers (You may need more or less, depending on how tightly you arrange them.)
¾ quart espresso, cooled
Cocoa powder
Powdered sugar

Whip egg yolks with ¼ cup sugar in a double boiler with hot water underneath until mixture becomes creamy. Let cool.

Whip ¼ cup sugar with heavy cream in a double boiler with ice on bottom. Add to yolk mixture. Add mascarpone cheese and whip together for approximately 8 minutes.

Add remaining 2 tablespoons sugar to espresso. Dip lady fingers in espresso one at a time. Arrange lady fingers evenly in the bottom of a 6 x 9-inch baking pan until the pan is covered. (Make sure lady fingers are all going the same way.). Cover lady fingers with a layer of half the mascarpone mixture. Sprinkle with cocoa powder. Dip more lady fingers in espresso and lay in an even layer over mascarpone with all lady fingers going the opposite direction of first layer. Spread on remaining mascarpone mixture. Sprinkle with cocoa powder and powdered sugar. Refrigerate, then serve.

Yields 6 servings

Ciro Lubrano Lavadera, Executive Chef
Lamberti's Cucina, Cherry Hill, NJ

Cappuccino Creams

1 vanilla bean, split lengthwise
1¾ cups whipping cream
2 ounces good quality white chocolate (such as Lindt or Ghiradelli), finely chopped
5 tablespoons plus 2 teaspoons sugar
4 large egg yolks
1 large whole egg
¼ cup sour cream
4 teaspoons white rum
Pinch of salt
4 teaspoons instant espresso powder
1 pint fresh raspberries, reserving 6 for garnish
1 tablespoon water
12 coffee beans for garnish

Preheat oven to 350°. Spray six ¾-cup ramekins or custard cups with nonstick spray. Place cups in a 13 x 9 x 2-inch baking pan.

Scrape seeds from vanilla bean into a small saucepan. Add bean. Mix in ½ cup cream and white chocolate. Stir over low heat until smooth. Set aside.

Whisk remaining 1¼ cups cream, 5 tablespoons sugar, yolks, whole egg, sour cream, rum, and salt in a medium bowl until smooth. Strain white chocolate mixture into egg mixture and whisk to blend. Pour ¼ cup custard mixture into each ramekin; reserve remaining custard. Pour enough hot water into baking pan to come halfway up the sides of ramekins. Bake until custards set, about 30 minutes. Let stand for 5 minutes in pan.

Add espresso powder to remaining custard mixture and stir until dissolved. Spoon espresso custard over baked custards, dividing equally. Bake until custards set, about 30 minutes. Remove from water. Chill uncovered until cold, about 3 hours.

Place raspberries in a small saucepan and crush with a fork. Add remaining 2 teaspoons sugar and water. Cook over medium heat until sugar dissolves and raspberries soften, approximately 5 to 7 minutes. Strain and chill.

Dip ramekins into warm water to loosen custards. Turn out onto plates. Top each custard with 2 coffee beans. Garnish with raspberry sauce and reserved raspberries.

Chef's note...Can be made 1 day ahead. Cover; keep chilled.

Yields 6 servings

**Robert Mansfield, Executive Chef
Porterhouse Steaks and Seafood, Cherry Hill, NJ**

Caramel Semifreddo

Davio's

Known for:
best veal chop

Year opened:
1999

Most requested table:
#10 by the fish tank
and #13 by the flowers

Menu:
northern Italian steakhouse

Pastry chef:
Kelly McGrath

Chef's training:
Community College of
Philadelphia and The
Restaurant School

**Chef's hobbies/
accomplishments:**
collecting cookbooks/member of
the Pastry Society of Philadelphia
and American Culinary
Federation; first place award:
"Kahlua Kookoff"; "2002
Delectable Desserts"; 2001 and
2002 "Pro-Choice/Pro-Chocolate"

Chef's favorite ingredient:
chocolate

Chef's favorite food:
anything chocolate!

6 egg yolks

1 cup granulated sugar

⅓ cup dark caramel (Dark caramel, available in gourmet stores, is preferred; but jarred caramel sauce can be substituted.)

4 egg whites, whipped to stiff peaks

2 cups heavy cream, whipped to soft peaks

Whipped cream and caramel sauce for garnish

Whisk together yolks, sugar, and caramel in a bowl. Place bowl over a water bath over medium heat and whisk until mixture is 160° and sugar is melted.

Remove bowl from heat and place mixture in the bowl of a mixer with a whisk attachment. Beat until cool.

Whisk ⅓ of whipped egg whites into yolk mixture to lighten. Add remaining whites, then add whipped cream in two stages.

Coat 12 plastic molds with nonstick spray. Pour mixture into molds and freeze overnight.

To unmold, run a knife around inside of molds and tap on a table to release. Serve with additional whipped cream and caramel sauce.

Yields 12 servings

Kelly McGrath, Pastry Chef
Davio's, Philadelphia, PA

Chocolate and Coconut Natilla

Cuba Libre

Known for:
colorful atmosphere — an escape to Havana

Year opened:
2000

Menu:
Cuban cuisine

Pastry chef:
Jennifer Martin

Chef's training:
Bachelor of Culinary Arts Management from The Culinary Institute of America

Chef's hobbies/ accomplishments:
cooking, wine, crafts

Chef's favorite ingredient:
Tahitian vanilla beans

Chef's favorite food:
risotto

1½ quarts whole milk

¾ pound sugar

¾ teaspoon salt

1 teaspoon vanilla extract

2 ounces cocoa

½ cup cornstarch

2 whole eggs

6 egg yolks

½ pound bittersweet chocolate, chopped

½ cup coconut milk

Place milk, about half of sugar, salt, and vanilla in a large pot. Heat mixture and bring just to a boil.

Combine remaining sugar, cocoa, and cornstarch in a medium bowl. In a separate bowl, combine eggs and egg yolks. When milk mixture has come to a boil, whisk eggs into sugar/cocoa mixture. Temper hot milk into egg mixture. (The term "temper" in this recipe means to add hot liquid to an egg mixture slowly so the eggs do not scramble with the heat of the liquid. Add just enough hot liquid to raise the temperature of the eggs.) Pour egg mixture into pot containing remaining hot milk. Return pot to high heat. Whisk constantly until mixture thickens and bubbles have just begun to break the surface of pudding.

Remove pudding from heat and stir in chopped chocolate and coconut milk and stir to combine. Strain pudding and pour into a bowl. Cover surface of pudding with plastic wrap. Cool to room temperature, then refrigerate. Best if chilled overnight.

Yields approximately 6 servings

Jennifer Martin, Pastry Chef
Cuba Libre Restaurant & Rum Bar, Philadelphia, PA

"Mom's" All-American Figgy Bread Pudding

Chef's Note

Most all ethnographic cuisines have a version of bread pudding. Some, such as German "red pudding (*rot grütze*) are heavy, dense, mostly-fruit affairs and have all but disappeared from modern repertoires. The French and English produce a "bread and butter 'pudding'" which is chiefly an egg custard with a few slices of toasted bread on top.

Bread pudding as "the kind Mom used to make" is understandably <u>the</u> favorite of any child of that mom. (It is well known that moms are very influential regarding the development of epicurean opinions.) In the north eastern United States the following recipe is fairly representative of what I call home-style bread pudding. Enjoy!

Fritz Blank, Chef de Cuisine

4 cups 1-inch bread cubes, cut from day-old Italian, French, or Viennese whole loaves or rolls
¼ cup melted butter
½ cup dried figs
¼ cup dry sherry
3 eggs
2 cups milk
¾ cup sugar
1 teaspoon vanilla
⅓ cup raisins
2 tablespoons butter
½ teaspoon cinnamon

Preheat oven to between 325° and 350°. Butter the inside of a 2-quart low-sided ovenproof casserole or baking dish.

Spread bread cubes onto a bun pan and sprinkle with melted butter. Place into oven and, turning cubes every 2 or 3 minutes, toast until golden.

Mix together figs and sherry to form a paste. Mix together fig paste, eggs, milk, sugar, and vanilla. In a separate bowl, toss together bread cubes and raisins. Pour egg-milk mixture over bread and allow several minutes for absorption.

Preheat oven to 350°. Place bread mixture into prepared baking dish. Dot top with butter and sprinkle with cinnamon. Place dish in a water bath and bake for "an hour or so" or until an inserted knife comes out clean.

Chef's note...Enjoy!

Yields 6 to 8 servings

Roger Johnson, Pastry Chef
Deux Cheminées, Philadelphia, PA

Raspberry Bread Pudding

Ristorante Panorama

Known for:
largest wine selection:
120 choices by the glass

Year opened:
1990

Most requested table:
#16

Menu:
Italian

Chef:
Rosario T. Romano, Jr.

Chef's training:
self taught

Chef's hobbies/ accomplishments:
drawing, sky diving, scuba diving, collecting belt buckles

Chef's favorite ingredient:
garlic

Chef's favorite food:
all seafood

2 cups heavy cream
1 cup whole milk
1 vanilla bean, split and scraped
6 egg yolks
2 whole eggs
¾ cup sugar
2 cups 1-inch cubed day-old bread, crusts removed
¾ pint fresh raspberries
1 teaspoon almond extract
1 teaspoon ground cinnamon
Pinch of salt
6 tablespoons light brown sugar, packed
Powdered sugar

Preheat oven to 350°. Butter six 8-ounce ramekins.

Bring heavy cream, milk, and vanilla bean to a boil in a heavy-bottomed saucepot. Remove from heat and allow to cool.

Whisk together eggs yolks, whole eggs, and sugar. Add cooled milk to egg mixture, making sure not to cook the eggs. Strain mixture into a clean bowl. Add bread, raspberries, almond extract, cinnamon, and salt. (For best results, let sit for about 45 minutes.)

Place 1 tablespoon brown sugar into each ramekin. Pour mixture into ramekins. Place ramekins in a shallow baking pan or hotel pan. Place pan in oven. Fill pan with enough water (about ½ gallon) to come up three-quarters on sides of ramekins. Bake for 45 to 50 minutes or until golden brown.

Allow to cool at least 1 hour. Run a small knife around sides of ramekin, then place pudding on a serving plate. Dust with powdered sugar and serve at room temperature.

Yields 6 servings

Rosario T. Romano, Jr., Executive Chef
Ristorante Panorama, Philadelphia, PA

Cherry Pistachio Bread Pudding

Happy Rooster

Year opened:
2000

Most requested table:
cockpit

Menu:
seasonal American bistro

Chef:
Steven Latona

Chef's training:
The Restaurant School,
Philadelphia

Chef's hobbies/ accomplishments:
water colors/children

Chef's favorite ingredient:
preserved lemon

Chef's favorite food:
veal Milanese

1 quart heavy cream
3 cups milk
2 teaspoons vanilla extract
14 egg yolks
2 cups sugar
Pinch of salt
4 pounds Italian bread loaves, crust removed and diced
2 cups dried cherries, soaked in bourbon
1 cup toasted and finely chopped pistachios
2 tablespoons cinnamon

Preheat oven to 300°. Grease a hotel pan or very large baking dish.

Scald cream and milk. Stir in vanilla.

In a large mixing bowl, beat egg yolks, sugar, and salt together until pale and extremely thick. (You'll know the mixture is thick enough when the beater is lifted and the batter falls onto the surface of the mixture, forming a ribbon-like pattern before sinking back into the batter.) Temper yolks into cream mixture by pouring a splash of hot cream into yolks and whisking thoroughly. Add hot yolk mixture to cream.

Combine bread cubes, dried cherries, pistachios, and cinnamon in pan. Pour cream yolk mixture over bread and soak. Cover and bake for approximately 2 hours. Serve alone or with a caramel sauce.

Yields 12 servings

Steven Latona, Chef
Happy Rooster, Philadelphia, PA

Rice Pudding

½ cup short-grain rice
2 cups water
4¼ cups whole milk
¼ cup heavy cream
¾ cup sugar
1 tablespoon cornstarch
Pinch of salt
1 tablespoon vanilla crystals or 1 tablespoon vanilla extract
Ground cinnamon

In a medium saucepan, bring rice to a boil in water over high heat. Lower heat, cover, and cook very gently for about 25 minutes until rice is tender and has absorbed water. Stir in 4 cups milk, cream, and sugar. Bring to a boil.

Dissolve cornstarch in remaining ¼ cup milk. Gradually add to boiling rice mixture, stirring constantly with a wooden spoon. Lower heat to medium. Add salt and vanilla crystals or extract and simmer for about 15 minutes, uncovered, stirring frequently.

Transfer mixture to individual serving dishes and let cool. Place in refrigerator for several hours. Sprinkle with ground cinnamon and serve.

Yields 6 servings

Melek Basaran, Chef
Authentic Turkish Cuisine, Voorhees, NJ

Vanilla Risotto

Spezia

Chef:
Kevin Couch, executive chef

Chef's training:
graduated from the Culinary Institute of America in Hyde Park, NY; worked in Washington, D.C. and Zurich

Chef's hobbies/ accomplishments:
ran the Philadelphia Marathon in 1998

Chef's favorite ingredient:
foie gras

Chef's favorite food:
the perfect cheeseburger

1 quart milk
1 vanilla bean
¾ cup Arborio rice
½ cup sugar
2 egg yolks

Bring milk and vanilla bean to a boil. Add rice to boiling milk. Cook, stirring constantly, over high heat for 15 minutes until rice grains are cooked through. (Constant stirring keeps the milk from scalding and also develops the gluten of the rice.)

In a mixing bowl, whisk sugar into egg yolks. When rice is cooked, temper yolks into rice-milk mixture by pouring a splash of hot milk into yolks and whisking thoroughly. Then add hot yolk mixture to rice. Stir for another 5 minutes to thicken.

Transfer to a bowl over an ice bath. Stir risotto while cooling. It will thicken further. Garnish with fresh fruit and serve.

Yields 4 servings

Monica Couch, Pastry Chef
Spezia, Bryn Mawr, PA

Vegan Chocolate Pudding

The Bakery at Essene Market & Cafe

Known for:
Essene is a natural foods store in Queen Village. Our bakery specializes in hand-crafted, organic, vegan baked goods. So tasty!

Year opened:
1969

Menu:
vegan baked goods

Bakery manager:
Lanie Meriwether

Chef's training:
H. Koskela School of Cooking and Handwork

Chef's hobbies/ accomplishments:
gardening

Chef's favorite ingredient:
chocolate, of course

Chef's favorite food:
anything fresh from the garden

1 pound silken tofu
⅓ cup maple syrup
1½ teaspoons vanilla
¾ cup sweetened chocolate chips, melted
Pinch of salt

Place tofu in a pot. Cover with water and bring to a boil. (This blanches the tofu and will later help the pudding "set up" or thicken.) When tofu comes to a boil, drain water and put tofu in a blender.

Add other ingredients. Blend for about 1 minute until all ingredients are incorporated and mixture is smooth. (Mixture will be runny.)

Pour into bowl or individual ramekins. Refrigerate for at least 2 hours.

Chef's note … This tasty pudding is easy to make and one of our most popular items.

Yields 4 servings

Lanie Meriwether, Bakery Manager
The Bakery at Essene Market & Cafe, Philadelphia, PA

Anthony's Baci Gelato

Anthony's Italian Coffee House

Known for:
home of Anastasio coffee

Year opened:
1995

Most requested table:
front window and by the fireplace

Menu:
Italian cafe featuring gelato, panini, and Italian pastries

Owner:
Anthony Anastasio

3½ cups toasted hazelnuts
4½ cups whole milk
6 ounces semi-sweet chocolate, chopped
½ cup sugar
5 egg yolks

Grind 3 cups hazelnuts in a blender. Reserve. Coarsely chop remaining ½ cup hazelnuts and reserve.

Heat milk in a saucepan over medium heat until bubbles form around edge of pan. Add ground hazelnuts. Remove from heat and let sit for at least 1 hour at room temperature.

Strain milk through a fine sieve lined with damp cheesecloth and press to extract as much milk as possible. Discard solids and return milk to saucepan. Add chocolate and simmer over low heat to melt chocolate.

Beat sugar and egg yolks in a blender until thick. Keep blender running and gradually add chocolate mixture to blender. Once combined, return entire mixture to saucepan.

Cook over medium heat, continually stirring with a wooden spoon, for 5 to 8 minutes or until thick. Remove from heat and place mixture into a stainless steel bowl. Cool immediately by placing bowl in a bowl of ice. Continue to stir mixture in ice bath until cool. Cover and refrigerate until thoroughly chilled, about 3 hours.

Transfer mixture to an ice cream maker and freeze according to manufacture's instruction.

Serve in small ice cream bowls and top with chopped hazelnuts.

Yields 6 servings

Anthony Anastasio, Owner
Anthony's Italian Coffee House, Philadelphia, PA

Amaretto Cherry Gelato

4 cups heavy cream
¾ cup sugar
1 tablespoon vanilla extract
4 ounces amaretto liqueur
8 ounces fresh cherries, pitted and coarsely chopped (or use frozen cherries)

Bring heavy cream, sugar, vanilla, and 2 ounces amaretto to a boil in a heavy saucepan. Cool down completely in refrigerator for about 2 hours.

Add cherries and remaining amaretto to cooled cream mixture. Transfer mixture to an ice cream maker and follow manufacture's instruction. Freeze for 1 hour.

Yields 1½ quarts

Jason McMullen, Chef/Owner
Valentes, Mt. Laurel, NJ

Baked Figs with Gorgonzola and Pine Nuts

Whisk Wisdom

Figs have been a main food source for humans since the beginning of our dietary history. According to legend, the Greek goddess Demeter was the first to show figs to mortals. She called it "the fruit of autumn." In the book of Genesis, figs provided clothes for Adam and Eve. Figs were also mentioned in a Babylonian hymn book about 2000 BC. Every inhabitant of Athens, including Plato, was a "philosykos": literally translated, "a friend of the fig." The prophet Mohammed once said: "If I should wish a fruit brought to Paradise, it would certainly be the fig."

4 large ripe figs, tops removed
2 teaspoons sweet Gorgonzola cheese
Pine nuts
6 sheets phyllo dough
Melted butter
1 cup port wine
Orange slices
Fresh mint leaves

Preheat oven to 425°.

Stuff each fig with ½ teaspoon cheese and a few pine nuts. Lay out 2 phyllo dough sheets on a clean work surface and cut in half. Brush one half sheet with melted butter. Cover with another half sheet. Brush with more butter and cover with a third half sheet. Wrap fig with layered phyllo dough. Repeat with remaining dough and figs. Place wrapped figs on a baking sheet and brush with more melted butter. Bake for 10 minutes.

Meanwhile, heat port wine in a pan over medium heat until volume is reduced by half, being careful not to burn.

Serve figs with port wine reduction and orange slices. Garnish with fresh mint.

Yields 4 servings

William W. Fischer, C.E.C., Executive Chef
Caffe Aldo Lamberti, Cherry Hill, NJ

Bananas Foster

Did you know?

— According to an old wives' tale, the inside of a banana peel makes a great shoe polish for patent leather shoes.

— The earliest dessert recipe ever written was a banana recipe—a mushy mixture of bananas, almonds, and honey.

— The average American eats 26 pounds of bananas per year, making it our most consumed fruit.

— The biggest banana split ever made was 4.55 miles long!

From *Family Fun Magazine*

¼ cup butter
1 cup dark brown sugar, packed
½ teaspoon ground cinnamon
¼ cup banana liqueur
4 bananas, cut in half lengthwise, then halved
¼ cup dark rum
4 scoops vanilla ice cream

Combine butter, sugar, and cinnamon in a flambé pan or skillet. Place pan over low heat and cook, stirring, until sugar dissolves. Carefully stir in banana liqueur. Place bananas in pan.

When banana sections soften and begin to brown, carefully add rum. Continue to cook until rum is hot, then tip pan slightly and ignite the rum. (You can skip this step if you are uncomfortable doing it.) When flames subside, lift bananas out of pan and place 4 pieces over each portion of ice cream.

Generously spoon warm sauce over top of ice cream and serve immediately.

Yields 4 servings

Victor Ossorio, Chef
The Prime Rib, Philadelphia, PA

Fresh Strawberry Sabayon

Did you know?

Sabayon is both a sauce and a dessert. In France it's called *sabayon* or *sabayon sauce*. It is made by beating egg yolks, wine, and sugar over simmering water. This causes the mixture to thicken and form a light, foamy custard. Sabayon may be sweet or savory and can be served warm or cold. It can stand alone as a dessert or the warm froth can be served as a sauce over cake, fruit, or ice cream.

1 quart water
1 ¾ cups sugar
¼ teaspoon vanilla extract
Rind of 1 lemon, white pith removed
3 pints fresh strawberries, washed, hulled, dried
4 egg yolks
4 tablespoons sugar
4 ounces Marsala wine

Combine water, sugar, vanilla, and lemon rind in a shallow saucepan over high heat. Boil for 5 minutes. Remove lemon rind. Add berries, cover, and bring to a brisk boil for about 1 minute. Drain in a colander. Spread berries in a shallow serving bowl and keep warm.

Bring a pot of water to boil. Place egg yolks, sugar, and wine in a stainless steel bowl; beat with a whisk until frothy. Place bowl as a double boiler over boiling water and beat constantly until foamy and peaks are formed. Spread over hot strawberries and serve.

Yields 6 servings

Ann-Michelle Albertson, Assistant Director
Albertson's Cooking School, Wynnewood, PA

Berry Martini

Bourbon Blue

Known for:
fine N'awlins style cuisine and a Mardi Gras like atmosphere; "Joie de Vie" (the joy of life)

Year opened:
2002

Most requested table:
table 1 with a Canal view (upstairs dining room). In the lower Canal Lounge, the table closest to the band is the most requested.

Menu:
a New Orleans inspired experience

5 strawberries, sliced into quarters
12 blueberries
5 blackberries
5 raspberries
1 tablespoon sugar
1 teaspoon cinnamon
½ ounce Grand Marnier (You may substitute your favorite liqueur.)
1 slice lemon
1 ounce whipped cream
Chocolate sauce
1 sprig fresh mint

Combine berries, sugar, and cinnamon with Grand Marnier in a mixing bowl and toss thoroughly. Press lemon around rim of a frozen martini glass and dip in sugar. Put berries in glass. Top with whipped cream and drizzle with chocolate sauce. Garnish with mint sprig.

Yields 1 serving

Brian Watson, Sous Chef
Bourbon Blue, Philadelphia, PA

Sweet Olde Torte (Antico Dolce Torte)

RoseLena's Coffee Bar/ Restaurant

Known for:
desserts, gourmet coffees, Art Nouveau atmosphere

Year opened:
1994

Most requested table:
bay windows in our turn-of-the-century dining rooms

Menu:
old-world European Continental with Italian flair; yesteryear with a bit of gourmet

Chefs:
Terry and Chris Masino

Chefs' training:
grandmother's recipes;hands-on learning from other chefs

Chefs' accomplishments:
rated #1 in nation by the Zagat survey for Desserts and Coffee/ at age 25 owning and operating our coffee bar and private dining rooms

3 cups white flour
½ cup sugar
1 egg yolk
6 tablespoons Crisco, melted
2 teaspoons crushed cinnamon
¾ cup bottled water
½ stick butter
3 cups coarsely crushed walnuts
2 cups raisins
¼ cup lemon and orange peels
3 teaspoons cinnamon
½ teaspoon fresh grated nutmeg
¼ cup honey

Combine first six ingredients. Refrigerate for at least 1 hour.

Melt butter in a pot. Add remaining ingredients, stirring until well combined.

Preheat oven to 350°. Cut off a 2½-inch strip of dough. Roll out to approximately 22 inches long. (You can use a macaroni machine, but we prefer doing it by hand with a floured rolling pin.) Cut into strips with a fancy-edged pizza cutter. Continue rolling out and cutting remaining dough.

Place a small amount of filling on one side of dough strip; close dough over filling; roll each piece, pinwheel style. Using thick cooking string, tie a knot so that each dough looks like a snail. Place "snails" on baking sheets.

Bake for 25 minutes or until bottoms are cooked. Cool and serve with string tied to preserve the rustic look.

Chef's note … This recipe comes from Calabria and is our signature dish. It is credited to Michael Angelo's mother. When we serve this at the restaurant, we heat it in the microwave for 30 seconds, then drizzle with honey and serve with small poached or fresh lemon slices and fresh whipped crème.

Terry and Chris Masino, Chef/Owners
RoseLena's Coffee Bar/Restaurant, Philadelphia, PA

Rum Pecan Meringues

Feast Your Eyes Catering

Known for:
cooking under any conditions!

Year opened:
1980

Menu:
beautifully handmade items
served as specialty foods

Chef:
Lynn Buono

Chef's training:
trained under many chefs both
locally and abroad in Europe

Chef's accomplishments:
being a mom to two daughters;
past president of Les Dames
Escoffier, Philadelphia; past
president of Philadelphia
Culinary Society; teaches at
Culinary Institute of America

Chef's favorite ingredient:
extra virgin olive oil

Chef's favorite food:
lobster and sea urchins

½ cup egg whites
¼ teaspoon cream of tartar
¼ teaspoon salt
1¼ cups brown sugar, packed
¾ teaspoon vanilla
¾ teaspoon rum
Pecan halves

Preheat oven to 250°.

Beat egg whites with cream of tartar and salt until frothy. Gradually add half the brown sugar, then vanilla and rum. Finally, add remaining brown sugar.

Fill a pastry bag with egg white mixture and pipe onto a baking sheet that has been greased or covered with parchment. Make the meringues approximately 1½ inches in diameter. Decorate each with a pecan half.

Bake for 45 minutes. Turn off oven and let meringues dry out (approximately 45 minutes longer). Carefully remove from baking sheet with a spatula and serve.

Yields 48 meringues

Lynn Buono, Chef/Owner
Feast Your Eyes Gourmet Catering, Philadelphia, PA

Pumpkin Raisin Squares

Did you know?

Almost half of all the raisins grown in the world come from California. In fact, Fresno, California, is the "Raisin Capital of the World." But it didn't intend to be. California discovered the commercial potential of raisins by accident. In 1873, a freak hot spell withered the grapes on the vine. An entrepreneurial grocer in San Francisco promoted these shriveled grapes as "Peruvian Delicacies." The rest is history … California is now the world's leading producer of raisins.

6 tablespoons unsalted butter, softened

⅔ cup light brown sugar, packed

1 large egg

½ cup canned pumpkin puree

½ cup all-purpose flour

½ teaspoon baking soda

½ teaspoon salt

¾ teaspoon ground cinnamon

½ teaspoon ground ginger

¼ teaspoon ground nutmeg

¼ teaspoon ground cloves

½ cup raisins

2 tablespoons cream cheese, softened

1 cup confectioners' sugar

Preheat oven to 350°. Butter an 8 × 8-inch baking pan.

In a large mixing bowl, beat 4 tablespoons butter and brown sugar until fluffy. Beat in egg and pumpkin.

In another bowl, whisk together flour, baking soda, salt, and spices. Beat dry mixture into butter mixture until just combined. Stir in raisins. Spread into prepared pan and bake for 20 to 25 minutes until a toothpick inserted in center comes out clean. Cool slightly in pan, then invert pan onto a rack and cool completely.

Blend remaining 2 tablespoons butter, cream cheese, and confectioners' sugar in a small bowl until smooth. (Add a little hot water, if necessary, to bring icing to a spreading consistency.) Spread icing over cooled cake and allow it to set up, about 10 minutes. Cut into 16 squares.

Chef's note … The squares, without icing, may be stored in an airtight container for up to 3 days.

Yields 16 servings

Donna Leahy, Chef/Owner
The Inn at Twin Linden, Churchtown, PA

Crispy Brown Rice Treats

The Bakery at Essene Market & Cafe

Known for:
delicious vegan baked goods

Year opened:
1969

Baker:
Tina Skibber

Baker's training:
apprenticeship at Essene

Chef's hobbies/ accomplishments:
massage therapist, music

Chef's favorite ingredient:
chocolate

Chef's favorite food:
dessert

1 10-ounce box brown rice cereal
1½ cups raisins and/or chocolate chips
1½ cups rice syrup
1¼ cups smooth peanut butter
1 tablespoon vanilla
Pinch of salt

Pour cereal and raisins and/or chips into a large mixing bowl.

In a saucepan, warm syrup over low heat until syrup is runny. (Do not allow it to boil, or you'll get crunchy, not chewy, treats.) Once warm, remove from heat and stir in peanut butter, vanilla, and salt. Pour syrup mixture over cereal mixture. Mix until well combined. Transfer mixture to a well-oiled 9 x 13-inch pan. Chill until firm. Cut into 12 bars.

Chef's note … This is an easy-to-make, crowd-pleasing dessert — one of our most popular items.

Yields 12 bars

Tina Skibber, Baker
The Bakery at Essene Market & Cafe, Philadelphia, PA

Chocolate-Zucchini Brownies

Chef's Notes

My mom used to send me to school with chocolate zucchini cake to share with all my friends. Here's a little twist on a favorite classic of mine. Also a great recipe for summertime when you're overwhelmed with zucchini from your garden!

2 cups all-purpose flour

½ cup sugar

2½ tablespoons cocoa

1½ teaspoons baking soda

½ teaspoon salt

2 cups finely grated zucchini

½ cup chopped walnuts or pecans

⅓ cup vegetable oil

1 teaspoon vanilla extract

2 1-ounce squares semi-sweet or unsweetened chocolate

¼ cup butter

2 tablespoons milk

2 cups sifted confectioners' sugar

⅛ teaspoon salt

½ teaspoon vanilla extract

Preheat oven to 350°. Grease and flour a 9 x 13-inch pan.

Mix flour, sugar, cocoa, baking soda, and salt. Add zucchini, nuts, oil, and vanilla. Mix well. Pour into prepared pan. Bake for 20 minutes or until a toothpick inserted into middle comes out clean.

Melt chocolate in top of a double boiler over boiling water. Blend in butter and milk. Remove from heat. Add sugar, salt, and vanilla. Blend until smooth. If necessary, thin with a few drops of milk. Cover brownies with chocolate frosting.

Yields 18 brownies

Kristin Albertson, Assistant Director
Albertson's Cooking School, Wynnewood, PA

Cranberry Orange Biscotti

The Bakery at Essene Market & Cafe

Known for:
delicious vegan baked goods

Year opened:
1969

Baker:
Scott MacDonald

Baker's training:
self trained, apprenticeships, mom

Chef's hobbies/ accomplishments:
in another life ... a music therapist

Chef's favorite ingredient:
for baking and desserts — caramel and cranberries (never tried them together)

Chef's favorite food:
things that transform stale bread

2½ cups spelt flour
1½ teaspoons baking powder
¼ teaspoon salt
½ cup safflower oil
½ cup maple syrup
¼ cup orange juice
1 teaspoon vanilla
Zest of 2 oranges
¾ cup dried cranberries or 1½ cups fresh/frozen cranberries, chopped briefly in a food processor

Preheat oven to 325°. Line a baking sheet with parchment paper.

Combine flour, baking powder, and salt in a large mixing bowl. In a separate bowl, combine oil, syrup, orange juice, vanilla, and zest. Add to dry ingredients and mix until ingredients are incorporated, but not too much. Fold in cranberries. (Dough should be somewhat firm and sticky if using fresh cranberries.)

Turn out dough onto prepared sheet and form into a 3 x 13-inch flattened slab, about 1 inch high. Bake for 35 minutes until golden. Remove from oven and let cool for 10 to 15 minutes. While still warm, use a serrated knife to cut biscotti on a slight bias into 1-inch pieces. Spread onto sheet and bake for 15 to 25 minutes. Biscotti will be done when no longer soft in middle. Let cool before serving.

Yields 12 to 14 pieces

Scott MacDonald, Baker
The Bakery at Essene Market & Cafe, Philadelphia, PA

Brunch

Broccoli Rabe Omelette 298

Zucchini Frittata with Sweet Basil 299

Peking Duck and Scrambled Egg Wrap 300

Philadelphia Style Breakfast Cakes 301

Shiitake Spinach Strudel 302

Souffléd Grits 303

Burgundy Poached Pear Crepes with Pecan Praline 304

Sweet Crepes 305

Baked French Toast with Apples and Cranberries 306

Butter Scones 307

Vegan Zucchini Walnut Bread 308

Bananapple Bread 309

Banana Bread 310

Molasses Granola 311

Broccoli Rabe Omelette

Carman's Country Kitchen

Known for:
Carman

Year opened:
1989

Most requested table:
back table #3

Menu:
breakfast/brunch

Chef:
Carman Luntzel

Chef's training:
self taught

Chef's hobbies/ accomplishments:
skiing, hiking, reading, dining

Chef's favorite ingredient:
pork

Chef's favorite food:
French

1 pound broccoli rabe, washed, drained, and chopped with stems
2 tablespoons olive oil
1 head garlic, chopped small
½ sweet onion, chopped small
¼ cup Pernod
16 extra large eggs, whisked
Salt and pepper to taste
Cheese of your choice

Steam broccoli rabe till tender and bright green.

Heat oil in a large skillet. Add broccoli rabe, garlic, and onion and sauté.

Carefully pour in Pernod. Add eggs, salt and pepper to taste. Cover. Cook till firm, then flip and crumble your favorite cheese over top. Cook until cheese melts.

Yields 4 servings

Carman Luntzel, Chef/Owner
Carman's Country Kitchen, Philadelphia, PA

Zucchini Frittata with Sweet Basil

Culinary Quote

"'When you wake up in the morning, Pooh,'
said Piglet at last,
'what's the first thing you say to yourself?'

'What's for breakfast?' said Pooh.
'What do you say, Piglet?'

I say, I wonder what's going to happen exciting today?'
said Piglet.

Pooh nodded thoughtfully.

'It's the same thing,' he said."

A. A. Milne,
in "The House at Pooh Corner"

⅔ cup olive oil

2 cloves garlic, minced

6 zucchini, cut into ¾-inch cubes

20 eggs

¾ cup milk

1 tablespoon salt

1 teaspoon freshly ground black pepper

½ cup chopped fresh basil

½ cup grated Parmesan cheese

Pinch of paprika

10 fresh basil leaves

Heat 1 tablespoon olive oil in a saucepan and sauté garlic for about 3 minutes over medium heat. Add zucchini and sauté until almost soft, about 10 minutes. Reserve.

In a large bowl, beat eggs well. Stir in milk, salt, pepper, and basil.

Put remaining olive oil in a 12-inch sauté pan suitable for serving. Add egg mixture and cook over moderate heat, folding as you would an omelet. When eggs are fluffy, stir in reserved zucchini and garlic. Continue to cook, without stirring, until semi-firm.

Top with Parmesan and sprinkle with paprika. Run frittata under the broiler for a few minutes until slightly brown on top. To serve, cut into pie-shaped wedges and garnish with fresh basil leaves.

Yields 10 servings

Jim Coleman, Executive Chef
Normandy Farm, Blue Bell, PA

Peking Duck and Scrambled Egg Wrap

Did you know?

Peking duck is an elaborately prepared Chinese dish. The duck is coated with honey and other ingredients and then hung until the skin is hard and dry. The duck is then roasted, and the skin becomes golden, very crisp, and amazingly delicious. (The meat's pretty incredible, too!)

4 tablespoons butter
10 extra large eggs, lightly beaten with a drop of water
1 bunch chives, finely minced
1 Peking duck, prepared and sliced into bite-size pieces
1 cup hoisin sauce
Juice of 2 limes
12 6-inch flour tortillas

Heat butter in a nonstick pan. Add eggs and cook until soft. Stir in chives and set aside.

Heat duck pieces with skin side down where possible in a nonstick pan.

Preheat oven to 350°. Combine hoisin sauce and lime juice. Drizzle half hoisin-lime mixture on tortillas. Place duck on tortillas and top with cooked eggs. Roll into cylinders and place on a baking sheet with seams down. Bake until heated through.

Garnish with remaining hoisin drizzle. Serve alone or with Roasted Mushroom and Golden Apple Salad (Recipe appears on page 66.).

Yields 6 servings

Bruce Cooper, Owner
Jake's, Philadelphia, PA

Philadelphia Style Breakfast Cakes

Did you know?

Many people outside the Delaware Valley have never heard of scrapple; and if they have heard of it, they often consider it to be a Philadelphia food. Although certainly popular in Philly, scrapple was created by the Pennsylvania Dutch living in the eastern Pennsylvania farmlands.

Scrapple — as defined by the Food Lover's Companion — is "cornmeal mush made with the meat and broth of pork, seasoned with onions, spices, and herbs and shaped into loaves for slicing and frying." The word scrapple comes from "scrap" or "scrappy," and that's because leftover pig scraps — skin, heart, liver, tongue, brains —were the original main ingredient. It's definitely one of those things that you either love or hate. (Personally, I love it!)

1 pound stiff mashed potatoes

1 pound cooked and chopped bacon

½ pound shredded ham

4 ounces cooked scrapple, chopped

½ pound shredded American cheese

¼ teaspoon Dijon mustard

Salt and pepper to taste

1 cup milk

3 eggs

1 cup seasoned flour

1 cup breadcrumbs

1 cup vegetable or canola oil

Dijon Mustard Béchamel Sauce (Recipe appears on page 319.)

Combine mashed potatoes, meats, cheese, mustard, and salt and pepper to taste. Form into 8 cakes. Whisk together milk and eggs. Place flour and breadcrumbs each in separate bowls. Dip cakes into flour first and then into milk mixture. Dredge in breadcrumbs.

Heat oil in a skillet to 325°. Panfry cakes on both sides until golden brown. Drain on paper towel. Serve with sauce.

Yields 8 cakes

Dan D'Angelo CEC AAC, Chef Instructor
Art Institute of Philadelphia, Philadelphia, PA

Shiitake Spinach Strudel

½ cup chopped shallots
1 tablespoon olive oil
1 pound shiitake mushrooms, sliced
½ teaspoon salt
¼ teaspoon black pepper
1 tablespoon finely minced garlic
1 tablespoon chopped fresh parsley
½ cup sherry
2 pounds spinach, chopped
4 sheets phyllo dough
¼ cup butter, melted

Preheat oven to 400°.

Sweat shallots in oil in a large sauté pan. Add mushrooms. Season with salt and pepper and cook until just tender. Add garlic, parsley, and sherry and cook until sherry is almost evaporated. Cool.

Glaze a separate pan with olive oil and heat over high heat. Add spinach and sauté until just wilted. Combine spinach and mushroom mixture.

Lay out 1 phyllo sheet on a work surface and brush with butter. Repeat with remaining 3 sheets, placing one sheet on top of another. Spread filling evenly on the phyllo and roll up. Brush top with butter. Bake on a baking sheet until golden brown, about 20 minutes. Slice to serve. Serve alone or with Herb Roasted Salmon (Recipe appears on page 155.).

Yields 12 servings

Meg Votta, Executive Chef
Joseph Ambler Inn, North Wales, PA

Souffléd Grits

2½ cups chicken broth
½ cup grits
1 teaspoon salt
3 eggs, separated
2 tablespoons butter
⅛ teaspoon cream of tartar

Bring broth to a boil in a medium pot. Slowly stir grits into boiling broth. Add salt, cover, and cook until grits are done: 3 to 5 minutes for quick grits and 20 to 30 minutes for regular grits.

Remove from heat. Beat in egg yolks and butter. Cool slightly.

Preheat oven to 400°. Generously butter a 1½-quart baking dish.

In a mixing bowl, beat egg whites with cream of tartar until stiff peaks form. Fold in grits and place in prepared baking dish. Bake for 30 minutes or until grits are puffed and browned. Serve immediately with butter.

Yields 4 to 6 servings

Jim Coleman, Executive Chef
Normandy Farm, Blue Bell, PA

Burgundy Poached Pear Crepes with Pecan Praline

Creperie Beau Monde

Known for:
sweet and savory crepes

Year opened:
1998

Most requested table:
outdoor deck

Menu:
French creperie

Chef:
David Salama

Chef's training:
self taught

Chef's hobbies/ accomplishments:
painter/artist

Chef's favorite ingredient:
vanilla beans

Chef's favorite food:
baby lamb racks

1 cup plus 4 cups sugar
¼ cup water
2 tablespoons melted butter
2 cups pecans
12 Bosc pairs, peeled and left whole
8 cups Burgundy
10 whole black peppercorns
Zest of 1 orange
Zest of 1 lemon
3-inch piece ginger, peeled and chopped
1 tablespoon vanilla extract
3 tablespoons pomegranate syrup, optional
Sweet Crepes (Recipe appears on page 305.)
Crème Anglaise (Recipe appears on page 349.)

Preheat oven to 350°. Combine 1 cup sugar, water, and melted butter in a mixing bowl. Toss in pecans. Spread on an oiled sheet pan and bake until sugar caramelizes. Remove from oven and cool. Chop into small pieces.

Combine remaining 4 cups sugar and the next eight ingredients (includes optional pomegranate syrup) in a saucepot. Simmer until pears are tender. Remove pears from liquid and cool. Strain liquid and cook until sauce is reduced by half and a syrup consistency.

Slice pears when cool enough to handle. Fill each crepe with pears and arrange on a baking sheet. Heat in a pre-heated 350° oven until warmed through.

Arrange crepes on a platter and sprinkle with chopped pecan praline. Pour crème anglaise around crepes.

Chef's notes ... You may substitute figs for pears and almonds for pecans.

Yields 6 to 8 servings

David Salama, Chef/Proprietor
Creperie Beau Monde, Philadelphia, PA

Sweet Crepes

1 cup milk
⅓ cup water
2 large eggs
1 tablespoon vanilla extract
1 tablespoon Grand Marnier, optional
1 cup white pastry flour
2 tablespoons sugar
2 tablespoons melted butter

Combine first five ingredients (includes optional Grand Marnier) in a mixing bowl. In a separate bowl, combine flour and sugar. Slowly add dry ingredients to wet ingredients until mixture is combined but not over mixed. Add butter and stir to incorporate thoroughly.

Heat a nonstick skillet until hot. Pour a 4-ounce ladle of batter into pan and tilt quickly until pan is completely covered. Cook until edges lift easily. Flip crepe and cook for 15 seconds. Reserve. Continue process with remaining batter.

Yields 6 to 8 servings

**David Salama, Chef/Proprietor
Creperie Beau Monde, Philadelphia, PA**

Baked French Toast with Apples and Cranberries

Chef's Notes

— Somewhere between traditional French toast and bread pudding, this French toast is perfect for entertaining. Toss the apples with a little lemon juice to prevent browning.

6 1-inch-thick slices challah
4 large eggs
½ cup heavy cream
½ cup milk
6 tablespoons granulated sugar
6 tablespoons light brown sugar, packed
¼ cup orange juice
1 cup fresh cranberries
2 tablespoons unsalted butter
3 apples, peeled, cored, and sliced
3 tablespoons mascarpone

Preheat oven to 350°. Butter six 3-inch-wide ramekins or soufflé dishes.

Cut challah into 1-inch cubes. In a large mixing bowl, whisk together eggs, cream, milk, 2 tablespoons granulated sugar, and 2 tablespoons brown sugar. Add challah cubes and toss to coat evenly. Divide mixture among ramekins. Place ramekins in a 9 × 13-inch glass baking pan. Add enough boiling water to reach midlevel of ramekins. Bake for 15 to 18 minutes until light brown and firm.

Meanwhile, combine remaining 4 tablespoons granulated sugar, orange juice, and cranberries in a small saucepan. Simmer over low heat, stirring often, until all cranberries "pop," about 4 to 5 minutes. Keep warm.

Melt butter in a medium skillet. Add apples and sprinkle with remaining 4 tablespoons brown sugar. Sauté until apples begin to soften and caramelize, about 4 to 5 minutes.

Invert ramekins onto individual plates so French toast is brown side up. Divide mascarpone among plates and spoon on apples and cranberry sauce.

Yields 6 servings

Donna Leahy, Chef/Owner
The Inn at Twin Linden, Churchtown, PA

Butter Scones

Chef's Notes

— While this recipe lists milk as one of the liquid ingredients, I personally prefer to use buttermilk, which gives the scones a slight, but distinctive, authentic tart bite. You could also use milk that has just started to sour as a substitute for the same effect.

3 cups all-purpose flour
½ cup sugar
½ teaspoon salt
3 teaspoons baking powder
½ cup butter
2 large eggs
6 tablespoons milk

Preheat oven to 425°. Lightly dust a cookie sheet with flour.
Sift together first four ingredients into a medium bowl.
Rub in or cut in butter until it resembles a sandy mixture.
In a separate bowl, whisk together eggs and milk. Add to flour mixture and blend to form a dough. Turn out dough onto a floured board and knead for 2 minutes. Roll dough into a long cylinder. Cut into 12 equal pieces. Shape each piece into a flat round. Brush with milk. Sprinkle with granulated sugar. Make a cut in each with a knife, cutting only halfway through the scone.

Place scones on prepared cookie sheet and bake for 10 to 12 minutes. Serve warm with butter, preserves, and whipped cream.

Yields 6 servings

Philip Pinkney CEC, CCE, Director of Culinary Arts
The Restaurant School at Walnut Hill College, Philadelphia, PA

Vegan Zucchini Walnut Bread

The Bakery at Essene Market & Cafe

Known for:
delicious vegan baked goods

Year opened:
1969

Baker:
Laura R. Grove

Baker's training:
The Restaurant School, Philadelphia, PA

Chef's hobbies/ accomplishments:
writing, reading, playing guitar, gardening

Chef's favorite ingredient:
chocolate, mango

Chef's favorite food:
Thai

2¼ cups whole spelt flour
3 tablespoons Cafix Crystals (a grain coffee substitute)
1 teaspoon baking powder
½ teaspoon sea salt
2 teaspoons cinnamon
½ cup chopped walnuts
¾ cup maple syrup
½ cup safflower oil
½ cup orange juice
1 tablespoon vanilla
¼ pound tofu
1 medium zucchini, grated

Preheat oven to 300°.

Combine flour, Cafix, baking powder, sea salt, cinnamon, and chopped walnuts. In a separate bowl, blend syrup, oil, orange juice, and vanilla with tofu until smooth. Stir in grated zucchini. Add dry ingredients to wet and stir until just combined.

Pour into a 9 x 4-inch loaf pan. Bake for 45 to 60 minutes until a tester comes out clean. Cool and remove from pan.

Chef's note ... Whole wheat pastry flour can be substituted for spelt flour, if desired.

Yields 8 slices

Laura R. Grove, Baker
The Bakery at Essene Market & Cafe, Philadelphia, PA

Bananapple Bread

Albertson's Cooking School

Known for:
Philadelphia's longest standing cooking school for home cooks

Year opened:
1973

Menu:
easy multi-cultural recipes for home cooks

Chef:
Kristin Albertson

Chef's training:
Culinary Institute of America; Johnson & Wales University

Chef's hobbies/ accomplishments:
teaching kids how to cook

Chef's favorite ingredient:
morels

Chef's favorite food:
any artisan cheese

½ cup butter or shortening, softened
2 eggs
½ cup sugar
½ cup dark brown sugar, packed
3 ripe bananas, mashed
1 small apple, peeled and grated
2 cups all-purpose flour
1 teaspoon baking soda
½ teaspoon baking powder
Pinch of salt

Topping:
½ cup dark brown sugar, packed
¾ cup chopped pecans or walnuts
¼ cup butter
1 teaspoon cinnamon

Preheat oven to 350°. Grease and flour a 9 x 5 x 3-inch loaf pan.

Blend shortening, eggs, sugars, banana, and apple together. In a separate bowl, mix flour, baking soda, baking powder, and salt with a whisk. Add to fruit mixture. Pour into pan. Bake on middle rack for 45 minutes (about 35 to 40 minutes if your pan is dark).

Combine topping ingredients in a saucepan. Cook until sugar dissolves. Spread on bread, covering top, using back of a large spoon. Return bread to oven for another 10 to 15 minutes.

Yields 8 servings

Kristin Albertson, Assistant Director
Albertson's Cooking School, Wynnewood, PA

Banana Bread

1 cup sugar
½ cup shortening
2 eggs
3 bananas, mashed
2 cups flour
½ teaspoon baking soda
½ teaspoon baking powder
½ teaspoon salt
1 cup chopped nuts

Preheat oven to 350°. Grease a 9 x 5-inch loaf pan.

Cream sugar and shortening. Add eggs and vanilla. Add mashed banana to mixture. Add dry ingredients and mix. Add nuts.

Pour into prepared pan. Bake for 1 hour or until done when tested.

Yields 1 loaf

Roz Bratt, Owner/Baker
Homemade Goodies by Roz, Philadelphia, PA

Molasses Granola

Spezia

Chef:
Monica Couch, pastry chef

Chef's training:
graduated from the French
Culinary Institute in New York
City; trained in Brussels,
Belgium, and worked in
Washington, DC

Chef's favorite ingredient:
Tahitian vanilla beans

Chef's favorite food:
"whatever Kevin is cooking,
honestly" (Kevin Couch is
Monica's husband and executive
chef at Spezia.)

¼ cup molasses
½ cup brown sugar
¼ cup honey
¼ cup butter
¼ cup cold water
3½ cups rolled oats
¼ cup sunflower seeds
¼ cup sesame seeds
½ cup shredded coconut
½ cup coarsely chopped walnuts
½ cup coarsely chopped pecans
½ cup coarsely chopped almonds
4 tablespoons ground cinnamon
½ cup golden raisins

Preheat oven to 350°.

Combine first five ingredients in a medium-size pot. Bring to a boil, stir, and remove from heat.

Combine remaining ingredients, except raisins, in a mixing bowl. Carefully pour hot liquid over mixed dry ingredients. Stir together until dry ingredients are well coated.

Spread evenly on a parchment or foil lined cookie sheet. Bake for 20 minutes until everything looks toasty.

Remove tray from oven and immediately sprinkle with golden raisins. Stir contents of tray with a large metal spoon. (This step incorporates the raisins without them drying up further in the oven and inhibits the formation of a single tray-shaped granola bar.)

Cool and break mix apart. Store in an airtight container. (This granola is both a yummy breakfast cereal and a crunchy ice cream topping.)

Yields 8 portions

Monica Couch, Pastry Chef
Spezia, Bryn Mawr, PA

Stocks, Sauces, Salsas and Such

Beef Stock

7 pounds meaty beef or veal bones, such as neck bones, shank crosscuts, short ribs, knuckles, or leg bones with marrow

1 cup red burgundy wine

4 celery ribs, diced

2 carrots, diced

1 large white onion, chopped

1 garlic clove, chopped

2 tablespoons unsalted butter

12 cups water

2 large ripe tomatoes, diced

1 teaspoon whole black peppercorns

1 bay leaf

Preheat oven to 350°.

In a high-sided roasting pan, array meaty bones. Roast for 1 to 1½ hours, until meat is well browned, turning the bones once.

Drain the fat from the roasting pan. Add the wine to deglaze the pan, loosening any browned bits with a wooden spoon. Set aside.

In an 8-quart (2-gallon) stockpot, sauté the celery, carrots, onion, and garlic in hot butter over medium heat for 5 minutes, until the onions are translucent. Add the water to the stockpot and bring to a boil. Add the tomatoes, peppercorns, bay leaf, and bone and wine mixture and bring to a boil. Reduce the heat and simmer, uncovered, for 4 hours, until reduced to about 4 cups (1 quart) of liquid.

Line a large colander or sieve with 2 layers of 100% cotton cheesecloth. Set colander in a large heat-proof bowl. Carefully pour hot mixture through it. Set aside to cool.

Transfer the stock to a storage container, cover, and refrigerate or freeze until ready for use. Stock will keep in the refrigerator for up to 1 week and in the freezer for up to 1 month, if well sealed.

Yields 1 quart

Walter Staib, Executive Chef/Proprietor
City Tavern, Philadelphia, PA

Lamb Stock

2 or 3 lamb shanks or 3 or 4 pounds bones
12 cloves garlic
2 carrots
1 stalk celery
2 or 3 springs fresh rosemary
2 sprigs thyme
1 tablespoon cracked black peppercorns
Salt
Leeks
Parsley

Place shanks or bones and other ingredients in a stockpot. Add enough cold water to cover 4 inches above level of bones. Bring to a full boil and then reduce heat to a simmer. Cook for 2 to 4 hours.

Discard bones and vegetables. Degrease; strain and chill.

**Fritz Blank, Chef de Cuisine/ Proprietor
Deux Cheminées, Philadelphia, PA**

Chicken Stock

3 celery ribs, chopped

2 carrots, chopped

2 medium onions, chopped

1 tablespoon unsalted butter

40 cups (2½ gallons) water

1 stewing hen (about 4½ pounds), whole or cut into eight pieces

1 cup white wine

4 sprigs fresh thyme

½ teaspoon whole black peppercorns

1 bay leaf

In a 12-quart (3-gallon) stockpot, sauté the celery, carrots, and onions in the butter over medium heat for 10 minutes, until the onions are translucent.

Add the water, hen, and wine and bring to a boil. Add the thyme, peppercorns, and bay leaf. Reduce the heat and simmer, uncovered, for 2 hours, until reduced to about 5 quarts of liquid.

Line a large colander or sieve with 2 layers of 100% cotton cheesecloth. Set colander in a large heat-proof bowl, carefully pour hot mixture through it. Return stock to stockpot. Continue cooking the stock for 4 hours, until reduced to about 10 cups (2½ quarts) of liquid.

Transfer the stock to a storage container, cover, and refrigerate or freeze until ready to use. Stock will keep in the refrigerator for up to 1 week, and in the freezer for up to 1 month, if well sealed.

Yields 10 cups (2½ quarts)

Walter Staib, Executive Chef/Proprietor
City Tavern, Philadelphia, PA

City Tavern Demi-glace

1 large shallot, chopped
1 teaspoon unsalted butter
1 cup red burgundy wine
1 bay leaf
1 whole black peppercorn
2 cups Beef Stock (Recipe appears on page 314.)

In a 2-quart saucepan, sauté the shallot in hot butter over medium heat for 5 minutes, until golden brown and translucent.

Add the red wine, bay leaf, and peppercorn and bring to a boil. Reduce the heat and simmer, uncovered, for 8 to 10 minutes, until reduced to about ½ cup liquid.

Add the Beef Stock and continue cooking for about 30 minutes, until reduced to about 1½ cups.

Line a large colander or sieve with 2 layers of 100% cotton cheesecloth. Set colander in a large heat-proof bowl. Carefully pour hot mixture through it.

Set aside to cool.

Transfer the stock to a storage container, cover, and refrigerate or freeze until ready to use. Stock will keep in the refrigerator for up to 1 month, if well sealed.

Yields 1½ cups

Walter Staib, Executive Chef/Proprietor
City Tavern, Philadelphia, PA

Scallop Jus

Savona

Known for:
cuisine of the Riviera — both French and Italian

Year opened:
1997

Most requested table:
on the patio

Menu:
French and Italian

Chef:
Dominique Filoni

Chef's training:
French Culinary School

Chef's hobbies/ accomplishments:
movies, traveling and dining

Chef's favorite ingredient:
black and white truffles

Chef's favorite food:
seafood and foie gras

2 cups blended oil
1 pound scallops, diced
2 shallots, thinly chopped
1 clove garlic, thinly chopped
1½ cups white wine
2 stems fresh thyme
3 or 4 parsley stems
1 bay leaf, fresh or dry
2 quarts water
1 cup heavy cream
½ pound butter

Heat 1 cup oil in a rondeau, brazier, or wide shallow pan with handles. When oil starts to smoke, add scallops and sweat until dry. Strain scallops and reserve. Reheat pan with remaining 1 cup oil. Return scallops to pan. Sweat until golden.

Add shallots and garlic. Deglaze almost immediately with white wine. Cook until liquid is almost all evaporated. Add thyme, parsley, bay leaf, and 1 quart water. Cook until liquid is reduced by three-fourths. Add ½ quart water. Cook until liquid is reduced by half. Add remaining ½ quart water and cook until liquid is reduced by half. Strain through a chinois or fine metal sieve, pressing well to extract all the liquid and flavor. Discard solids.

Add liquid to a clean pot and cook for 15 minutes, skimming the surface regularly. Add cream and bring to a boil. Add butter. Strain again through chinois and season to taste.

Dominique Filoni, Chef/Partner
Savona Restaurant, Gulph Mills, PA

Dijon Mustard Béchamel Sauce

Chef's Note

Béchamel is white French sauce traditionally made of butter, milk, and flour. It was named after its inventor, Louis XIV's steward Louis de Béchamel. One of the "five mother sauces," béchamel is often used the base of many other sauces.

In his 1891 cookbook, *The Art of Eating Well,* Pellegrino Artusi says a good béchamel sauce and a properly cooked meat sauce are the principal secrets of refined cooking.

¾ cup onion
½ cup butter
2¼ tablespoons flour
2 cups milk
2 cloves
1 teaspoon Dijon mustard

Sauté onion in butter. Add flour and stir. Add milk and cloves. Continue to stir until thick. Add mustard. Strain and serve.

**Dan D'Angelo CEC AAC, Chef Instructor
Art Institute of Philadelphia, Philadelphia, PA**

Choron Sauce

Whisk Wisdom

Alexander Etienne Choron, a French chef from Caen, created Choron sauce. He was chef de cuisine at the famous Voisin restaurant in Paris in the late 19th century. Choron sauce is a béarnaise or hollandaise sauce with tomato puree added to give it a pink tint. It can be served with poultry, meat, or fish.

1 medium shallot, minced
¼ cup white wine
1 teaspoon minced tarragon
¼ teaspoon fresh ground pepper
2 tablespoons water
2 egg yolks
½ cup sweet butter, clarified
1 teaspoon tomato paste
½ teaspoon salt
Ground cayenne pepper, otional
Tabasco sauce, optional

Place shallots, wine, tarragon, and pepper in a medium saucepan and bring to a simmer over medium heat. Cook until liquid is reduced about 80 percent or until nearly dry. Add 1 tablespoon water. Strain out solids.

Transfer remaining liquid to a metal bowl placed over a pot of barely simmering water (or the top of a double boiler). Gently whisk in egg yolks until tripled in volume and mixture forms "ribbons" as it falls from the whisk. Add butter and whisk constantly until sauce is thick.

Thin tomato paste with remaining 1 tablespoon water. Add mixture and salt to egg mixture and continue to whisk until deep pink in color. Set aside and keep warm, whisking frequently to keep from separating. A dash of ground cayenne pepper or Tabasco sauce may be added, if desired.

Victor Ossorio, Chef
The Prime Rib, Philadelphia, PA

Smoked Red Pepper Sauce

Chef's Notes

This is the technique I recommend for roasting and smoking peppers. Cut peppers in half lengthwise. Remove and discard stem, core, and seeds. Lightly rub skin with oil and place on a sheet pan, skin side up. Place sheet pan directly under hot broiler and broil until skin becomes charred and black, approximately 5 minutes. Remove and let cool to room temperature. (This can also be done in a preheated 400° oven or skin side down on an outdoor grill.) While peppers are cooling, place soaked hickory chips in a smoker. Close lid and place on medium-high flame until smoke develops, about 10 minutes. Peel charred skin from peppers as soon as they are cool enough to handle, using a pairing knife, if necessary. (Do not rinse with water.) When the smoker is heated up, turn off heat and place the peppers inside. Leave the lid a little ajar for 1 minute. Remove at once and check the smoke flavor.

6 large smoked roasted red peppers
½ tablespoon olive oil
½ large Vidalia onion, sliced
3 cloves garlic, sliced
½ cup extra dry white vermouth
8 ounces chicken stock
½ teaspoon fresh thyme
Salt to taste
Cracked black pepper to taste
1 tablespoon whole butter

Puree peppers and reserve.

Heat olive oil in a sauté pan over medium heat. Add onion and garlic and sweat for 3 minutes. Do not brown. Add vermouth and deglaze pan. Add chicken stock and cook for 3 minutes. Add pureed peppers and thyme and return to a boil. Lower heat and simmer for 5 minutes.

Strain through a china cap and a chinois, if needed. Adjust seasoning with salt and pepper. Whisk in butter until emulsified.

Vince Alberici, Executive Chef
Marker Restaurant at Adam's Mark Hotel
Philadelphia, PA

Sun-dried Tomato Cream Sauce

2 cloves cloves, finely chopped

1 medium shallot, finely chopped

½ cup white wine

1½ cups heavy cream

⅓ cup sun-dried tomatoes

½ teaspoon salt

⅛ teaspoon white pepper

In medium saucepan, heat garlic and shallot over medium heat until fragrant. Add white wine and cook until wine is almost completely evaporated. Add heavy cream and cook until thick enough to coat back of a spoon.

Transfer to a blender or food processor. Add sun-dried tomatoes and blend until smooth. Season with salt and pepper. Strain and keep warm. Serve with Panko Crusted Sea Bass (Recipe appears on page 166.).

Yields 2 cups

Robert Mansfield, Executive Chef
Porterhouse Steaks and Seafood, Cherry Hill, NJ

DD's Meatless Tomato Sauce

32 ounces ground peeled tomatoes
3 ounces water
3 tablespoons chopped fresh sweet basil
1 tablespoon marjoram
1 tablespoon salt (2 tablespoons if kosher)
¼ teaspoon ground black pepper
1 tablespoon chopped fresh parsley
½ cup olive oil
5 cloves garlic, coarsely chopped

Combine all ingredients, except oil and garlic, in a saucepan. Simmer for 1 hour. In a separate pan, combine oil and garlic and sauté garlic until golden brown. (Be careful not to burn garlic. If you do, discard and start over.) Strain and discard garlic. Turn heat off under tomatoes. Add oil and whip until well incorporated. Serve immediately or freeze.

Yields 1 quart

Dan D'Angelo CEC AAC, Chef Instructor
Art Institute of Philadelphia, Philadelphia, PA

Coconut Soy Sauce

Did you know?

Man can use every part of the coconut. The white nut-meat can be eaten raw or shredded and dried and used in most cooking recipes. A single coconut has as much protein as a quarter pound of beefsteak. Copra, the dried meat of the kernels, when crushed, is the source of coconut oil. The husks, known as coir, are short, coarse, elastic fibers used to make an excellent thatch roofing material for houses. A coconut shell is also an excellent charcoal that works as a cooking fuel and in the production of gas masks and air filters. The outer part of the trunk of the coconut palm furnishes a construction lumber known as porcupine wood used for houses and furniture. The swollen base of the trunk, when hollowed, can be turned into a hula drum that the Hawaiians use for entertainment. These are just a few examples of how the extraordinary coconut palm can be utilized.

Southern Illinois University
Carbondale / Ethnobotanical Leaflets

1½ ounces ginger, peeled and grated
4 cloves garlic, minced
1½ cups soy sauce
¼ cup sherry
1½ cups water
¾ cup sesame oil
1 13.5-ounce can coconut milk
1 15-ounce can crème of coconut
2 stalks lemon grass
1 teaspoon chili garlic

Blend ginger, garlic, soy sauce, sherry, and water in a blender on high. Slowly drizzle in sesame oil until emulsified.

Combine emulsion and remaining ingredients in a pan and bring to a boil. Lower heat and simmer for about 30 minutes. Strain and serve.

Yields about 6 cups

Laura Kaplan, Chef/Owner
Emerald Fish, Cherry Hill, NJ

Soy Basil Dipping Sauce

Did you know?

There are many varieties of sweet basil available for cooking and ornamental purposes. Experiment! They can add exciting color, texture, flavor, and fragrance to your garden and your cooking.

Cinnamon basil has brownish stems and purple flowers tinged with bronze. The dark green leaves have a cinnamon taste and fragrance.

Dark Opal has lovely red-purple leaves and stems. Its pink flowers are a nice addition to gardens and walkways.

Genovese (or "Genova") is a flat-leafed Italian basil often used in pesto.

Lemon basil has small light green leaves and a lemony fragrance. It is often used in Indonesian cuisine.

Magical Michael has small purple and white flowers that are attractive to bees in the garden and as a garnish in salads.

Purple Ruffles has large, shiny purple-black fringed leaves and pink flowers. It adds color and contrast to flower beds, container gardens, and culinary dishes.

University of Wisconsin-Madison
Department of Horticulture

½ cup soy sauce
½ cup balsamic vinegar
¼ cup chicken stock
2 teaspoons finely chopped fresh basil
2 teaspoons peeled and finely chopped ginger root

Combine all ingredients. Serve with Scallop and Shrimp Dumplings (Recipe appears on page 14.).

Yields 2 servings

Michael M. Wei, Executive Chef/Owner
Yangming, Bryn Mawr, PA

Guava Barbecue Sauce

3 quarts prepared barbecue sauce
2 pounds guava paste
1 cup Worcestershire sauce
1 cup hot sauce

Combine all ingredients in a nonreactive saucepan. Cook over slow heat, allowing guava paste to completely melt. Simmer to combine all flavors.

Guillermo Veloso, Executive Chef
Cuba Libre Restaurant & Rum Bar, Philadelphia, PA

Green Curry Barbecue

Blue Sage Vegetarian Grille

Year opened:
2000

Most requested table:
W3

Menu:
vegetarian, New American

Executive Chef:
Mike Jackson

Chef's training:
self taught

**Chef's hobbies/
accomplishments:**
Hobbies? Maybe some day!/
Blue Sage named
"Best of Philly" 2002

Chef's favorite ingredient:
fresh figs — black mission
and brown turkey

Chef's favorite food:
Chinese

4 green bell peppers
1 small red onion, peeled and cut into ¼-inch slices
2 tablespoons fresh ginger
2 tablespoons fresh garlic
1 bunch cilantro, roughly chopped
1 bunch basil, roughly chopped
6 ounces canned coconut milk
1 ounce soy sauce
Salt and pepper to taste

Lightly oil sides of bell peppers and onion. Char all sides on a grill pan or oven broiler. Let cool. Remove stems and seed pods from peppers. Leave on blackened skins. (No need to worry about any seeds that remain.)

Place all ingredients in a blender and blend well. Season to taste.

Chef's note... Canned coconut milk can be found in the ethnic section in most grocery stores. Be careful not to confuse coconut milk with cream of coconut.

Yields 1 quart

**Mike Jackson, Chef/Owner
Blue Sage Vegetarian Grille, Southampton, PA**

Red Curry Barbecue

Chef's Note

— This recipe calls for dried chiles: use Ancho, Pasilla, or New Mexican red. Almost any grocery store has at least one variety in the produce section.

— This sauce and Green Curry Barbecue sauce are easily made at the same time due to many common ingredients. Both freeze well and are great in Asian or Indian dishes. They can be added to broth to enhance flavor or be a finishing glaze for barbecue.

4 medium-large dried chiles, destemmed
4 red bell peppers
1 small red onion, peeled and cut into ¼-inch slices
2 tablespoons fresh ginger
2 tablespoons fresh garlic
2 tablespoons brown sugar, packed or pure maple syrup
2 tablespoons soy sauce
1 canned chipotle pepper
Salt and pepper to taste

Soak chiles in hot water for 30 minutes.
    Lightly oil sides of bell peppers and onion. Char all sides on a grill pan or oven broiler. Let cool. Remove stems and seed pods from peppers. Leave on blackened skins. (No need to worry about any seeds that remain.)
    Place soaked chiles in a blender with all other ingredients. Blend well and season to taste.

Yields 1 quart

Mike Jackson, Chef/Owner
Blue Sage Vegetarian Grille, Southampton, PA

Mojito Marinade

⅔ cup fresh citrus juice (sour orange, lime, grapefruit, or any combo)
⅓ cup olive oil
6 to 8 cloves garlic, minced
1 fresh jalapeño pepper, chopped
3 bay leaves
½ teaspoon ground cumin
¼ teaspoon dry oregano
Salt and pepper to taste

Combine all ingredients in a saucepan and mix well. Cook over low heat for about 10 minutes or use raw (as is) as a marinade.

Yields 1 cup

**Susanna Goihman, Chef/Owner
Azafran, Philadelphia, PA**

Roasted Garlic Aïoli

Whisk Wisdom

Aïoli, a strongly flavored garlic mayonnaise, is one of the primary sauces in the south of France, especially in Provence. As the artist Frederic Mistral put it, "Aïoli intoxicates slightly, saturates the body with warmth, and bathes the soul with enthusiasm." It's a popular accompaniment for fish, meats, and vegetables, both hot and cold. Once you taste it, you may never go back to plain old mayo again.

1 large head garlic
2 tablespoons plus 1 cup extra virgin olive oil, divided
Salt and pepper to taste
3 egg yolks
1 tablespoon champagne vinegar or lemon juice

Preheat oven to 500°. Slice off top of garlic head to expose cloves. Place head on a sheet of aluminum foil in a shallow baking dish. Drizzle with 2 tablespoons olive oil and season with salt and pepper. Cover with foil and roast until garlic is very soft, 30 to 40 minutes (or roast in a preheated 350° oven for 1 hour).

Remove garlic from oven and let stand until cool enough to handle. Squeeze pulp from cloves and set pulp aside.

In a food processor or blender, process egg yolks, vinegar, and garlic pulp, adding remaining cup of oil in a slow stream until a thick mayonnaise-like emulsion forms. Use as a spread on Lobster Hoagie (Recipe appears on page 242.).

Yields about 1½ cups

Gene Betz, Executive Chef
The Saloon, Philadelphia, PA

Lemon Aïoli

Chlöe

Known for:
herb tabletops and handmade candle votives

Year opened:
2000

Most requested table:
"the nook" — tables 7 and 8

Menu:
American eclectic

Chef's training:
The Restaurant School

Chef's hobbies/ accomplishments:
aggressive skating, backpacking, reading, homebrewing

Chef's favorite ingredient:
avocados — I love their texture.

Chef's favorite food:
foie gras

3 egg yolks
Juice of 2 lemons
1 tablespoon Dijon mustard
⅔ cup blended oil
⅓ cup olive oil
Salt and pepper to taste

Combine egg yolks, lemon juice, and mustard in a blender. Blend on low speed. Slowly add blended oil, drop by drop, slowly blending to start emulsion. Increase speed and add olive oil. When all oil is incorporated, season with salt and pepper. Chill until ready to use.

Daniel Grimes, Co-Chef/Co-Owner
Chlöe, Philadelphia, PA

Chipotle Aïoli

Culinary Quote

"Aïoli (garlic mayonnaise) epitomizes the heat, the power, and the joy of the Provençal sun, but it has another virtue - it drives away flies."

Frédéric Mistral
Nobel Prize winning
French writer

1 cup mayonnaise (Any high-quality commercial brand you prefer is suitable.)
4 medium cloves garlic, roasted, peeled, and pureed
½ teaspoon dark brown sugar
1 chipotle chile (Chipotle is a smoked jalapeño pepper.)
Salt and pepper to taste

Place all ingredients into a food processor or blender and puree until smooth and well blended. Serve with fish, meats, and vegetables.

Yields 2 servings

David Grear, Executive Chef
La Terrasse, Philadelphia, PA

Saffron Aïoli

Pinch of saffron
¼ cup warm water
1 cup mayonnaise
3 cloves garlic, minced
½ bunch parsley
Salt and pepper to taste

Combine saffron and water in a blender and pulse for 1 minute. Add remaining ingredients and blend for 3 minutes. Refrigerate until ready to serve. (This is best if made 2 days in advance to release saffron flavor and color.)

Yields 1½ cups

Jon C. Hallowell, Chef/Owner
Mixmaster Café, Malvern , PA

Creole Tartar Sauce

1 cup mayonnaise
⅛ cup Dijon mustard
Juice of 1 lemon
2 plum tomatoes, seeded and chopped
1 red onion, minced
½ bunch fresh parsley, chopped
1 teaspoon Old Bay Seasoning
½ teaspoon paprika
Dash of cayenne pepper

Combine all ingredients. Add more cayenne pepper for a bit more of a bite.

Laura Kaplan, Chef/Owner
Emerald Fish, Cherry Hill, NJ

Classic Rouille

Chef's Note

— Rouille is a spicy, garlic mayonnaise from France. It is often used for fish dishes, fish soups and stews, and is the traditional accompaniment to bouillabaisse.

1 egg yolk
4 sprigs parsley
1 teaspoon paprika
½ cup olive oil
1 red bell pepper, roasted, core and seeds removed
7 large cloves garlic, peeled
3 teaspoons fresh lemon juice

Process yolk, parsley, and paprika in a food processor. While machine is running, drizzle in oil so that mixture emulsifies and gets creamy. Add remaining ingredients and blend again until well combined. Pour mixture into a small container and cover with lid. Let sit several hours in refrigerator so that flavors blend together well.

Yields about 1 cup

Justin Sanders, Chef/Culinary Student

Pasilla Chile Salsa

Whisk Wisdom

Pasilla chiles are narrow, wrinkled chiles measuring up to 6 inches long. They have a rich, spicy flavor with hints of fruit and impart a deep, moderately hot flavor to stews, salsas, soups, and casseroles. Fresh chiles are called "pasilla." When dried, they are called "chile negro."

When handling chiles, wear kitchen gloves to prevent any cuts or abrasions on hands from contacting the volatile oils. Wash your hands well with warm, soapy water after handling the chiles, and do not touch your eyes or other sensitive areas.

3 pasilla chiles, cut open, seeds removed
¼ small white onion, diced and rinsed
2 tablespoons tomato sauce
1 tablespoon apple cider vinegar
½ teaspoon salt
¼ teaspoon cumin
1 tablespoon vegetable oil

Soak chiles in boiling water for 20 minutes. Drain chiles and place in a food processor or blender with onion, tomato sauce, vinegar, salt, and cumin. Blend until smooth.

Heat oil in a small saucepan. When oil is hot, add to puree all at once and stir for 3 minutes until salsa begins to thicken.

Mark E. Smith, Chef/Owner
The Tortilla Press, Collingswood, NJ

Tomato-Habañero Salsa

4 plum tomatoes, halved, deeded, and diced
½ small Spanish onion, diced
1 habañero chile, minced
1 clove garlic, minced
1 tablespoon chopped cilantro
Juice of 1 lime
Kosher salt

Combine tomatoes, onion, habañero, and garlic in a bowl. Stir in cilantro and juice. Season with kosher salt and mix thoroughly.

**Daniel Bethard, Executive Chef/Operating Partner
Iron Hill Brewery and Restaurant, West Chester, PA**

Pineapple-Chile Pequin Salsa

Chef's Note

— Chile pequin, also called chiltepe, is a tiny, oval dried chile. It is powerfully hot with a rich flavor.

1 tablespoon chopped fresh pineapple
1 teaspoon fresh lime juice
2 teaspoons pickled chile pequin, or dried chile pequin soaked in 2 tablespoons cider vinegar
4 teaspoons honey
2 tablespoons extra virgin olive oil
1 teaspoon kosher salt

In a blender jar or in a bowl with an immersion blender, combine all the salsa ingredients and puree until creamy.

Yields about ½ cup

Guillermo Pernot, Executive Chef/Owner
¡Pasión!, Philadelphia, PA

Justin's Salsa

Chef's Note

I would like to thank some people for being there and helping me along my culinary journey:

... my parents and my family for always being there and being the judges of my food

... Edward Austrian and his family along with Kevin MacMillian. I will always remember the fun times cooking with such great friends

... Axelsson's Blue Claw Restaurant, including Kurt Sr., Cecil, Michael, and Kurt Jr. Axelsson; head chef Christian Rife; chef George MacFeat, and chef Terri MacFeat

...Chef Tony Clark— special thanks

... Connie Correia Fisher for inviting me to be a part of this wonderful cookbook

Without these people and more, I would not have my culinary journey be where it is today. So again, I thank you all.

2 large ripe yellow tomatoes
3 large ripe red tomatoes
2 tablespoons finely minced red onion
1½ teaspoons finely chopped cilantro
1 medium clove garlic, finely minced
½ jalapeño pepper, seeds removed and finely minced
4 tablespoons rice wine vinegar
1 tablespoon extra virgin olive oil
Zest of 1 lime
Salt and pepper to taste

Cut an 'x' into the bottom of each tomato. Carefully submerge tomatoes into boiling water for about 1 minute or just until skins start coming off. Quickly transfer to an ice bath. When cool enough to touch, gently peel away outer skins and squeeze the juices from tomatoes. Discard juices. Cut all tomatoes into a small dice and place in a metal bowl.

Add red onion, cilantro, garlic, jalapeño, rice wine vinegar, oil, and lime zest. Gently fold ingredients together with a rubber spatula until well blended. Season with salt and pepper. Refrigerate until ready to serve.

Yields approximately 3 cups

Justin Sanders, Chef/Culinary Student

Grilled Pineapple-Mango Salsa

Whisk Wisdom

Fresh, ripe pineapples should have green, fresh-looking leaves in a small, compact crown, and a leaf should be easy to remove if fully ripe. It should feel heavy and have a strong, sweet, but not fermented, smell. Feel the bottom. It should yield to medium pressure and have no indication of mold. Avoid pineapples that appear dry or look old and wrinkly. Dark eyes, soft spots, and yellowed leaves are all indicators that the pineapple is past its prime. Pineapples will not ripen on your counter. Without any starch reserves to convert to sugar, they will simply begin to rot and ferment.

Choose mangoes that yield to gentle pressure, with no dark spots or blemishes. Although most are yellow to red in color, color alone is not always an indicator of maturity: some varieties are greenish. A ripe mango will have a very fragrant aroma. If the mangoes are still hard and too green, place them in a brown paper bag on your counter for a few days to ripen. Ripe mangoes can be stored in a plastic bag in the refrigerator for two to three days.

½ pineapple, cored, peeled, and sliced into ¼-inch rings
1 mango, peeled, pitted, and chopped
½ red bell pepper, cored, seeded, and chopped
½ green bell pepper, cored, seeded, and chopped
½ red onion, chopped
3 tablespoons chopped cilantro
3 tablespoons olive oil
1 tablespoon peeled minced fresh ginger
1 jalapeño pepper or to taste, chopped
Juice of 1 or 2 limes
Kosher salt and freshly ground black pepper to taste

Preheat a grill pan over high heat. Grill pineapple rings, turning once, until charred. Transfer rings to a cutting board and chop.

Place chopped pineapple and remaining ingredients in a bowl and thoroughly combine.

Chef's note ... Salsa can be prepared up to 2 days in advance.

Susanna Goihman, Chef/Owner
Azafran, Philadelphia, PA

Grilled Pineapple and Crabmeat Salsa

Christopher's

Known for:
the neighborhood place
that is ALWAYS open
(storms, holidays, all the time)

Year opened:
2001

Most requested table:
the booths

Menu:
American comfort foods

Chef:
Ryan McCauley

Chef's training:
The Restaurant School,
Philadelphia

**Chef's hobbies/
accomplishments:**
fishing, boating, collecting wine

Chef's favorite ingredient:
mushrooms

Chef's favorite food:
any type of pork product

1 pineapple, cored and cut into ½-inch-thick slices
½ medium red onion, cut into ½-inch-thick slices
1 red pepper
½ pound lump crabmeat, shells removed
¼ cup chopped cilantro
Salt and pepper

Grill pineapple and onion slices for 2 to 3 minutes per side on a preheated grill. Reserve.

Grill whole red pepper until black and charred. Peel, seed, and cut into small cubes. Cut pineapple and onion into pieces slightly larger than the pepper pieces.

Place all ingredients in a large mixing bowl. Stir carefully to avoid breaking the lumps of crab. Season with salt and pepper to taste. Serve with your favorite grilled fish.

Yields 8 servings

**Ryan McCauley, Head Chef
Christopher's, A Neighborhood Place, Wayne, PA**

Mango Habañero Salsa

Did you know?

Habañeros are the hottest of chiles in the world. Their heat comes from a compound called capsaicin that causes acrid vapors and a burning taste. Capsaicin is located inside the glands of the chile, with the most intense heat located in the placenta that attaches the seeds to the pod. Unwise handling of hot chiles can cause a medical condition known as "Hunan Hand," where the capsaicin enters tiny cracks in the skin and produces a profound burning sensation that lasts quite a while. (Vinegar supposedly helps relieve the pain.) If it's your mouth that's burning, immediately consume some kind of dairy product like milk, sour cream, or ice cream. The more fat in the product, the better. Starchy foods may also absorb the heat, but water won't ease your burning tongue because capsaicin is insoluble in cold water.

1 fresh mango, diced
3 plum tomatoes, diced
1 habañero pepper, minced
½ medium red onion, chopped
2 tablespoons cilantro, cut into ribbons
Juice of 1 lime
Juice of 1 orange
Salt and pepper

Combine all ingredients. Season highly with salt and pepper.
　　Chef's note … The key to a good salsa is a very sharp knife and precise cuts.

Carlo deMarco, Chef/Owner
333 Belrose Bar & Grill, Radnor, PA

Roasted Red Pepper Coulis

Whisk Wisdom

You may have noticed that the term "coulis" keeps popping up on restaurant menus. What's a coulis? Originally, it was a term to describe the juices from cooked meat. Coulis now refers more to any thick puree. A vegetable or fruit sauce without cream is also often labled a coulis. So raspberry coulis is a trendy way of saying raspberry sauce. Mystery solved.

1 tablespoon olive oil
2 red bell peppers
1 tablespoon rice vinegar
1 teaspoon sugar
4 tablespoons canola oil
Salt and pepper to taste

Smear olive oil over peppers and roast in oven until skins are blistered. Remove and place in a bowl. Cover with plastic wrap for a few minutes while cooling. Peel and deseed.

Place peppers, rice vinegar, and sugar in a blender. While machine is running, drizzle in canola oil. Season with salt and pepper.

**Daniel Bethard, Executive Chef/Operating Partner
Iron Hill Brewery and Restaurant, West Chester, PA**

Creamy Cucumber Relish

1 cucumber, seeded and diced
1 tablespoon plus 1 teaspoon kosher salt
1 plum tomato, diced
1 teaspoon blended oil
½ cup champagne vinegar
½ cup sugar
½ teaspoon black mustard seeds
½ cup crème fraîche
3 teaspoons minced chives

Sprinkle cucumbers with 1 tablespoon kosher salt. Drain for 1 hour. Rinse, then gently squeeze dry. Reserve.

Season tomato with oil and remaining 1 teaspoon kosher salt. Dry in 250° oven for 1 hour.

Cook vinegar, sugar, and mustard seed over medium heat until a syrup forms. Cool.

Combine cooled syrup and remaining ingredients and stir to combine. Chill for 1 hour.

Yields 4 to 6 servings

Tracey A. Hopkins, Sr., Executive Chef
Museum Restaurant at the Philadelphia Museum of
Art, Philadelphia, PA

Oven-Dried Grape and Ginger Relish

Chef's Notes

You may add a bit of thin-sliced fennel and grilled red or white onion to the relish. It will add to both the flavor and the appearance.

¼ cup kosher salt

¼ cup granulated sugar

1 medium bunch red seedless table grapes, stems removed

3 cups port wine (An inexpensive brand is fine.)

1 cup light Karo Corn Syrup

5 whole black peppercorns

2 bay leaves

3 teaspoons ginger preserves

Salt and pepper to taste

1 bulb fennel, peeled and sliced thin, optional

1 medium red or white onion, peeled and sliced thin, optional

Preheat oven to 200° F.

In a mixing bowl, combine salt and sugar. Add grapes and toss until well coated. Place coated grapes on a cookie sheet and bake for 12 to 15 hours (depending upon your oven) until grapes are dry but still retain shape and color without shriveling.

In a medium saucepan, combine port wine, Karo syrup, peppercorns, and bay leaves. Reduce over a low flame until mixture reaches the consistency of a thick syrup (but thinner than molasses).

Stir in ginger preserves. Add grapes and toss until completely coated. Add salt and pepper to taste.

Yields 2 servings

David Greer, Executive Chef
La Terrasse, Philadelphia

Tomato Jam

The Global Dish Caterers

Known for:
creating a custom "restaurant" for each client's event, upscale boutique catering

Year opened:
1997

Most requested table:
the one in your own dining room

Menu:
custom created menus: We have never served the same menu twice.

Chef:
Mitchell Prensky

Chef's training:
Bachelor of Music from Wm. Paterson University; graduate and former employee of the French Culinary Institute, NYC

Chef's hobbies/ accomplishments:
playing music, sports spectating, big Flyers fan!

Chef's favorite ingredient:
truffles

Chef's favorite food:
my mom's brisket

2 tablespoons extra virgin olive oil

¼ cup minced ginger

3 cloves garlic, minced

¼ cup cider vinegar

2 cinnamon sticks

4 large ripe tomatoes, peeled, seeded, and diced

⅓ cup brown sugar, packed

1 teaspoon toasted cumin

¼ teaspoon cayenne pepper

⅛ teaspoon ground cloves

Salt and pepper

¼ cup honey

Heat oil in a saucepot. Add ginger and garlic and cook for 2 to 3 minutes. Add vinegar and cinnamon and cook until reduced by half. Add tomatoes, brown sugar, cumin, cayenne, and cloves.

Simmer low for 1½ hours, stirring occasionally, until all juices have evaporated. Season with salt and pepper. Add honey and remove from heat.

Chef's note … This Moroccan spiced tomato condiment is great on fish, chicken, and lamb. Make a big batch. It freezes well!

Yields 2 cups

Mitch Prensky, Chef/Owner
The Global Dish Caterers, Philadelphia, PA

Slow-Roasted Garlic Oil

¡Pasion!

Known for:
ceviches

Year opened:
1998

Most requested table:
ceviche bar

Menu:
Latino

Executive chef:
Guillermo Pernot

Chef's training:
self taught

Chef's hobbies/ accomplishments:
Chef of the Year, *Esquire* magazine 1999; James Beard Best Chef of the Mid-Atlantic 1999; one of America's Ten Best New Chef's 1998 by *Food and Wine* magazine

Chef's favorite ingredient:
chiles

Chef's favorite food:
ceviche

1 pound container peeled garlic cloves
2 cups mild vegetable oil, or 1 cup each vegetable oil and olive oil
½ cup water
2 teaspoons kosher salt
½ teaspoon freshly ground black pepper

Preheat the oven to 300°. Place the garlic, oil, water, salt, and pepper in a baking dish with a lid. Cover and bake for 45 minutes. The oil should be gently bubbling. Remove from the oven and cool. Refrigerate in a covered container for up to 1 month.

Yields 2 cups

Guillermo Pernot, Executive Chef/Owner ¡Pasión!, Philadelphia, PA

Joe's Cajun Seasoning

3 tablespoons garlic powder
2½ tablespoons paprika
2 tablespoons salt
1 tablespoon black pepper
1 tablespoon cayenne pepper
1 tablespoon onion powder
1 tablespoon ground oregano
1 tablespoon ground thyme

Combine all ingredients. Store in an airtight container in a cool, dry place. Shake or stir to recombine before each use. Seasoning can be stored for up to 3 months.

Joe Brown, Chef/Owner
Melange Cafe, Cherry Hill, NJ

Crème Anglaise

6 egg yolks
½ cup sugar
2 cups heavy cream
1 tablespoon vanilla extract

Beat egg yolks and sugar in a mixing bowl until pale yellow in color. Reserve.

Bring heavy cream and vanilla extract to a simmer in a medium-size saucepan. Slowly pour hot cream into yolk mixture.

Return mixture to pan. Cook over a very low flame, stirring constantly, until thick. (Do not allow eggs to scramble.) Chill immediately until ready to serve.

David Salama, Chef/Proprietor
Creperie Beau Monde, Philadelphia, PA

Cocktails

Pineapple and Vanilla Bean Infused Margarita

Whisk Wisdom

If we've learned one thing in over twenty years in the catering business, it's that the first thing guests do at a party is head straight for the bar. Maybe all they want is a sparkling water, but their number one priority is to get a drink in their hand. Then they feel comfortable. So be sure your bar features a special drink or two, something your guests haven't seen before and will find intriguing, and your party's on the way to being a big hit.

1 gold pineapple

1 750-milliliter bottle clear tequila

3 tablespoons superfine sugar

1 vanilla bean, split

1 cup Triple Sec

½ cup fresh squeezed lime juice (approximately 5 to 6 limes)

Peel and core pineapple and place in a clean container. Add tequila, sugar, and vanilla bean. Let sit overnight.

Remove one-third of the pineapple and puree in a blender, adding a little infused tequila as needed. Strain remaining tequila. Add pureed pineapple, Triple Sec, and lime juice. Pour everything into a pitcher with a few ice cubes. Serve in a martini glass with a pineapple wedge garnish.

Chef's note ... Don't bother with the traditional salt rim for this margarita: it's not a good mix. Trust us on this.

Lynn Buono, Chef
Feast Your Eyes Gourmet Catering, Philadelphia, PA

Eclipse Margarita

Whisk Wisdom

El Tesoro de Don Felipe is still produced entirely in the old traditional method: by hand. Agave plants of the proper maturity and quality are slowly steamed in brick ovens and crushed with a stone wheel. They are then fermented in wood tanks and distilled to exactly 80 proof so that water is never added to dilute the tequila. The Cabo Good Times Web page says "The aroma exhibits moderate wet cement with sweet roasted agave overtones and a refreshing lack of floral components while slightly volatile. Softly pungent on the attack, its thick and oily body weighs heavy on the tongue. Taste is very similar to the aroma with a nice balance. The finish is tingly warm with slight pepper, citrus, and lasting sweetness." Yummy!

5½ ounces El Tesoro Silver Tequila
¾ ounce fresh pineapple puree
¾ ounce pineapple schnapps
¼ ounce fresh lime juice
Splash of Blue Curacao
Splash of sour mix
1 red serrano chile pepper

Pour all ingredients, except chile pepper, over ice in a cocktail shaker. Shake well and strain into a chilled "up" glass. Garnish with chile pepper.

Yields 1 serving

Nick Georigi, General Manager
Eclipse Restaurant, Wilmington, DE

Thommy G's Espresso Martini

Thommy G's

Bartender:
Willy Melendez

Signature drink or most recommended wine:
Espresso Martini and
Mac Murray Pinto Noir 2001

Hobbies/accomplishments:
constant observer

Favorite ingredient:
Van Gogh Pineapple Vodka

Best advice I ever gave:
Why don't you let me
call you a cab!

1 ounce vanilla vodka
¼ ounce Kahlua
1 ounce chilled espresso

Fill a martini glass with ice and water to thoroughly chill glass. Remove water and ice. Combine all ingredients in a cocktail shaker and shake until you think your hands should fall off. Strain into chilled glass and enjoy! (Feel free to adjust the above amounts so long as they remain in proportion.)

Yields 1 serving

Willy Melendez, Bartender
Thommy G's, Burlington, NJ

Espresso Martini

Toto

Bartender:
Erika West

Signature drink or most recommended wine:
Espresso Martini

Hobbies/accomplishments:
won 1st prize in recent "Iron Bartender Competition"

Favorite ingredient:
amaretto

Best advice I ever gave:
You can always make a second drink, but you can never make a second impression.

4 ounces freshly made espresso coffee
1 ounce Stoli Vanilla vodka
1 ounce Baileys Irish cream liqueur
Splash of amaretto

Pour all ingredients into an ice cube laden shaker. Pour into a chilled martini glass and serve.

Yields 1 serving

Erika West, Head Bartender
Toto, Philadelphia, PA

Bourbon Blue Appletini Martini

Bourbon Blue

Beverage manager:
Edward Sotherden

Signature drink:
Bourbon Blue Appletini

Hobbies/accomplishments:
lived in Belize, Central America
for four months. This influenced
my palate as well as my bartend-
ing style. I have worked all front of
the house positions from busboy
to my current position of Manager/
Marketing Coordinator. I have a
bachelor's degree in Intercultural
Communication with a focus on
Marketing. I love all aspects of
the restaurant business, but I am
most knowledgeable, and I have
the most fun, when I am working
or promoting the bar.

Favorite ingredient:
fresh fruit, fresh fruit juices, and
rum. This stems back from my
time in Belize. I believe every bar
should have a juice machine
behind the bar.

Best advice I ever gave:
My restaurant business mentor
told me "whenever you're working
in a restaurant, you have to take
off all your blinders." What he
meant was you have to be on top
of everything, without letting
individual tasks get in the way of
the bigger picture.

4 ounces Chopin Vodka
2 ounces DeKuyper Sour Apple Schnapps
2 ounces Blue Curacao
1 orange wedge

In a mixing glass full of ice, combine vodka, schnapps, and
Blue Curacao. Vigorously shake for 10 seconds. Strain into
a large frozen martini glass and garnish with orange wedge.

Yields 1 serving

**Edward Sotherden, Restaurant/Bar Manager
Bourbon Blue, Philadelphia, PA**

Chunk Martini

1½ ounces Greygoose vodka
½ ounce Bailey's Irish Cream
½ ounce Butterscotch Schnapps
1½ ounces cream
1 maraschino cherry
Grated nutmeg

Fill mixture glass with ice cubes and ingredients. Shake 30 times. Strain into a martini glass. Garnish with cherry and nutmeg.

Yields 1 serving

Yardley Inn, Yardley, PA

Raspberry Chocolate Martini

Dome Restaurant & Bar

Beverage manager:
Bryan Jariwala

Signature drink or most recommended wine:
Raspberry Chocolate Martini

Hobbies/accomplishments:
days off/bachelor's degree in Hotel Restaurant Management

Favorite ingredient:
simple syrup

Best advice I ever gave:
Take a moment and put yourself in their shoes.

3½ ounces Godiva white chocolate liqueur
2½ ounces Stoli raspberry vodka
Splash of grenadine
Splash of fresh raspberry puree

Pour liqueur, vodka, and grenadine into a cocktail shaker filled with ice. Stir until cold. Strain into a chilled martini glass. Swirl raspberry puree on top to garnish.

Yields 1 serving

Bryan Jariwala, Beverage Manager
Dome Restaurant & Bar, Hockessin, DE

Sandito Mojito

Cuba Libre

Bar manager:
Pete Rossi

Signature drink or most recommended wine:
Mojito and 2000 Mumanthia Toro

Hobbies/accomplishments:
golf, cooking, wine, baseball

Favorite ingredient:
guarapo

1¼ ounces white rum
1¼ ounces fresh lime juice
1¼ ounces guarapo (sugar cane juice)
1¼ ounces fresh watermelon juice
4 to 6 herba buena leaves
Splash of lemon-lime soda
Lime wedge

Combine rum, lime juice, watermelon juice, guarapo, and leaves in a shaker glass. Add ice and shake well. Pour into a 10-ounce glass. Top with lemon-lime soda. Garnish with lime.

Chef's note ... Simple syrup may be substituted for guarapo.

Yields 1 serving

Pete Rossi, Bar Manager
Cuba Libre Restaurant & Rum Bar, Philadelphia, PA

Tropical Mojito

Mixto Restaurant

General manager:
Mark Sylva

Signature drink or most recommended wine:
Tropical Mojito

Hobbies/accomplishments:
working out

Favorite ingredient:
maraschino cherries

Best advice I ever gave:
Don't mix business with pleasure!

2 slices lime
3 or 4 mint leaves plus extra for garnish
1 ounce sugar syrup
½ ounce banana rum
½ ounce pineapple rum
½ ounce mango rum
6 ounces Sprite soda
1 pineapple slice

In a shaker glass, mash limes, mint leaves, and sugar syrup. Add ice and rums and shake. Add Sprite. Pour drink, including ice, into a tall glass. Garnish glass with mint leaves and a pineapple slice.

Yields 1 serving

**Mark Sylva, General Manager
Mixto Restaurant, Philadelphia, PA**

4 PM Shift

Caribou Café

Bartender:
Bill Gat

Signature drink or most recommended wine:
4 PM Shift

Hobbies/accomplishments:
music

Favorite ingredient:
dark liquors

Best advice I ever gave:
Don't take my advice.

Dry vermouth
Sugar
3 ounces Ketel One vodka (Any vodka with a lesser sugar
  content can be used.)
½ ounce Pernod Ricard
½ ounce Grand Marnier

Slightly chill a cocktail glass. Splash cocktail glass with a swirl of vermouth. Rim glass with sugar.

Mix vodka and Pernod over ice in a shaker glass and gently shake. Strain ingredients into prepared glass and top with Grand Marnier.

Yields 1 serving

Bill Gat, Bartender
Caribou Café, Philadelphia, PA

Caipirinha ¡Pasión!

Chef's Note

— Caipirinha is a drink that is popular everywhere is Brazil, but especially at the beaches. It is based on cachaça, the potent white Brazilian liquor distilled from sugar cane. The two brands most frequently available in the United States are Cachaça 51 and Pitu. While a caipirinha always contains limes and sugar, at ¡Pasión! we use every tropical fruit from pineapple to passion fruit.

½ lime, scrubbed and cut into 3 or 4 wedges
1 tablespoon sugar
1 ounce passion fruit purée
2½ ounces cachaça

Cut each lime wedge in half crosswise. Chill an 8-ounce rocks glass by swirling it with crushed ice, then discard the ice. Add the lime wedges and sugar to the glass. Using a wooden muddler or the back of a heavy spoon, crush the wedges with the sugar to release the fragrant oils from the rind. Add the passion fruit purée. Fill the glass with ice, pour in the cachaça, and serve.

Yields 1 serving

Guillermo Pernot, Executive Chef/Owner
¡Pasión!, Philadelphia, PA

Carlito

¼ lime, sliced
2 ounces tequila (any kind you prefer)
3 ounces club soda

Fill a 10-ounce glass (or any size you prefer) with ice. Squeeze slice of lime into glass. Pour in tequila, then club soda. Stir and serve.

Yields 1 serving

Carlo Sena, Manager
Le Castagne, Philadelphia, PA

City Tavern Cooler

Whisk Wisdom

Although Madeira was the drink of choice in the City Tavern, rum from Jamaica, French brandy, and English whiskey were also consumed in healthy quantities. This recipe for a refreshing summer drink combines all three with another common beverage, apple cider.

Ice cubes
2 tablespoons peach brandy
1 tablespoon Appleton rum
1½ teaspoons whiskey
1 cup fresh apple cider

Fill a 12-ounce highball glass half full with ice cubes. Add peach brandy, Appleton rum, and whiskey. Add apple cider. Mix well and serve.

Yields 1 10-ounce serving

Walter Staib, Chef/Proprietor
City Tavern, Philadelphia, PA

Citrus

Denim Lounge

Sommelier:
Chris Robin

Signature drink or most recommended wine:
Citrus

Hobbies/accomplishments:
drinking wine, cooking

Favorite ingredient:
Grand Marnier

Best advice I ever gave:
Kill them with kindness

1½ shots Solichnaya Ohranji
1 shot Grand Marnier
Splash of cranberry juice
Splash of sour mix
Splash of orange juice

Fill mixture glass with ice cubes and ingredients. Shake and strain into a martini glass and serve straight up.

Yields 1 serving

Chris Robin, Sommelier
Denim Lounge, Philadelphia, PA

Hurricane Cocktail

Did you know?

The Hurricane became popular during the 1940s when traveling to the Caribbean and Cuba became popular. It is of Caribbean decent and is based on rum influences. Traditionally, only fresh juices should be used, and the hurricane should always be garnished with an orange wheel and cherries.

3 ounces quality rum
¼ cup passion fruit juice
3 tablespoons water
1 teaspoon superfine sugar
½ teaspoon grenadine
Juice of 1 lime
Ice cubes
Cherries and orange slice

In a cocktail shaker, mix rum, passion fruit juice, water, and sugar until sugar is dissolved. Add grenadine and lime juice and stir to combine. Add ice cubes and shake. Strain Hurricane into a cocktail glass. Garnish with cherries and orange slice.

Yields 1 serving

Jim Coleman, Executive Chef
Normandy Farm, Blue Bell, PA

Peach Bellini

Spezia

Known for:
upscale BYOB on the Main Line

Year opened:
2001

Most requested table:
The Chef's Table #10

Menu:
contemporary American influenced by French and Italian cuisine, heavily featuring local and seasonal produce

1 ounce peach nectar (Looza is a good brand and readily available in most grocery stores.)
1 ounce peach schnapps
4 ounces sparkling wine (I recommend Prosecco.)

Place peach nectar and schnapps in the bottom of a champagne flute. Top off with sparkling wine and stir gently. Enjoy immediately. (We might be a BYOB, but we adore our bubbly.)

Yields 1 serving

Monica Couch, Pastry Chef
Spezia, Bryn Mawr, PA

Pinata

Fountain Restaurant

Sommelier:
Melissa Monosoff

Signature drink or most recommended wine:
I can never say "no" to champagne.

Hobbies/accomplishments:
My job is my hobby! I am also a runner and have run a few marathons.

Favorite ingredient:
fresh lime juice

Best advice I ever gave:
Work hard and stay true to yourself.

1½ ounces Absolut Vanil
1½ ounces pineapple juice
Splash of Triple Sec
Juice of 2 limes

Shake over ice until frothy. Serve in a martini glass.

Yields 1 serving

Melissa Monosoff, Sommelier
Fountain Restaurant, Philadelphia, PA

Scarlet Pansy

Cresheim Cottage Cafe

Wine steward:
Adina Silberstein

Signature drink or most recommended wine:
drink: Scarlet Pansy
wine: Wild Horse Malvasia Bianca, California

Hobbies/accomplishments:
endurance cyclist

Favorite ingredient:
Chambord

2 ounces Ketel One vodka
½ ounce Chambord
1 ounce soda water
2 slices lime

Fill a highball glass with ice. Add vodka, Chambord, and soda water. Float one slice of lime and garnish with the other.

Yields 1 drink

**Adina Silberstein, Wine Steward
Cresheim Cottage Cafe, Philadelphia, PA**

Contributors

333 Belrose
Albertson's Cooking School
Alex Long New Asian Cuisine
Amish Barn
Anjou
Anthony's
Anthony's Italian Coffee House
Art Institute of New York
Art Institute of Philadelphia
Authentic Turkish Cuisine
Azafran
Blue Sage Vegetarian Grille
Bourbon Blue
Braddock's Tavern
Brasserie Perrier
Bravo Bistro
Buffalo Bill's BBQ Restaurant
Cafe Spice
Caffe Aldo Lamberti
Caribou Café
Carman's Country Kitchen
Catelli Ristorante
Caviar Assouline
Chadds Ford Inn
Chez Colette in the Hotel Sofitel
Chlöe
Christopher's
Cin Cin
City Tavern
Company's Coming Catering
Copabanana
Creative Cuisine Catering
Creperie Beau Monde
Cresheim Cottage Cafe
Criniti
Cuba Libre
Custom Cuisine Cooking
D'Angelo's Summit Caterers
Davio's Northern Italian
    Steakhouse
Denim Lounge
Deux Chemineés

Diane's La Patisserie
DiBruno Bros. House of Cheese
Dome
Eclipse
El Sarape
Elements Cafe
Emerald Fish
Essene Cafe
Feast Your Eyes Catering
Fork
Fountain
Frog Commissary Catering
GG's
Happy Rooster
Harry's Savoy Grill
Homemade Goodies by Roz
Iron Hill Brewery and Restaurant
Jack Kramer's Catering
Jake's
Jamaican Jerk Hut
Jeffrey Miller Catering
Jimmy Rubino's Ralph's of
    South Philadelphia
Joseph Ambler Inn
Joseph Poon Asian Restaurant
Justin Sanders
La Bonne Auberge
La Campagne
La Terrasse
Lamberti's Cucina
Le Bec-Fin
Le Castagne
Maggiano's Little Italy
Manayunk Brewery & Restaurant
Marigold Dining Room
Marker at Adams Mark Hotel
Max's Fine Dining
McCrossen'sTavern
Melange Cafe
Metropolitan Bakery
Miel Patisserie
Mixmaster Café

Mixto
Mom's Bake at Home Pizza
Monk's Café
Morton's the Steakhouse
Museum Restaurant
Nodding Head Brewery
Nola on Head House Square
Normandy Farm
Novelty Restaurant
Paradigm
¡Pasión!
Pat's King of Steaks
Philadelphia Fish & Co.
Pinziminio Trattoria
Porterhouse Steaks and Seafood
Ralph's Italian Restaurant
Rangoon Burmese
Ravenna
Rembrandt's
Restaurant Passerelle
Ristorante Panorama
RoseLena's
Rouge
Rx
Sansom Street Oyster House
Savona
Severino Homemade Pasta
Solaris Grille
Sotto Varalli
Spezia
Stella Notte
The Chef Did It
The Global Dish Caterers
The Greatest Grub Ever
The Hotel DuPont
The Inn at Twin Linden
The Little Tuna
The Night Kitchen Bakery
The Prime Rib
The Red Hen Cafe
The Restaurant School at
    Walnut Hill College

The Saloon
The Spaghetti Warehouse
The Terrace at Greenhill
Thommy G's
Tony Luke's
Tortilla Press
Toto

Trax Cafe
Trust
Twenty Manning
Ulana's
Upstares at Varalli
Valentes

What's for Dinner...It's a Mystery
White Dog Cafe
Wild Tuna
Yangming
Yardley Inn
Your Private Chef
Zanzibar Blue

Wine Experts

Corkscrewed
Village Walk Shopping Center #15, 1990 Marlton Pike (Route 70), Cherry Hill, NJ 08003
856-874-1090, Fax 856-874-1092, www.eatwelldrinkbetter.com

John McNulty is the co-owner of Corkscrewed. A popular wine educator, John hosts "On the Town with John McNulty," a radio program about wine, food, dining, and travel which is heard every Saturday from 3 to 5 p.m. on WNWR Radio 1540 AM. John has contributed to national publications, such as *The Wine News* and *The Wine Spectator*.

Moore Brothers Wine Company
7200 N. Park Drive, Pennsauken, NJ 08109, 856-317-1177, www.moorebros.com
1416 N. Dupont Street, Wilmington, DE 19806, 302-498-0360, www.moorebrosde.com

The staff at Moore Brothers Wine Company looked over each of these recipes, discussed the possibilities, disagreed (around here, if you ask two of our people what wine to serve with a particular dish, you're likely to get three opinions), discussed some more, tested a couple of the recipes to make sure they were on the right track, and came up with the suggestions in this book. Participants included Brian Healy, Jonathan Read, and Dale Belville, all of whom eat and drink to excess.

Old Wines LLC
710 Chestnut Street, Philadelphia, PA 19106, 215-351-9985, www.marnieold.com

Marnie Old is the Philadelphia-area's leading wine educator and highest profile sommelier. At 33, she is one of the youngest women to be sought after as a speaker on wine both nationally and internationally. She is certified by the *Court of Master Sommeliers* and is the only wine professional in the region enrolled in their Master Sommelier program. Old launched her independent venture, Old Wines, in 2001, offering sommelier services and wine education to both consumers and the wine trade. Old spent five years as the Executive Beverage Director for Philadelphia's premier restaurant group, Meal Ticket Inc., operators of Striped Bass, Avenue B, Rouge, and Bleu. She has been honored by *Food and Wine* magazine as having created one of the country's "Ten Best New Wine Lists of 2001" at Avenue B. *Philadelphia magazine* also named Marnie their "Best of Philly Sommelier 2001." She served as the founding education chair of the *American Sommelier Association* and has taught award-winning wine classes to both consumers and her peers in the industry since 1995.

Index

Symbols

¡Pasión! 41, 45, 229, 338, 347, 362
333 Belrose Bar & Grill 204, 226, 342
4 PM Shift 361

A

African Peanut Yams 227
Aïoli
　Chipotle 332
　Lemon 331
　Roasted Garlic 330
　Saffron 333
Alberici, Vince 67, 178, 234, 321
Albertson, Ann-Michelle 69, 288
Albertson, Charlotte Ann 100, 138
Albertson, Kristin 23, 294, 309
Albertson's Cooking School 23, 69,
　100 138, 288, 294, 309
Alex Long New Asian Cuisine 157
Almond Financier with Diced Apples 268
Amaranth
　Grilled Asparagus, Amaranth, and
　　Wild Watercress Salad 67
Amaretto Cherry Gelato 285
Amish Barn Restaurant 96
Anastasio, Anthony 284
Ancho chili pepper
　Creative's Award-winning Black Bean
　　Chile 106
　Filete Toluca 192
　Savory Black Beans 231
Anchovy
　Sautéed Wild Mushrooms 222
　Sea Bass Baccala Style 165
Anderson, John 62
Anjou Restaurant 44
Anthony's Baci Gelato 284
Anthony's Creative Italian Cuisine
　92, 123, 205, 220
Anthony's Italian Coffee House 284
Antico Dolce Torte 290
Apple
　Almond Financier with Diced Apples
　　268
　Baked French Toast with Apples and
　　Cranberries 306
　Bananapple Bread 309
　Grilled Gruyere Cheese and Apple
　　Currant Chutney 248
　Pear Ginger Pie 267
　Pork Normandy 202
　Roasted Mushroom and Golden Apple
　　Salad 66
　Shortbread Triangles with Apple
　　Chutney Filling 270
Apricot
　Sun-dried Apricot Vinaigrette 50
Arborio rice. *See* Rice
Art Institute of Philadelphia 301, 319
　323

Artichoke
　about 218
　and Crab Bisque 88
　Criniti Appetizer 53
　Stuffed Artichokes 218
　Veal Oscar 198
Arugula
　Insalata di Tonno con Arugula 73
　Maine Lobster Asparagus Salad 78
　Pan Seared Diver Scallops with
　　Herbed Goat Cheese 38
Asparagi Parmigiano e Tartufi Nero 219
Asparagus
　Asparagi Parmigiano e Tartufi Nero
　　219
　Grilled Asparagus, Amaranth, and
　　Wild Watercress Salad 67
　Insalata di Tonno con Arugula 73
　Ivory King Salmon with Black and
　　White Truffle Butter 158
　Maine Lobster Asparagus Salad 78
　Maine Lobster Risotto with Sweet
　　Corn and Basil 131
　Pan Seared Foie Gras with Fingerling
　　Potato Salad 74
　Puffed Asparagus Spears 25
　Solaris Chopped Vegetable Salad 62
Assouline, Joel 247
Authentic Turkish Cuisine 213, 228, 281
Avocado
　about 10
　Blue Crab Jumbo Lump "Tamale" 32
　Copa Guacamole and Chips 11
　Crab and Avocado Salad 77
　Grilled Chicken and Sweet Potato
　　Burrito 249
　Grilled Shrimp with Mango and
　　Avocado Salads 79
　Jamaican Jerk Chicken Napoleon 143
　Lenguado Handroll 45
　Salad 63
　Seared Alaskan Halibut with Grilled
　　Pineapple-Mango Salsa 174
　Solaris Chopped Vegetable Salad 62
　Tortilla Press Guacamole 10
Azafran 174, 230, 235, 340

B

Bacon
　Bourbon Grilled Shrimp Skewers 21
　Chicken Casserole 147
　El Sarape Cortadillo 193
　Open-faced Salmon BLT 246
　Philadelphia Style Breakfast Cakes 301
　Purple Potato Salad with Crispy Bacon
　　69
　Smoked Sea Scallop Chowder 101
　Solaris Chopped Vegetable Salad 62
　Tony Luke's Belly Buster 245
Baguette
　Georges Perrier's Hoagie Francais 244

Lobster Hoagie 242
Muffuletta Hoagie 243
White Dog Cafe's Philly Cheese Steak
　241
Baked Figs with Gorgonzola and Pine
　Nuts 286
Baked French Toast with Apples and
　Cranberries 306
Balsamic
　Brown's Balsamic Dressing 75
　Grilled Calves Liver 50
　Jamaican Jerk Chicken Napoleon 143
　Pan Seared Diver Scallops with
　　Herbed Goat Cheese 38
　Portobello Napoleon 65
　Soy Basil Dipping Sauce 325
　Vinaigrette 82
Banana
　Bananapple Bread 309
　Bread 310
　Foster 287
　Red Snapper Creole with Grilled
　　Mangoes and Bananas 176
Bananapple Bread 309
Banh, Kiong 17, 59, 81
Bank, David Leo 246
Barbecue
　BBQ Beef Tips 195
　Ginger-Soy Barbecued Chicken Breast
　　138
　Green Curry Barbecue 327
　Guava Barbecue Sauce 326
　Guava Barbeque Ribs 208
　Pulled BBQ Pork Pot Stickers 12
　Red Curry Barbecue 328
　Salmon with Cucumber Salad 160
Barbuto, Dan 222
Barrett, James 248
Basaran, Melek 213, 228, 281
Basil
　-Dijon Vinaigrette 39
　Green Curry Barbecue 327
　Pistachio and Basil Battered Salmon
　　Fillet 159
　Polenta Crusted Halibut with Lobster
　　Basil Sauce 172
　Soy Basil Dipping Sauce 325
　Spicy Beef with Basil 194
　Zucchini Frittata with Sweet Basil 299
BBQ Beef Tips 195
Beans
　Black Beans 230
　Broccoli Rabe with White Beans and
　　Tomato 221
　Carolyn's Crab Chile 105
　Creative's Award-winning Black Bean
　　Chile 106
　Drunken SoCo Chicken 142
　Nicola Shirley's Rice and Beans 232
　Salmon with Black Bean Sauce 157
　Savory Black Beans 231
Béchamel Sauce, Dijon Mustard 319

About the Authors

Connie Correia Fisher is the president of Small Potatoes Press,
a company that specializes in cookbook publishing and provides editorial, design,
and public relations support for restaurants and food-related businesses.
A graduate of Johnson & Wales University, Connie is the coauthor of five
cookbooks and served as editor and designer of the award-winning cookbook
Joe Brown's Melange Cafe Cookbook. She is the founding publisher/editor
of *Cuizine* magazine. Connie lives in Collingswood, New Jersey,
with her husband and amazing toddler son.

Joanne Correia is Connie's mom and the former executive editor of
Cuizine magazine. She and Connie are the authors of five cookbooks, including
Cape May Cooks. Joanne is a full-time employee of the Cherry Hill Board of Education,
sings in a local choir, and — according to her daughter — is a fabulous mother.
Joanne lives in Cherry Hill, New Jersey, with her husband.